The Third Ear

On Listening to the World

Joachim-Ernst
Berendt

TRANSLATED BY TIM NEVILL

Foreword by Yehudi Menuhin

An Owl Book
Henry Holt and Company
New York

Henry Holt and Company, Inc.
Publishers since 1866
115 West 18th Street
New York, New York 10011

Henry Holt® is a registered trademark
of Henry Holt and Company, Inc.

Published in Canada by Fitzhenry & Whiteside Ltd.,
195 Allstate Parkway, Markham, Ontario L3R 4T8.

Originally published in Germany in 1985
under the title *Das Dritte Ohr.*

Library of Congress Catalog Card Number: 91-58829

ISBN 0-8050-2007-1

Henry Holt books are available for special promotions
and premiums. For details contact: Director, Special Markets.

First Owl Book / American Edition—1992

Designed by Clarke Williams

Printed in the United States of America
All first editions are printed on acid-free paper.∞

3   5   7   9   10   8   6   4

IN MEMORY OF

Gregory Bateson
(1904–1980)
ethnologist, biologist, and systems researcher,
who once said that any living thing which triumphs in the
struggle against its environment destroys itself.

Georg von Békésy
(1899–1972)
physiologist and biologist,
who taught us to understand the miracle
of the human ear more completely.

Niels Bohr
(1885–1962)
atomic physicist, who was the first person to note the
similarity between the concept of *Field* in Chinese Taoism
and theoretical physics.

Albert Einstein
(1879–1955)
who created the theory of relativity, uncovering
the deceptive nature of our sense of time.

Richard Fester
(1910–1982)
researcher into languages and originator of palaeo-linguistics,
who demonstrated the truth of the Tower of Babel myth.

Heraclitus
(*c*. 550–*c*. 480 BC)
philosopher, who bid us discover harmony where it is most
deeply concealed.

Carl Gustav Jung
(1875–1961)
psychologist and analyst, who made men aware of their
anima and women of their *animus*.

Johannes Kepler
(1571–1630)
astronomer, mathematician, and musician, who heard and
calculated 'world harmonics' in planetary orbits.

Ramana Maharshi
(1879–1950)
Indian sage, who taught us to ask anew: Who am I?

Pythagoras
(*c.* 570–*c.* 480 BC)
philosopher, astronomer, mathematician, theoretician of
music, who discovered the harmony of the spheres and was
the first man to travel the way we are once again learning
today: from the Orient to the Occident – and thereby
established Western Science.

Maulana Jalaluddin Rumi
(1207–1273)
the Persian poet in whose verses
the wisdom of Sufism became sound.

Colin Walcott
(1945–1984)
musician and percussionist, who played and lived World
Music so marvellously.

CONTENTS

2   Contents

4 Contents

Hear, and your soul shall live.
Isaiah

Merely looking at something cannot develop us.
Goethe

Hidden harmony is mightier than what is revealed.
Heraclitus

Our tradition teaches us that sound
is God – Nada Brahma.
The highest aim of our music is to reveal
the essence of the universe it reflects.
Ravi Shankar

The eye takes a person into the world.
The ear brings the world into a human being.
Lorenz Oken

The ear is the way
The Upanishads

FOREWORD

The reader will soon understand why this book fills me with admiration and wonder for its author, a kindred spirit who corroborates my conviction that the magic of listening brings us closer to the central core of the universe. To begin to comprehend the mystery of life it is not sufficient to touch and to see – we need to hear, to listen, and thus to unite heart and mind and soul. The softer the sound, the more important it is that we perceive it. We have, I fear, become a deaf people, and the cries of pain of the flora and fauna around us, the very air we breathe, the suffering of our fellow human beings in our urban deserts, in parts of the globe we have subjected to war, to famine and flood, through greed and selfishness, have become inaudible. The media encourage us to read, to view, to hear, but that does not mean we listen.

Until we can create a still centre within ourselves we will be unable to attune the 'third ear' to the messages that are broadcast to us, loud and clear for the most part, but rendered futile due to our incapacity to listen. This handicap is more than deafness; it is blindness as well – and our only hope as we reach the end of the twentieth century is to heed that childhood rhyme we all learned – a key to finding the 'third ear':

> A wise old owl lived in an oak
> The more he saw, the less he spoke;
> The less he spoke, the more he heard –
> Why can't we be like that wise old bird?

Sir Yehudi Menuhin

1

EAR AND EYE

'One of the most remarkable manifestations of the degeneration of
modern man is an increasing weakening of his acoustic sense.'

Marius Schneider

I
BLOCKED EARS

Odysseus: Scarcely any other figure in world literature has so often
and so imperatively been viewed over the centuries as the prototype
of Western man, seeking, investigating, going astray – as a human
being striving upwards along that λόγος which thenceforth radiated
sun-like over the Occident for two millennia.

When Odysseus and his comrades approached the land of the
Sirens, Circe, the sorceress, warned them that 'There is no home-
coming for the man who hears the Sirens' voices – no welcome from
his wife, no little children brightening at their father's return.' She
told them of the mouldering skeletons, withered skin still clinging to
the bone, of those who had succumbed to the Sirens.

Odysseus understood. He and his companions would not be able to
resist. The Sirens' song was overwhelmingly tempting because in
reality it came from within themselves, from within their own blood.
'*It* sings' – says Rilke in a poem about the Sirens.

The Sirens, who sing 'like Angels', were bewitchingly, divinely
beautiful but the sea largely concealed their bestial lower limbs,
ending in claws apparently rooted in the rocks on which they were
sitting. Odysseus therefore followed Circe's advice, and ordered his
ship's oarsmen to block their ears with 'softened bees-wax'. That was
to prevent them from hearing both the Sirens' alluring, seductive
song and also their leader's orders. He knew that he would weaken.
He might have ordered his men not to row towards the shore under
any circumstances, but he knew himself. Once he heard the song of
the Sirens, he would scream that they should make for land.

Nevertheless Odysseus himself wants to hear. He orders the crew
to bind him to the mast so that he does not succumb to what he
hears, seizing the oars and heading for the shore.

Odysseus escapes the Sirens and thus remains what he is and what
he has been depicted as being throughout European intellectual
history from Duns Scotus by way of the troubadors to Adorno: a

listener in chains. For Kafka the man who sees stuffs wax into his own ears, 'blocking' himself as well as his companions – 'in innocent pleasure over his limited resources'. Joy is fear. Odysseus wanted to be sure of not having to yield to the song of the Sirens come what may – and the price paid was high as will be seen.

From the very beginning the Church Fathers saw the Sirens as women rather than as goddesses, female demons, or animal-like creatures. Ambrose, for instance, wrote: 'These Sirens are to be viewed as symbolising singing voluptuousness and cajolement through which the flesh experiences temptation and turmoil.' They are 'lovely ladies of lust', standing for what from then on would be 'enchained' and 'blocked', and symbolising the sex to which man, at that time establishing the patriarchy (and everything fits together), no longer wished to listen.

Kafka believed that the Sirens did not sing at all during this encounter. 'The look of bliss on the face of Odysseus, who was thinking of nothing but wax and chains, made them forget all about their singing.' 'The Sirens vanished in the face of his determination . . . Lovelier than ever, they stretched and turned, allowing their terrifying hair to blow in the wind and stretching their claws on the rocks. They no longer wanted to lead astray. They merely wished to grab the splendour reflected in Odysseus's great eyes for as long as possible.'

What Odysseus calls his 'determination' is basically nothing but the deafness he imposes on himself, thereby excluding and thwarting a genuine encounter with all its possibilities of seduction and resistance, victory and defeat.

A later tradition adds to that. The desperate Sirens plunge into the sea so as to die. It is surprising that Homer did not hit on that solution too. Whosoever sings and is not listened to dies. The singer who sings to deaf ears loses the reason for existence. Who can say whether someone has sung if no one listened? Is that the reason why song becomes silence for so many of those who sought to understand myth?

For Kafka silence is 'an even more terrible weapon than song'. 'It may be conceivable' – he reflects with subtle humour in the language of the insurance expert that he was – 'that someone could have escaped from their singing but certainly not from their silence.' Even Bertolt Brecht – and much of the Occident seems to have drawn on this myth – was fascinated by the idea of silent Sirens and their absolutely unproletarian arrogance, refusing the 'squandering' of their art on people 'lacking freedom of movement'. He maliciously asked whether that was 'the essential nature of art', but since he was not sure of his case he referred to Kafka, not to Homer.

Even the very first writer to comment on this myth wonderously silences the Sirens by transporting them to Heaven. According to Plato, they continue to sing there but earthly ears cannot hear them. In his *Politeia* they – eight in number and each a planet – no longer sit on the shore of the seas through which Odysseus ploughed. They are to be found in 'starry orbits' with 'a harmony resounding from all eight Sirens'. Aristotle indicates – in appropriately encoded fashion since his source was the secret knowledge of the Pythagoreans – that this heavenly harmony was 'the Tetrachord, the mode in which the Sirens sing'. There are two views about the nature of the Tetrachord governing the Pythagorean oath, seeing it as relating either a fourth, fifth, octave, and double octave, or an octave, fifth, fourth, and whole-tone.

The possibilities and variants – and there are a dozen more, not mentioned here – are 'numberless'. What is at issue is the fact that the heroes extolled by Homer were deaf and in chains, 'transmitters of looks'. The man who retold, and possibly invented, the myth was, however, according to legend blind. The blind singer Homer, a human being completely dependent on hearing. A 'receptive' person who 'absorbed' song his life long. Someone who knew what he wanted and what conflict he caused when he had the Sirens sing, made Odysseus's comrades deaf, and bound their captain.

Can we comprehend the 'bees-wax' in the ears of Odysseus's sailors and the ear-muffs stuffed over the heads of maintainers of aircraft and factory workers as the beginning and end of a development? Anyone who is shocked by that question should consider it at a later stage – perhaps at the end of the chapter on noise.

II
PLAYS FOR LISTENING AND SILENT FILMS

Let us attempt to proceed contrapunctually, for instance contrasting the 'scything eye' evoked by poet Saint-John Perse, like Homer 'by vocation a seaman' (Paul Claudel), with the 'particular tenderness of hearing' referred to by Jakob and Wilhelm Grimm. Let us take that as a starting-point, attempting to find our way from there towards our theme – and more besides.

Lorenz Oken, the nineteenth-century scientific researcher and philosopher, once wrote: 'The eye takes a person into the world. The ear brings the world into a human being.' The eye took Odysseus, the mariner, across the sea. The ear would have brought him to women, making him a lover.

Anthroposophist Diether Rudloff was of the opinion that

> . . . The eye is a peripheral sense because it is directed outwards and only comprehends the external person. The ear on the other hand is a central sense since the outer world enters the human soul through the ear, apprehending the concealed inner being. That can be demonstrated at any time in everyday experience since blind people are usually more inwardly sensitive, focused, and spiritual than those who can see. They are less easily deceived because they concentrate on the essential rather than being distracted. The deaf on the other hand are often much more distrustful, stolid, and isolated. They may see everything, but something that the blind possess in more concentrated form evades them. The deaf person may seem to possess the world but it has become silent, speechless, because he does not feel that world as an expression of his self. A blind man appears to have lost the world, but he lives wholly within himself and from there can feel his way out into the world.

Aristotle long ago observed that 'the blind are more understanding than the deaf because hearing exerts a direct influence on the formation of moral character, which is not immediately true of what is seen. The human soul can also become diffused by way of the eye whereas what is heard results in focus and concentration.'

Modern psychologists and neurologists confirm that very finding. A psychiatrist who first worked in a home for the deaf and dumb and then in an institution for the blind – and wishes to remain anonymous because of the personal nature of what follows – reports:

> It was a relief to come to the home for the blind. The institution for the deaf and dumb erupted with aggressions. You wouldn't believe what those people did to one another. How they were constantly charged with anger and fury. How murderous their looks were. The blind were much more reserved, cautious, ready to help, and sensitive, and tried much more intensely to understand and accept their fellows.

Helmut Reinold, who has devoted particularly careful thought and research to 'Problems in Hearing', speaks of 'the immeasurably greater psychological impact of deafness as opposed to blindness'. 'The blind man', writes Dr F. W. Koeppel, a specialist in ear, nose, and throat medicine, 'who excites all our compassion is ten times better off – because he is in contact with the world around and can seek sympathy there – than someone who may still see but no longer hear, feels himself misunderstood, and forced to creep back into his shell . . . Of the communicative senses hearing is clearly superior to vision.' One of the main reasons for that is that hearing picks up language, which is our most important communicative ability.

Let us compare the radio play (the German word means 'play for listening') and the silent film. Even the great masters of the silent film in the twenties did not succeed in putting across the totality of their works' message by exclusively cinematic means. They could not do without the occasional title conveying information about time ('Twenty years later') or place ('Back at home') otherwise impossible to communicate. Such titles were almost always important, making it possible to understand the story.

The radio play, on the other hand, transmits the entire story and all the information without resorting to non-acoustic assistance. Doesn't that signify that our ears can perceive more of the world than our eyes? Even great creative artists, such as Charlie Chaplin, were unable to compensate for that revelation of vision's inferiority, no matter how hard they tried.

Also worthy of mention in that connection is the fact that during the era of the silent film it was usual for the action to be accompanied, more or less dramatically, by pre-selected pieces of music or an improvising pianist or organist. The audience 'needed' an aural stimulus to complete an experience that would otherwise have been deficient. But no listener to radio plays would hit on the idea of looking at pictures so as to round off that experience.

III

COUNTING BY EAR

We see a colour and say *blue*, or perhaps more precisely *marine* or *indigo*. We can attempt to describe colour impressions as exactly as possible through differentiated use of words: carmine, maize yellow, tobacco brown, moss green, khaki, pink, cornflower blue, purple, Prussian blue. We can also try and define such colour tones in long and detailed sentences, but the spectrum of frequencies thus circumscribed rather than described is many times greater than in the acoustic sphere so that the inaccuracy of the eye is correspondingly greater.

We hear a note and – if we possess 'absolute pitch' – say: 'F sharp' or 'C', thereby precisely determining its frequency. Even if we do not have absolute pitch, or if we are 'unmusical', we immediately hear whether an octave is correct or not. We can register that the highest note within an octave vibrates exactly twice as fast as the lowest.

Our eyes cannot, however, inform us that, for instance, the wavelength of purple (760 nm) is twice that of violet (around 380 nm). If we want to know that, we must use complicated technical equipment to measure it. With sounds though our ear can measure for itself.

It must be of evolutionary significance that we have a capacity for 'absolute hearing' within the acoustic sphere whereas even the visually talented lack anything approaching an 'absolute visual sense'. The eye can only compare and estimate; the ear measures.

Linguistic capacity in the acoustic realm is accordingly much further developed than in the visual sphere. Language reflects what our senses supply. The eye yields incomplete information, which is why colour words are imprecise and cannot attain exactitude through additional description. When language has to express something vague, imprecise, or ostensible, it time and again resorts to words from the optical sphere: imagined (from the Latin *imago* = picture), illusory (from the Latin *lux* = light), semblance, etc. The ear, on the other hand, supplies data based on measurement, so language can be more exact when it reflects what has been heard.

'We can only speak of precise measurement, based on perception, in the acoustic sphere but not in the optical realm,' writes J. Handschin in his important book on *The Nature of Sound*, pointing to the fact that 'the correspondence between numerical and psychological reality . . . seems miraculous to us.'

To summarise: Both the ear and the eye can evaluate, supplying us with intellectual, psychological, and emotional information of qualitative relevance. But only the ear can measure, thereby mediating quantitative and numerically precise information. If the eye wants to operate quantitatively it can at most estimate, but – as we all know – it is only able to provide approximations, and very often miscalculates.

That is why the term 'optical illusion' exists in our language. Every painter, every physiologist, every interior designer, every illustrator, has experienced the many ways in which the eye deceives. In fact every single human being knows the necessity of that term. That is why language established it. There are also a few acoustic illusions but they are so rare that language did not develop any appropriate term. It is not needed.

Music therapists and music teachers often conduct the following experiment. A participant in their group is asked to estimate the length of a string in, say, a monochord. The teacher tells him first to estimate by eye where the mid-point of the string is. Measurement almost always shows that the visual estimate is inaccurate. Then the pupil is blindfolded and he is asked to judge by ear. He plucks the string – first the longer, deeper-sounding half, and then the shorter, higher section, moving the bridge until his hearing tells him that both parts sound the same. He puts the bridge there, and measurement usually demonstrates that the ear assesses more accurately than the eye.

Music, in Leibniz's opinion, is 'the concealed art of computation for a soul unaware of its counting'. No other locus, no other *topos*, within the senses at man's disposal is so directly linked with mathematics as the ear. We have two arms and two legs, two eyes and two ears, and twice five fingers and toes. The number two is the most striking of those incorporated in our body, symbolising sexual duality, preparing every human being for that right from the start, and informing us how we have to cope with it: $1 + 1 = 2$.

When the ear hears a note, it also takes in the associated harmonics, an infinite series of whole numbers (see Chapter 9) and their ratios: 1:2 with every heard octave (and also in many conversations between men and women), 2:3 with every fifth, 3:4 with fourths, 3:5 with the major sixth, 4:5 with the major third, 5:6 with the minor third, 5:8 with the minor sixth, and so on. The fact that this process takes place unconsciously does not affect its permanent presence. In fact it becomes all the more important for that very reason. The immediacy with which the ear transforms what is unconscious into consciousness – in every aspect of hearing – will be shown in the chapters that follow.

Nowhere else do numbers – the simple whole numbers with which we all start counting – penetrate us to the extent involved in the process of hearing. They physically enter the *cochlea* of the inner ear. With every sound that we hear we learn numbers. Early man knew that, perceiving it in the holistic, wise way which knowledge entailed for him. The old Indian and Indo-European linguistic root *ar-* signifies both harmony and number as in the Greek ἁρμονία (*harmonia*) = harmony, joining together, concord – and, on the other hand, ἀριθμός (*arithmos*) = series, number.

For hundreds of thousands of years sounds have fed us with numbers – with an immediacy and directness unparalleled in our other senses. It is inconceivable that this should not have become a genetic impulse, and – like all such impulses – have to be refined and differentiated. With such 'codes', refinement and differentiation inevitably entail mathematics. The ear thus 'taught' us counting, calculating, mathematical curves, and progressions.

This was one of the most difficult learning processes to which man was subjected during the course of his evolution, so the ear thereby taught us 'how to learn'. That is why – as Alfred A. Tomatis, the great French researcher into the ear and hearing, has shown – there are three times as many nerve connections between the ear and the brain as between the eye and the brain. Everyone finds out during their schooldays that we learn more through the ear than through the eye. Blackboards and all that film and video can offer in the way of educational aids are ultimately nothing but aids. The decisive factor is what the teacher says and what we take in through our ears.

That is no longer disputed now that the various techniques of 'Superlearning' are available. All of them – including the Losanov method developed at Sofia University in 1966 – function through the ear when the auditory sense develops its greatest capacity and our other senses are switched off (because they would distract us) rather than being set to work to 'help' us. That occurs in a state of complete relaxation, initiated by suitable music (usually Baroque music), so that our brainwaves are in an *Alpha* state. Neurologists agree that 'Alpha rhythms' are primarily an 'ear state', constituting the best condition for learning. It is also fun to learn in that way. It relaxes, refreshes, and regenerates.

More and more teachers and psychologists complain about the 'restlessness' and lack of capacity for concentration apparent among today's children. A connection probably exists between the greater focus of previous generations of schoolchildren and the fact that their input of information was primarily through the ear and listening to what their teachers said. It is in the nature of the eye to 'roam around', scanning rather than taking in. That is why excessive emphasis on eye-input causes restlessness, especially when eye and ear are simultaneously – and often divergently – appealed to.

We must, however, bear in mind that both hearing and seeing only provide us with partial aspects of the whole. Physiologists are of the opinion that they filter information about the world. They only tell us about what is absolutely necessary, about what the human species really needed in order to be able to survive and develop within the evolutionary process. The area our eye informs us about is also ten times more restricted than the auditory sphere. The deepest sound we can hear is around 16 hertz (1 hz = one frequency per second). If we double that frequency ten times – i.e. add ten octaves, we attain 16,000 hertz, thereby approaching the area where our capacity for hearing comes to an end.

The electromagnetic waves of the visual sphere are measured in nanometres (nm = one thousand-millionth of a metre) – and previously also in angstroms. Sound and electromagnetic waves differ, and measurements are not directly compatible. We can, however, establish a comparison by raising the octave level and hertz reading of the auditory sphere until we reach the realm of the visible. For that we require 35 octaves, reaching the beginning of the visual sphere at around 380 billion hertz. If we double that frequency just once, we attain 760 billion hertz where visibility comes to an end again.

The ear thus registers ten octaves and the eye just one.

All our senses are miraculous – and what the eye derives from its octave in the way of information and abundant experience is also marvellous. The eye would nevertheless have to be around ten times more efficient than the ear in order to make up for the limitations of its range – but, as we have seen, that is certainly not the case.

That also provides a partial explanation of why the ear, but not the eye, is capable of measurement. The frequency range of visibility is so limited that the eye does not need to deploy it for measurements. It can assess things at a glance. The ear, on the other hand, with a range ten times greater requires a capacity for measurement so as to find its way around, or else there would be a danger of failing to hear essential differentiations.

It is, however, that very capacity for measurement which makes the ear superior – and the eye cannot compensate for that superiority despite a remarkable gift for differentiation within its limited sphere.

IV
SEEING = SEEKING

Ear physiologist Manfred Spreng points out that the eye can put up with its greater inaccuracy. 'Unlike the eye the ear does not possess the possibility of scanning something several times. The spoken word is a rapid singular event, and can practically never be repeated in exactly the same way.' In its mode of working and decoding mechanisms the ear has to be sure immediately whereas the eye can look again – two, three, or four times – if there is uncertainty. The possibility of making a mistake has in fact become such a standard experience for the eye that it has got used to multiple scanning of objects of perception.

In the majority of cases the outcome of a specific act of seeing amounts to an approximate mean, based on the various scanning processes. The ear, on the other hand, has no such possibility. Hearing something once has to suffice since in the next second the speaker has moved several words further. That is to be experienced in any conversation – and we can even hear what is happening behind the words, picking up the slightest fluctuation of mood without ever having the possibility of rechecking.

It is thus all the more amazing that people today are so seldom aware of their ears' ability to measure and the accuracy of their hearing. Almost anyone asked about that would instinctively assume that the eyes are of course more accurate than the ears. Wherever modern technology sets about mastering acoustic phenomena and problems, it first expresses these in visually graspable tables and graphs, i.e. in the less precise – and for the auditory sphere inappropriate – realm of optical dimensions.

When I established the Berlin Jazz Festival at the start of the sixties, it became clear during the first concerts that the city's Philharmonie was only suitable for symphonic and chamber music, and not for jazz – despite all the time and money expended by such a celebrated architect as Scharoun. The civil servant responsible for such matters said that aspect had been 'overlooked', and brought me together with a group of acousticians who were commissioned to 'refurbish' the much-praised concert hall for jazz, folk, and rock. That was only achieved after various false starts and the passing of a number of years. I spent a long time working together with those experts, but only once was a sound actually to be heard – and that was the clapping of our hands so as to measure echo times rather than music. Those specialists – said to be the best in the Federal Republic of Germany at the time – represented the 'acoustic situation' in the Philharmonie by way of charts, graphs, diagrams, and statistics, and worked purely visually despite being concerned with something supposed to be heard. I assume that was the main reason why they took so long to solve the problem.

The Japanese acousticians who are supposed to measure and keep under control the 'noise pollution' around Shinjuku railway station, Tokyo's busiest and noisiest area, also operate optically, producing drawings, diagrams, and graphs – perhaps because they want to protect their own ears! They point to a graph and tell their visitors:

'Here you can *see* that the noise reaches a peak between 16.30 and 17.30.'

Anyone who has to deal with acousticians – say in radio stations – knows that most of them operate visually. Just imagine though what would happen if the designer of a stage set or a big department store's display areas were to rely primarily on acoustic data when endeavouring to please the eye. The hypertrophy of the visual in our time truly leads to strange absurdities!

A Swiss painter – and it had to be a painter – reminds us that we can see with the speed of light, i.e. with the greatest possible speed in this universe (300,000 km per second), but can only hear with the speed of sound (330 metres per second). The eye is everywhere! It has no specific location within the dimensions of our planet. That may also be one reason for its volatility, restlessness, and homelessness.

The ear, however, is unhurried – a thousand times slower than the eye. It takes time. It knows that speed is not significant since everything is 'here and now'. That is why it is more thorough and accurate. The ear finds. The eye seeks.

We live in a predominantly visual civilisation, so we tend to 'visualise' our senses. We even try and influence our taste nerves optically. That is why food is artistically 'embellished' in shop windows and restaurants. The advertising industry knows that average-quality, or even sub-standard, foodstuffs can be sold with great success – and especially to children – if skill is devoted to giving the 'product' an attractive appearance. Visualisation is even of significance in the realm of the modern gramophone record where optical criteria (brilliance, transparency, etc.) now predominate.

V
LOVE THROUGH THE EAR

Let us try to discover more about the 'particular tenderness of hearing'. For some twenty years now ethnologists have been marvelling at the Kalinga, a primeval people living on the Philippines. They marvel at them because the Kalinga experience so few social tensions, and lovers and marital partners are so remarkably gentle and considerate towards one another. There are certainly other peoples of whom that is also true – such as the Balinese or the Dogons of Mali in West Africa. In those cases, however, it was soon possible to determine why social tensions were so low. Gregory

Bateson, for instance, demonstrated the importance the Balinese assigned to 'problems of balance', 'diminishing the child's tendencies towards competitive and rivalrous behaviour', 'the substitution of a plateau for a climax', and the wish not to change or endanger social ranking, or to influence anyone socially. Above all, the Balinese strove to do things for their own sake rather than for money or prestige.

The Dogon – according to Swiss psychologists Paul Parin, Fritz Morgenthaler, and Goldi Parin-Matthey – are less aggressive than other peoples because they spare their children the trauma of weaning. The baby is carried on the hip and several women are usually available for breast-feeding, so it scarcely knows which its 'real' mother is. It calls all the women in the family 'mother', and moves from one hip and one woman to another. A naked, milk-giving breast is always within reach until the child – often only at the age of 3 or 4 – takes the initiative in seeking other contacts and forms of nutrition. From the very beginning the child relates to a group of people rather than to one or two individuals.

For many years, however, no explanation was found for the harmonious social behaviour prevalent among the Kalinga until they were by chance observed making love. For the Kalinga the ear – and particularly the male ear – is the most important secondary sex organ whose sensitivity by far exceeds what is felt by Western lovers. Kalingan love begins with touching, stroking, and kissing the ear, not with a kiss on the mouth.

Psychologists have shown that every time we kiss, we fall back into the orality of early childhood. When the first Western men came to Japan, they noted with astonishment that Japanese girls and women were unaware of the kiss. They had remained in ignorance for hundreds of years until they saw kissing in American films. Then they learnt to kiss within ten or twenty years – as quickly as they took up all the other 'blessings' the West brought them.

We also know that for Eskimos love is initiated with a rubbing of noses. Kalinga couples can get so excited about ear contact – without touching any primary sex organ – that they even attain orgasm. It could be said that they 'listen' to one another in the most intimate and precise way possible before doing anything else. Ethnologists ask whether that is the reason why they treat one another so gently and considerately. Is this a society where the commonplace Western reproach between husband and wife or lovers – 'You never listen to what I say!' – is almost unknown?

VI
PETRARCH ON MONT VENTOUX

It is not just since the arrival of television that Western man has
existed in an eye culture. Television is only a degenerate form.
Western culture has been 'visual' from the start – ever since the wax
in the ears of Odysseus's oarsmen. The Greek gods are gods of light.
Plato viewed 'seeing' as the 'highest sense', and in the fourth book of
The Republic extolled the eye as the most beautiful part of the body.

Leonardo da Vinci, the Renaissance man who believed in the
primacy of the eye, wrote what is perhaps the most beautiful among
many wonderful hymns to the eye:

> *Quanta bellezza al cor per gli occhi*. What beauty enters the heart
> through the eye! . . . See you not that the eye comprehends the
> worldly miracle entire, ruling astronomy, founding cosmography,
> and counselling all human arts . . . begetting architecture, perspective,
> and, at last, divine painting. Oh thou most excellent eye, elevated
> above all that God created! What exalted praises are capable of
> expressing thy nobility? What peoples, what tongues, can describe
> thy abilities? Through the window of the eye the soul regards the
> world's beauty. For the eye endureth the soul the prison of human
> form. Without the eye that prison were its torment.

Philosopher Jean Gebser sees Petrarch's ascent of Mont Ventoux
in Provence in the year 1336 as a key event in the development of eye
dominance in Europe, far beyond what had already been initiated
by the Greeks. At that time the Italian poet lived north-east of
Avignon near Vaucluse, which has become celebrated for its fountain
emerging so mysteriously out of the rocks. Petrarch loved and
extolled Laura who was 12 or 13 when he first saw her in an Avignon
church on Good Friday 1327, and until the end of his life he
commemorated that sighting as the epitome of purity and innocence.

Petrarch constantly had Mont Ventoux before his eyes. That
mighty mountain arose miraculously out of the hilly landscape
between the Alps and the Massif Central into what was already a
Mediterranean sky. No one 'expects' such a monumental peak there,
which is why the challenge of climbing it is so great. Petrarch
accepted that challenge. It is scarcely comprehensible that no one
had done so long before, but an old shepherd, who encountered the
poet and his brother Gherardo in a gorge at the foot of the mountain,
said he 'had never heard of anyone embarking on such a venture'.
The shepherd warned Petrarch against what he was undertaking.

One must have stood on top of Mont Ventoux oneself to appreciate what Petrarch's achievement signified. Gebser calls it 'epoch-making', and the poet himself spoke of 'a shock' where he felt 'as if petrified with terror' and 'transported out of space into time'.

From Mont Ventoux you look out onto a major European landscape: from the Alps in the north-east to the Mediterranean in the south – and even as far as the island of Corsica on days before the Mistral arises, and to the Pyrenees in the west. *Europa in nuce*. Somewhere in the haze the Atlantic is to be sensed. And the Mistral comes from Africa. Whenever I return to Goethe's 'watchman on the tower' in *Faust II*, 'born to see, ordered to look', I think of Petrarch on Mont Ventoux.

Jean Gebser has shown that awareness of perspective in seeing, painting, and drawing is profoundly connected with Petrarch's initial conquest of this mountain in Provence. It was at any rate at that time that a new awareness of space began to make its way in painting – as a synchronistically linked development rather than as a causal outcome of the mountain having at last been climbed. At that time, poets, painters, and also thinkers started to conquer space; and even musicians joined in – if one thinks of the way in which, say, Venetian composers set about 'playing' with the acoustics in San Marco a little later. For painters conquering space entailed confining three dimensions within two and forcing them onto a flat surface, i.e. painting in perspective.

In the whole of Greek and Roman literature – with the possible exception of Ovid – there are hardly any poetic descriptions of landscapes; and where they do exist they are just attempts and mostly inventories – 'a means of surveying a specific area for administrative and practical reasons' (Gebser). Not even that was to be found in the Middle Ages. Petrarch's climbing of Mont Ventoux was a triumph for the eye-dominated man. We know what landscape is ever since that day in the year 1336. Even Petrarch had some idea of the importance of his deed since in a celebrated letter to another brother he wrote that his ascent would 'certainly be of benefit for many'. Gebser views that day as marking the beginning of 'a new way of regarding nature, realistic, individual, and rational'.

As so often in the history of ideas, however, a 'deficiency' lay embedded in that development right from the start. 'From that day onwards human responsibility grew to such an extent that, confronted by the contemporary situation, we must doubt whether man was able to cope with it.' When he was on top of Mont Ventoux, Petrarch opened at random Augustine's *Confessions* – a heavy pigskin-bound volume he had carried up to the summit – so as to see what the Church Father had to say to him there, and reported: 'As God be my witness, my gaze fell on the following passage: "Men travel to wonder at the height of mountains, at the huge waves of the sea, at the long courses of rivers, at the vast compass of the ocean, at the orbits of the stars, and they pass by themselves without wondering." ' Petrarch was awe-struck.

Just two hundred years later, with the advent of Descartes and Bacon, people began to get some idea of why Petrarch had been so awe-struck, and why man was perhaps 'giving up' and had to be asked whether he could 'cope' with the situation. The space that the poet had caught a glimpse of as if it were a marvel, experienced as a mystery, transformed itself into the three-dimensionality of physical space, into the demand that we rely solely on what our eyes can see and measure within that space – as if man had banished the miraculous from the prospect from Mont Ventoux without asking whether anything then remained of the space concealing that wonder.

The development of European scientific thinking, launched by Descartes, Galileo, and Bacon, can be traced back to Mont Ventoux and the year 1336. That development took place within the visible, three-dimensional arena of space until time was added by Einstein six centuries later as a fourth invisible spatial dimension, leading to the unfolding of new ways of thinking, new ideas about space and matter, beyond what can be merely seen.

What began with Petrarch as a wonder and an unanticipated enrichment of human perspectives has become Gebser's 'deficiency' and degeneration. Space became more and more empty. The world became more and more empty. We all became more and more empty. The mystery vanished from space. The world lost its magic.

What got under way with *measuring* ended with *missing* – and once again one is shocked by the profundities of language since both those words derive from the same root, are basically still a single word originating in *metra* (womb), which is also the source of *mother*.

VII
HEAR, AND YOUR SOUL LIVES NOW

The unfolding of eye culture, the constantly intensifying dominance of seeing and the seeable, has despiritualised our existence. That runs parallel to the development towards rationalism and material-ism. People became ever less aware that our 'inner eyes' are just as important as the 'outer' organs, and that 'looking within' is as crucial as what we see externally. Plotinus, Plato's hellenistic descendant, reminded us that a human being cannot see the beautiful if the eyes have not previously been 'purified'. Goethe called for 'spiritual eyes', writing in the foreword to his *Theory of Colours* that 'Merely looking at something cannot develop us.'

For centuries we have only employed the ear as a 'subsidiary organ' utilised by the eye. Hearing is none the less the most spiritual of our senses – even physically as will become clear later.

Sesshin is the Zen name for six to ten days of meditation from 5 or 6 in the morning to around 10 in the evening with little sleep and even less to eat. No other practice promotes such powerful inner develop-ment, allowing us to experience the Sound of Being so intensely.

In the Japanese ideogram for *Sesshin* (page 25) it is immediately apparent that the three symbols at the top right are all the same. They all signify 'Ear'. The top left symbol stands for 'Hand', and the lower part of the ideogram signifies 'Heart'. Zen meditation thus entails: 'Listen! Listen! Listen! With Hand and with Heart!'

Humanity's great spiritual books – the Upanishads, the Koran, the Bible – are full of exhortations and instructions about listening. Jesus said: 'He that hath ears to hear, let him hear.' The words that serve as motto for this book, 'Hear, and your soul shall live', also apply to their mouthpiece, the prophet Isaiah, the 'greatest listener' among the Bible's great men. I see Isaiah as being naked when he spoke those words since that is how he preached after God told him: 'Go and loose the sackcloth from off thy loins . . . naked and barefoot' (Isaiah 20:2).

'Hearing' is referred to no fewer than ninety-one times in the first five books of the Old Testament. Time and again one reads: 'Now therefore hearken, O Israel.' The first mention of hearing in the Bible runs: 'And they heard the voice of the Lord God . . .' (Genesis 3:8) – and the last: 'And let him that heareth say, Come' (Revelation 22:17).

The Psalms proclaim: 'Today if ye will hear his voice', and 'Cause me to hear thy loving kindness in the morning'; but they conclude: 'They have ears, but they hear not.' Jeremiah urges: 'O earth, earth, earth, hear the word of the Lord.' And finally St John in the New Testament: 'Every one that is of the truth heareth my voice.'

That voice was there from the very beginning: the *primal voice*. It was that divine, creative voice which moved upon the face of the waters when God created the world.

EAR

HAND   EAR   EAR

HEART

The Japanese ideogram for *Sesshin*

According to the Cabbala, the ego feeds itself on visual images. People pray: 'O Lord, free us from the power of images.' God calls us to our vocation, and such a call cannot be seen but must be heard.

A verse in the Rig-Veda, the ancient book of Indian wisdom, runs:

> Breath of the Gods
> and life-cell of the world,
> He freely wanders.
> We devote
> our veneration
> to Him
> whose voice we hear
> but whose form
> no one sees.

The Upanishads tersely say: 'The Ear is the Way.' There is also frequent mention of Light and the eye, but the ear is the way.

The teachings about chakras in the Indian tradition put seeing in the third Manipura chakra in the navel area. That is the fire chakra which regulates our ego and will-power. Hearing, however, is centred in the Vishuddha chakra at the lower end of the neck, which is also responsible for communication and the voice. The ear is thus assigned to one of the higher chakras, and the eye to one of the lower chakras. The Kundalini energy must mount up the chakras from the lower to the higher.

Many spiritual traditions – Judaism, Islam, Zen, and many shamans – expressly forbid the making of an image of God and the divine since images and the eye excessively direct the attention outwards. Instead they say: Listen to the divine voice. You can hear what is within. Listen to the inner voice. People are not told: Look outwards – but possibly: Close the eyes and look inwards.

Listening words became less frequent as the West increasingly pursued rationalism. Seeing words predominated everywhere. Listeners constituted a minority, and were usually spiritual beings such as Sören Kierkegaard:

> As my prayer became more attentive and inward
> I had less and less to say.
> I finally became completely silent.
> I started to listen
> – which is even further removed from speaking.
> I first thought that praying entailed speaking.
> I then learnt that praying is hearing,
> not merely being silent.
> This is how it is.
> To pray does not mean to listen to oneself speaking.
> Prayer involves becoming silent,
> and being silent,
> and waiting until God is heard.

And Nietzsche declared in his main work, *Thus Spake Zarathustra*:

> Awaken and listen, you solitary ones!
> Winds are coming from the future
> with mysteriously beating wings,
> and good news is reaching sensitive ears.

Listen to all those declarations – to Isaiah for instance: 'Hear, and your soul shall live.' A young woman once asked me during a seminar: Why did the prophet Isaiah express that as a future event? Why are such consolations always in the future? Why not now? In fact all the great expressions of hearing and exhortations to listen within humanity's spiritual traditions amount to:

> *Hear, and your soul lives now!*

VIII
THE EYE SAYS I

For the Chinese the eye is a *yang* sense expressing the sun and masculinity whilst the ear is a *yin* sense embodying the moon and femininity. That is also apparent in the Western world. The eye thrusts out into the world, and in many cultures is symbolised by an arrow which has long been a phallic symbol. The ear is receptive, often compared with a shell, which in turn evokes the female sexual organ.

Eye culture – and its drawbacks – developed alongside the rise of patriarchy, and is also experiencing the latter's degeneration and decline. Early humans, living in a matriarchy, were – as Jakob Bachhofen (1815–1887) first pointed out – primarily focused on hearing. Viewed 'historically' the eye is the 'winner'. It is, however, appropriate that the culture of hearing and the miracle of the ear should be rediscovered at a time when patriarchy is losing power.

The sense of dominance associated with the eye-directed man has been most concisely expressed by Jakob Grimm: 'The eye is a master, the ear a servant.' It is clear that Grimm himself was one of the masters and did not consider reflecting on the negative implications of his declaration, which could be interpreted as: The eye coerces, the ear serves; the eye gives orders, the ear listens and obeys. In *Nada Brahma* I referred to the relationship between the human eye and the eye of the eagle, so passionately lauded as symbolising intense acuity of vision. It is not just chance that the eagle is so often to be found in the coats of arms and emblems of power-conscious states and cities.

In the English language the words *eye* and *I* sound absolutely similar, and can only be distinguished according to context. As Krishnamurti has stated: 'The eye says I.'

My eye may say I but it cannot see me; it cannot see my face, standing for my 'I'. Hardly anyone thinks about that. We can hear ourselves (especially as there is a direct channel from the throat to the inner ear so that sound does not have to travel out of the mouth and in through the outer ear); we can feel, smell, and taste ourselves; but in order to see myself, to see my face, I need a mirror, or a photograph of myself. The eye may say 'I! I! I!', but it says that to other people. It knows very little about me myself.

The 'I' is confronted by the 'Self', our essential being, called *Atman* in the Indian spiritual tradition. Know Thyself: that is the great task with which we are all faced – both in Eastern traditions (the Upanishads, Buddhism, Zen) and in Western thought from Socrates to C. G. Jung. The contribution that the eye makes towards fulfilment of this task is less than that of our other senses. The fact that the eye constantly thrusts outwards distracts us from self-knowledge and the way inwards. It dissipates attention.

I discovered in the language charts contained in the works of palaeo-linguist Richard Fester that the words for *eye* and *I* are directly related in many other languages – including the primal tongues of South American Indians and Australian aborigines.

The eye says I. We sense when someone is looking at us. Their gaze insists: Pay attention to me! Almost everyone is also aware of that when the observer is standing behind us. We notice after a while. Someone is there. Who is it? We would not, however, know if someone were listening to us if he or she did not say so.

The listener does not put the emphasis on himself or even the other person. He does not insist on a separation between subject and object. The ear establishes a 'more correct' relationship between ourselves and others. It implies unity rather than division.

IX
EYE AND EAR NEED ONE ANOTHER

Ear and eye are not alternatives. The objective remains what Rajneesh so marvellously calls 'democracy of the senses'. That has been lost as a result of the dominance of the eye. The eye has become a 'dictator'. I am only attacking the *hyper*trophy of seeing, the over-emphasis on the optical, and its degeneration, in our culture. I am shocked by the *hypo*trophy, the undervaluation, of the ear and hearing over the course of many centuries.

We think in terms of relationships. We see and hear in terms of relationships. The decisive, all-inclusive relationship for the ear is the relationship to the eye – and vice versa. Little or nothing is gained by merely enumerating the ear's many possibilities and capabilities without at the same time making clear (and demonstrating) their relationship to those of the eye.

A few examples. Reference to the auditory sphere's remarkable frequency range of ten octaves only becomes meaningful through computation in terms of the single octave available to the visual realm. Discussion of the ear's ability to evaluate subjectively and measure objectively only takes on significance in view of the fact that the eye can merely assess and comes no closer to mathematical accuracy than rough guesses. The significance of the ear's possession of three other important abilities apart from hearing – regulation of our sense of balance, 'feeding' mathematics into our sense organs, and the capacity for transcendence – will only become fully apparent when that relationship is clear. Our vision does not possess anything comparable.

Of course we can become aware that most of our languages derive precision, affinities, and safeguards from words concerned with hearing, but that only really becomes significant when a diametric-ally opposed trend towards superficiality, vagueness, and deception is found among seeing words: overlook, insincerity, fantasy, etc. The aggressiveness that psychologists have observed as an outcome of excessive emphasis on seeing only takes on its true aspect when contrasted with what our civilisation would gain if hearing were treated as being equally important. The outcome would be an intensification of receptivity, gentleness, femininity, understanding, discretion, openness, and tolerance.

I establish relationships because that is the only way of making meaningful statements – and not because I am against the eye. As always we need an Archimedian point. For the eye that is the ear; and for the ear the eye. In other words, establishment of a relationship is necessary. The ear is nothing without the eye, and the eye nothing without the ear.

We must make comparisons and reflect on what is involved – and not merely in utilitarian and evolutionary terms – when, dazzled by brightness, I can only see a lark, ascending up into the heavens on hot summer days, as a distant dot, but can hear its song as close and clear as a shower of notes pouring down on me. Or what does it signify that I can rarely see the nightingale, hidden amid leaves shimmering in the moonlight, but hear its song as if the moonbeams and the green of the wood were predestined for that.

I cannot help establishing relationships, although strictly speaking I do not in fact establish them: they already exist. And they are relationships, not alternatives. The directness of eye-dominated man also involves the belief that every relationship demands a decision from him, and that any choice in favour of something inevitably also involves a decision against the other pole, which is however only – and we will resort to this image time and again – the other side of the same coin. We can – and should – make use of both sides of the coin.

In my lectures and seminars I often encounter people who react aggressively to such assertions. They seem ready to accept anything – except any calling into question of the eye's dominance. I long asked myself why that was so before the answer became clear to me. It is the aggressiveness of the eye-person that answers me there, the aggressiveness of someone who knows that he is still dominant and does not want to lose control. The aggression of those who feel attacked confirms that finding. If that were not the case, something would be wrong.

Eye people taking part in discussions display strikingly more aggressiveness than ear-orientated participants, who are more 'tranquil', reflective, and patient, consider what they say more carefully, and are generally balanced.

People who mainly depend on what they see feel that everything they believe in has been undermined if seeing and hearing are compared to the advantage of the latter. The opposite reaction does not occur. For centuries ear people have had to undergo the ear's submission to the eye, and yet there are no reports of their having succumbed to aggression.

Eye people think causally – in those straight lines demonstrated to them by light; and it is that kind of thinking which results in the mistaken conclusion that an either/or is at issue, as if we should close our eyes and henceforth only open our ears. We want to perceive and experience more, not less. We want to extend and deepen our awareness, not restrict it.

There is no question of suppressing our visual sense as hearing was stifled for centuries. What is important is at long last to explore, develop, and cultivate the potentialities of the ear and of hearing to the same degree as the possibilities inherent in seeing have been developed in our culture for centuries – up to the point of hypertrophy in the television age.

What is important is to be a participant rather than continuing to be merely a spectator – a participant as comprehended by theoretical physics, which has demonstrated that we perceive reality wrongly if we believe we can observe it as onlookers. We are in its midst, and we take part in it. That too is a discovery which was made as long ago as the twenties so one must time and again ask: Why do we not draw the obvious conclusions? We otherwise pounce on all of modern science's achievements, incorporating them in our thinking and our lives within three or four years. But we resist those discoveries in the New Physics that tell us: You must change the way you perceive things. Ways of perception after all always entail ways of living.

We have not even *incorporated* the dual character of light – as a wave and as a corpuscle – in our body-sense and consciousness. We are still subject to the eye man's illusion that a decision has to be made between wave and particle. We would become gentler and more receptive, 'listening' more completely, if we were to comprehend – in our deepest being rather than intellectually – that the particle can change into a wave, and the wave can solidify into a corpuscle and then dissolve again; and that all these processes are dependent on the perception of the observer whom the very fact of perception makes into a participant who can make waves of particles and particles of waves.

For that we must of course once again learn to see anew. We cannot, however, achieve that by continuing to give precedence to seeing while suppressing our other senses. We possess a venerable tradition of seeing, going back by way of Goethe, Newton, and the Renaissance to the Greeks – but we do not have any comparable Western tradition as far as hearing and the ear are concerned. That must still be created, bearing in mind that the fact of being primarily eye people brought us to our present crisis.

Futurologists and physicists join spiritual people in saying that we need a new consciousness, a new perception of the world, if we want to survive. We can acquire that consciousness in a variety of ways. In the sixties when it started to unfold, many of us got there through LSD, cannabis, etc. For many people that was important, and they thereby came to realise the existence of another reality 'beyond' and 'within' which had previously been unknown to them. Today we no longer need drugs to transcend our everyday dimensions. An abundance of better procedures has become available, and for that very reason it is now clear that there is no more plausible, 'more natural', way towards a new consciousness than at long last opening up the ear and hearing in the same way as the eye and seeing have already been developed in our culture.

In the existing situation greater emphasis must be put on the ear and hearing than on the eye and seeing. Such one-sidedness is always necessary in the case of new departures. In the same way feminism must exaggerate its arguments if there is to be the slightest chance of ultimate attainment of equality of rights. Socialism had to be over-emphasised too in order to eliminate at least the worst exploitation in the industrial civilisation of capitalism. No idea would ever have been implemented if it had not initially been exaggerated.

Ever since the age of Newton and Descartes we have existed in a culture that put excessive emphasis on the eye. The time has now come to over-accentuate the ear for a couple of generations. We will perhaps then end up by achieving a 'democracy of the senses'.

X
HE WHO HAS EARS TO HEAR SEES!

When we have learnt to hear we will also be able to correct our eyes' hypertrophy.

The Indian spiritual world has far more to offer than the West with regard to interconnections between the ear and the eye, and between seeing and hearing. Prajapati, the primal creator, is 'singing Light', a 'singing sun', and 'the sound of Light'. Radiant Light is also transformed into sound in the Tibetan Book of the Dead:

> O nobly-born, when thy body and mind were separating, thou must have experienced a glimpse of the Pure Truth, subtle, sparkling, bright, dazzling, glorious, and radiantly awesome, in appearance like a mirage . . . From the midst of that radiance, the natural sound of Reality, reverberating like a thousand thunders simultaneously sounding, will come. That is the natural sound of thine own real self. Be not daunted thereby, nor terrified, nor awed.

'The world began with a sound.' Anthropologist and musicologist Marius Schneider discovered that truth in the myths and legends of many peoples, but – he stresses – this sound often has 'the character of light'. 'All light is merely a passing manifestation of the sound of creation. The sun is . . . only a sound that has become luminous and hot.'

Kabir knows no higher praise for Krishna's flute than to affirm that its song is 'as light as a thousand suns'.

The idea of an intermingling of lights and sounds, of inner seeing and inner hearing, has time and again suddenly appeared across the millennia. That is an archetypal concept, instilled in us from the very beginning.

The further we penetrate into humanity's early history, the more important inner hearing and inner seeing become, and the more frequently seeing and hearing come together. In many of humanity's languages there are words whose meaning is ambivalent, embracing both light and sound as well as seeing and hearing.

The word enlightenment signifies an expanded form of perception dependent on neither ear nor eye, a form of perception that penetrates the deceptive filter our senses impose between ourselves and reality. Japanese Zen monks call that *Kensho* (meaning inner vision and gazing on the essence) whose root *kan* in many languages entails aspects of hearing and in others also of seeing.

For Jakob Böhme, the German mystic, the light manifesting in enlightenment was a resounding sound. He experienced enlightenment as a filling with inner sound. The 'eyes of the spirit' about which so many sages speak were at the same time also 'ears of the spirit'.

He who has ears to hear sees!

The word *mystic* comes from the Greek *myein* = close the eyes. Ever since ancient times mystics have, however, been viewed as human beings who see more.

According to Sufi tradition 'Seers are blind'. They really are too. Not only Homer was blind. Oedipus was as well after he really understood what he had done. Some people believe that Pythia, the Oracle's prophetess at Delphi, Cassandra at Troy, and Calchas with whom the Iliad begins were also blind. There have been blind seers in many cultures – in India's Brahmanic tradition, among Taoists and Zen sages, among Sufis and in Eastern European Jewry, among Germanic peoples and the Celts – both in ancient times and even today. At the beginning of the sixties, for instance, a blind 'prophet' was much in demand on Bali.

Time and again, across millennia, the seer is said to be a seer *because* he is blind. Blindness intensifies the gift of prophecy. It is impossible to imagine a corresponding situation with any of the other senses. It would be absurd to say that a gourmet lacked any sense of taste, a connoisseur any sense of scent, or that a listener was deaf – but seers are blind.

As we have seen, Homer, the blind singer, was a man who listened. That is the reason why he was one of 'the most seeing' of men and could describe Odysseus, the eye man, as if he, Homer, could see with his hero's eyes. And that is certainly what he did, gaining vision through and in Odysseus. That is the objective – and it is marvellous to experience how everything suddenly once again becomes visible and attainable, seeing as a listener and listening as a man who sees. The new Odysseus no longer needs any chains. His companions do not require any wax in their ears. They hear what they want and travel where they wish.

2

WE SEE THREE DIMENSIONS BUT HOW MANY DO WE HEAR ?

'The human eye cannot see most of the lights in this world. What we perceive of surrounding reality is distorted and weakened by our organ of vision.'

Lincoln Barnett

I
RELATIVITY ISNT A PROBLEM FOR THE EAR

The most convincing demonstration of the eye's fallibility and the illusions to which looking is liable comes from modern theoretical physics. Ever since Planck, Einstein, and Heisenberg – in other words for over three quarters of a century now – we know that we perceive the world wrongly. It is not restricted to the three dimensions – length, breadth, and height – we see, but is multi-dimensional.

Many physicists today take six dimensions as their starting-point; some say that time is a miscomprehended spatial dimension; others surmise that there are as many temporal as spatial dimensions; and still others speak of '*n* dimensions', not wanting to specify the actual number involved.

At any rate, the world is not as we see it, as it 'appears' to us. But which sense is it that mediates that wrong image of the world?

The answer is absolutely certain. Most of the relatively misleading information comes from our most outwardly directed sense – the eye. The more our potential for perception is directed inwards, the less incorrect information we receive. The ear therefore provides a relatively low level of misinformation – viewed both subjectively and in terms of the findings of modern theoretical physics. It is true that we can hear 'spatially' (as indicated by the term *stereo*, which derives from the realm of vision) but spatial hearing is only a side-effect, as it were – a concession to the eyes confirming their functioning: what we heard there comes from the right or left, above or below, in front or behind. Those points of *view* are not of great importance as far as the actual experience of hearing is concerned. What the ears hear is not dependent on whether the world is – as our eyes think – three-dimensional or whether it is – as the New Physics believes – four-, five-, or even more multi-dimensional. When we consider that this also applies to our senses for taste and smell, we can measure the extent of the misinformation that our eyes give us about the dimensionality of our world.

Music has long been viewed as an 'art in time'. All our auditory impressions occur within a temporal continuum, and yet also unfold in spatial dimensions (see also Chapter 3). To measure amplitudes and frequencies we need spatial dimensions, but we nevertheless perceive them in music as temporal phenomena.

What we hear thus occurs in a multi-dimensional world of space and time, comparable with what we know from the theory of relativity and the Minkowski equations, which we find so difficult to approach when we rely solely on seeing. For our ears, on the other hand, such a world is everyday reality.

II
INFINITY AND THE EAR

As early as 1908, Elsie von Cyon, the Russian scientist, showed in his trail-blazing work *The Labyrinth of the Ear as an Organ for Expression of the Mathematical Senses in Space and Time* that the ear is capable of perceiving both space *and* time:

> The spatial and temporal qualities of the sense of hearing are of much greater importance – thanks to the inner ear's sensitivity to location – than their counterparts in the spheres of touch and vision. We owe . . . the concept of the infinitude of space to those perceptions. Direction is in its very nature indivisible and unlimited. It is to perceptions of sound or resonance, supplying us with knowledge about numbers, that we owe our concept of the infinity of time since numbers can essentially be developed infinitely.

In his *Definition of Life and the Organism*, Jakob von Uexküll characterised as a 'concept of genius' what Cyon described in sober scientific language. The ear is seen as the central switchboard for our sense of space and time, *and* for going beyond that to infinity. The wheel thus comes full circle, linking the insights and knowledge of wise men from many cultures. For them the ear has for thousands of years been our 'gateway to other worlds'.

The ear takes in music as an art in time but it also locates us in space. In the labyrinth of the inner ear, known as the semicircular canal, is to be found the most important of our receptors of balance. It regulates all the others distributed throughout the body, and is the only receptor that can measure angular velocity and never sleeps. It is thanks to this function that when we wake up, we immediately know how we are lying, even when still half asleep. The inner ear even remains on the alert when we are sleeping – unlike all the other senses which switch off then.

It is indisputable – summarised Cyon back in 1908 – that 'the ear is the most important of our sense organs'. Helmut Reinold commented: 'The fact that such a decisive discovery, establishing hearing as man's most central and highest sense, was not accepted or suitably acknowledged by anatomists, physiologists, and psychologists, let alone musicologists, can only surprise someone unfamiliar with the mechanistic emphasis within nineteenth-century scientific development.' However Reinold also draws attention to recent changes in otiatry (medicine of the ear), biology, anatomy, and physiology, and reminds us how Marius Schneider's musicological research demonstrated 'the central significance of the ear in primal cultures' view of the world', and how in Chinese philosophy hearing is 'the only sense endowed with capacity for comprehension'.

Our hearing comes closer than any other sense to at least the possibility of perceiving even the *n*-dimensional space in the most recent physics. Perhaps it does perceive that. We cannot know. We do, however, know of the eye that it cannot do so since it only sees three dimensions and feels – as anyone experiences who tries to think in terms of the relativity theory – that multi-dimensionality is absurd and 'illogical'.

III
BABY IN THE EAR

Austrian composer Josef Matthias Hauer, who developed a 'twelve-note system' even before Schoenberg, once declared that 'The man who listens is from the outset a spiritual being compared with the person who merely speaks, sees, and grasps. Hearing and taking in are spiritual activities: hearing the unchangeable, the untouchable, the incomprehensible, the constant, the eternal within the Melos. Only someone who listens can also recognise, interpret, think, speak, apprehend, and comprehend.'

We can be totally within our ear – as is not possible with our other senses. We can be our ear. We are our ear. In the words of *Shiatsu* teacher Wataru Ohashi: 'If you look at the ear, you will see that it is formed exactly like an embryo, which is why it can be viewed as a microcosm for the entire body.' In shape the ear is like an upturned 'little human being'. It is fitting that – as ear physiologist S. S. Stevens has shown – the organ of Corti, the most important element in our hearing, developed directly from the embryo's skin. Morphologically the ear *must* therefore possess the same potential for full human development as the embryo. The ear even intensifies that possibility since the cochlea in the inner ear – as Carl Gustav Carus (1789–1869) demonstrated in his *Symbolism of the Human Form* – again repeats the shape of the auricle, and thus of the embryo. Carus wrote that one cannot observe the 'characteristically convoluted structure' of the auricle 'without seeing it as a kind of symbolic repetition of the cochlea, the most deeply concealed and mysterious organ of hearing'.

It is logical that the embryo should be similar to the ear. The embryo *wants* to hear. Alfred A. Tomatis, the great French ear specialist, points out that the embryo starts to develop rudimentary ears within a few days of impregnation when it is just 0.9 mm long. It still derives everything from the mother but wants to have its own ears. The cochlea, the organ of hearing, is fully developed and has reached its ultimate size four and a half months after fertilisation. We grow until we are 17, 18 or 19 years old but the cochlea completes its growth before we are even born – 135 days after impregnation. During the first months of existence, the most important thing for the embryonic creature is to be able to hear for itself – to be all ears.

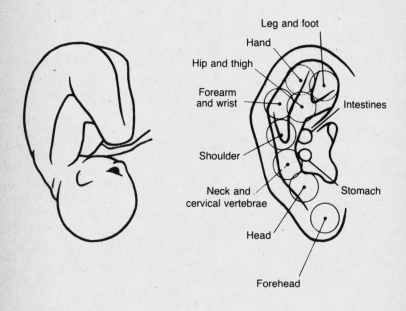

Embryo and diagram of acupuncture points in the ear (after Ohashi)

3

THE EAR GOES BEYOND

On the Miracle of Hearing

I
THE EAR AS HALL OF MIRRORS

Transcendence entails going beyond. It is a favourite word among Christian theologians who employ it with reference to the metaphysical and the hereafter. The implication is of a crossing from one sphere to another – as for instance from the audible to the inaudible.

The ear goes beyond. It hears and *is* ear because it goes beyond – in a never-ending succession of processes of going beyond, starting with the impact of sound on the cochlea and leading to transcendence of the finite into the infinite. All those processes dovetail together. No other organ offers anything comparable. The impression is that every going beyond stands – morphologically as well as symbolically – for any other, as if the ear 'reflected' such transcendences. They behave as if they were in a hall of mirrors where everything multiplies itself with its own reflections. That which reflects and that which is reflected are so interlinked that they cannot be distinguished from one another.

II
WE HEAR MORE THAN WE BELIEVE

The realm of the audible lies between 16 and 16,000 hertz, but René Chocholle, the French physiologist, shows in his study of 'Qualitative Hearing' that those figures are 'highly theoretical'. 'The upper limit is difficult to ascertain since capacity to distinguish between high frequencies differs greatly.' Experiments demonstrated that ultrasound from 30,000 to 50,000 hertz can, 'if sufficiently intense', actually produce experiences of hearing, albeit 'painful and unpleasant'. Chocholle compares that pain with what can be caused by a high-pressure steam jet. He and other acousticians are of the opinion that the fact that this sensation is painful 'calls into question its acoustic character . . . It could just as well be a feeling of pain caused within the ear, similar to what results from audible high-intensity sounds.'

Other researchers have expressed the view that ultrasound can be perceived because it derives from the existence of 'undertones', i.e. of 'whole number fractions of the basic frequency'. The traditional idea that only overtones can be heard has been abandoned. Many acousticians believe that the existence of a series of audible harmonics demands a parallel series of 'undertones' which are 'too faint to be established experimentally even though their absolute value could be high enough to make them audible' (Chocholle). As early as 1856 in a lecture to the Paris Academy of Sciences, Duhamel pointed out that sounds deeper than the bottom note on the deepest string could be produced on the violin . . . Later 'electro-acoustic examination revealed up to four notes in the undertone series on the G string, and up to twenty in an unbroken series on the E string.' Henri Bouasse attained similar results for wind instruments in 1929. Martin Vogel summarises in his *Theory of Sound Relationships*: 'Undertones really do exist, comparable with the harmonics found everywhere, but their intensity and frequency of occurrence in no way match that of the overtone series.'

The realms of the audible vary subjectively. For older people – and often from the 50th year onwards – the upper limit moves appreciably downwards. Others are capable – through training or natural ability – of considerably extending the limit upwards. Anyone who works a lot in sound studios constantly meets people who hear aspects of music that others are unable to perceive. If that is checked, it usually turns out that such tonal vibrations really are present where they were heard. Sometimes they are important and must be emphasised so that they become audible for others.

It is also difficult to determine the lower limit to hearing. Here too it becomes clear that the sensation of hearing does not simply vanish – as does the perception of light in specific, relatively determinable frequency ranges – but is instead transformed into a vibratory sensation 'such as one can also bring about in any other part of the body through contact with a vibrating object . . . One thus moves without noticing from a predominantly but not exclusively acoustic sensation to a predominantly and even exclusively vibratory sensation. Distinguishing between these two modalities in this transitional area is scarcely possible and highly subjective . . .' (Chocholle).

III
BRIDGING THE GAP

It is already apparent that one should not speak about 'audibility' without being aware that audibility and inaudibility overlap (see Chapter 11). A very low and no longer audible sound generates higher vibrations so that we also hear the harmonics of what is no longer perceptible. Interestingly the lowest audible sound in such a harmonic series can take on – in strangely irrational fashion – the character of a base note from which an additional series can develop. We thus take as a 'base' something that in 'reality' (and what *is* reality in this 'hall of mirrors'?) is not one.

A corresponding process creeps in at the other end of the scale. If we start out from a sound which is so high that it is no longer audible, assuming that this sound generates lower vibrations, then the harmonic series thus created must at some stage enter the realm of the audible. We then hear – physically rather than merely figuratively – traces of the inaudible.

IV
MICROSCOPIC PRECISION

Even morphologically the ear's dimensions symbolise the fluctuating frontiers between, on the one hand, what is perceptible and can be measured, and, on the other, the imperceptible and immeasurable. The actual organ for the distribution of sensations within the cochlea – with the organ of Corti, the basilar membrane, and the inner and outer hair cells – is 'a system only a few cubic millimetres in size whose minute scale and vulnerability have up to now resisted examination to a very much greater extent than the relatively large and easily investigated human or animal eyeball' (W. D. Keidel). Some 30,000 nerve fibres and as many nerve cells are at work in the human inner ear. The activities of the tympanic membrane 'operate at an order of magnitude of 19^{-9} . . . which is below the wavelength of viable light and even less than the diameter of a hydrogen atom. The energy threshold of the sensitivity of hair cells and auditory fibres fluctuates around 10^{-11} *erg*, and is thus many times greater than that of the eye but also much more durable. It can in fact vary between still tolerable intensities and the greatest noise levels by a factor of 10^6, a magnitude of millions.' If we were to similarly increase the eye's lowest tolerance, we would be so dazzled as to immediately go blind.

Experts still cannot explain how it is possible that movements of the head or jolting when walking do not affect the auditory ossicles in such a highly sensitive organ, thereby setting off mistaken perceptions of hearing. Some scientists are of the opinion that the malleus, incus, and stapes, three small interlocking bones in the inner ear, are so delicately positioned (their support lines run through their own centres of gravity) that they are perfectly cushioned. Nature has strikingly separated the cochlea – and above all the organ of Corti – from the body's usual lines of supply. Other specialists point to the fact that an organ which can register amplitudes even less than the diameter of a hydrogen atom must pick up both movements of the head and the vibrations constantly produced through all our activities, but possesses a kind of 'secret intelligence' for filtering out whatever is disruptive or irrelevant.

V
SOUND EXALTS TIME

Let us devote attention now to what happens when sound vibrations penetrate the ear. They encounter the eardrum, which starts to vibrate, as does the air affecting the thin membrane between the auditory canal and the inner ear. The tympanic membrane projects and transports sound into the interior of the ear where it meets the auditory ossicles, which are the smallest bones in the human body. They are linked by joints, and actually correspond to the bone structures of legs and feet strangely miniaturised. The organs within the inner ear lie in the petrous part of the temporal bones, the hardest and least alive bones in the entire human body. That is the location of the bony cochlea in whose fluid the membranous cochlea is suspended. Both cochlea are spiral-shaped, and these are logarithmic spirals which the dictionary defines as 'transcendental open curves starting out from a single point and ending in infinity'. This form is of importance because the ratio between the intervals and the associated numerical frequencies (ultimately between musical and acoustic laws) precisely matches the ratio between the logarithms' additive regularity and the multiplicative regularity of the underlying *Numeri*. The cochlea spirals in our ear constantly allow logarithmic processes to take their course, transforming the frequency of oscillations in sounds or music into intervals.

The fact that the cochlea is a spiral means that it transports perceptible vibrations out of the material world by way of open, mounting curves – ultimately into infinity. The existence of two cochlea constantly enables the membranous organ to reflect even the scarcely measurable vibrations of its bony counterpart, intensifying them into something beyond physical registration.

Sounds – writes German physiologist Ernst-Michael Kranich – penetrate 'the depths of the cochlea like a breaking wave' but then – as shown in experiments by Georg von Békésy (1899–1972), the Hungarian-American physiologist who won the Nobel Prize for Biology in 1961 and is probably the most important researcher into human hearing – there occurs 'an exceptionally significant process. The "travelling wave" breaks up . . . It is as if the wave that penetrated the inner ear were all of a sudden to lose its strength.' Something very strange happens. The power, which only millimetres previously on the short stretch between the tympanic membrane and what is known as the oval window was around 90 times greater, liberates itself from its physical substance. 'The sound frees itself from its physical impact . . .'

I refer here only to sounds with a musical component. In the cochlea such sounds liberate themselves from the physical body. From then onwards their purely musical and purely artistic quality is transcended in a spiritual sphere 'beyond the senses' which 'establishes' this process in such compelling fashion that it can be said to 'prove' it.

VI
MUSIC - ART IN TIME?

We have seen that music is art in time. The eye has long been said to be concerned with space and the ear with time. That is correct – and yet also incorrect. It is correct with regard to the spatial nature of seeing, but a spatial element is also present in what can be heard, and particularly in music. For a start it is present in sound vibrations, which occur in space. Music transforms them into time. But distinctions must be made when the concept of time is applied to sounds. Imagine the following: We hear a note when a bell is struck, allowing it to persist, and then we hear another note when a second bell is struck. We observe that we do not just perceive the two different notes but also the interval between them – for instance, a third or a fifth. Ernst-Michael Kranich sensitively perceived that:

> This does not entail musical memory . . . First you hear one note and then another. That is how you regard the succession of notes within the usual concept of time. This does not, however, yield a complete description of the phenomenon since the first note is somehow involved in the experience of the second note. Otherwise you could not recognise it as a third or fifth. The first note has faded away into the past, and yet out of that past, where it experienced full tonal reality, it exerts an influence on the presence of the second note.

We also see from this example that music does not merely take place within time. It also exalts and surmounts time. It is not just that the past and present merge. The future is also involved to the extent that within the harmonious progression of music the note sounding 'now' anticipates the future note in which it will be resolved. The note to come is, as it were, contained in the present note, which could not otherwise 'summon' it. Anyone musical knows that it is hardly possible to break off certain cadences before the final note. The final note is 'there' whether it is played or not. It may sound out later – or not at all – but, viewed in a higher sense, it was to be heard much earlier. Time only completes what became necessary outside of time. It merely makes manifest what would otherwise have remained hidden.

Kranich says that musical events are not to be grasped by way of our customary concept of time.

> Even in the simplest of musical phenomena man experiences that higher reality otherwise only to be found in encountering the spiritual world. A man thus experiences the lawfulness of the super-sensory when an interval leads him to perceive that the previous note is exerting an influence on the present one. If a previous experience did not exert such an influence, there would only be an unrelated succession of sounds.

What has been said with regard to individual notes also applies to more extended passages of music. All previous notes play a part in the current one. The fact that we can hear a succession of notes as a melody is only possible because in perceiving this melody we surmount time. Harmony and melody result from the influence exerted by what is past on an ever-new present.

In a poem about the music of a flute-player, Hermann Hesse wrote: 'And all time became present,' and in a letter written shortly afterwards he spoke of that line being 'the final outcome of many years of speculation about the essential nature of music. It seems to me that, viewed philosophically, music is time made aesthetically perceptible. As the present. And the identity of the present moment and eternity once again becomes apparent.'

Music is only art in time in a superficial sense. Viewed more profoundly it is the art of surmounting time in time.

Our visual sense leaves what we see where it is. It comes to terms with space. It merely looks. Our experience of hearing does not, however, acquiesce in time. It hears time but simultaneously more than time. It can hear what is past and what is future as something present. It thus accords with the demands of many great spiritual traditions – such as Zen or Tantrism – that one should live 'Now' because past and future are *Maya*, are illusions. For theoretical physics too they are also frequently illusions.

VII

HEARING ENTAILS QUANTISING

It might be asked whether the reader is fully aware of how many processes of going beyond we have encountered on the few pages of this and the previous chapter. Implicit in such processes is a capacity for self-transcendence, so the total number of 'goings beyond' in our hearing's 'hall of mirrors' is infinite. That basically only depends on where I allow one to end and another to begin. Perhaps everything is a single transcendence that goes beyond and beyond and beyond itself, reflecting, reflecting, reflecting itself: what can be felt into what can be heard, the audible into the inaudible, the additive into the logarithmic, the measurable into the immeasurable, the physical into the mental, the sensory into the supersensory, the material into the vital, the bodily into the spiritual, time into space, past into future and both into the present, three-dimensionality into multi-dimensionality, the aperiodic into the periodic, the symmetrical into the asymmetrical, and of course always vice versa.

And yet anyone who generalises that it is simply the 'absence of leaps' which characterises the essence of the hearing process deceives himself. Interestingly, the ear only establishes such transitions where and when transcendence is involved in terms of the transformation of one sphere into another. Before that stage is reached the ear constantly resists smooth transitions, so that the 'linking function' between areas which to the mechanical understanding are almost totally unrelated becomes all the more important. Where the ear cannot transcend it insists on 'quantising'. In the most favourable condition 231 different notes can be registered in an octave, but our ear insists on hearing them as the usual seven notes in the scale plus the linking semitones. Discrepancies may amount to as much as 40 per cent, i.e. we can hear a completely 'different' note but our ear gently forces us to perceive that as the appropriately 'correct' note. The ear 'quantises'.

It is important to be aware of the fact that there is no optical equivalent of 'compensatory hearing'. We see colour impressions as what they are with smooth transitions from one to another, but we hear notes as leaps without such gradual changes.

For centuries we were told *Natura non saltat*, but our ears, basic research into harmonics, nuclear physics, and music convince us of the opposite. In the decisive processes nature makes nothing but abrupt transitions. The old belief was another of the illusions resulting from dominance of the visual. It must have been eye men who thought up the maxim 'Nature does not proceed in leaps'. That idea was in fact only 'valid' in 'self-evident' spheres at a time when man was primarily visually orientated. We would have long ago recognised the crudity and imprecision of that view if we had not denied the ear its due for three centuries.

VIII
The Ear Finds Crossing-Places

It is very important to recognise the difference between the ear's capacity to go beyond and its supposed lack of ability to differentiate. The eye needs to deploy spectral analysis in order to ascertain the colours contained within an overall impression. It could not cope with that task by relying solely on its own resources. A good musician can, however, both take in the overall sound and also – without resorting to any technical assistance – state precisely what notes and instruments produce the chord at issue. The ear's ability to go beyond does not therefore in any way eliminate distinctions or reduce the capacity to differentiate.

No scientist has to date been able to explain how it is possible, on the one hand, for the sum total of sound vibrations surrounding us to impinge on our eardrum, and, on the other, for our ear to be able to 'sort out' all those vibrations, locating and measuring them even in a noisy café. Fragments of conversation come from the table diagonally behind me and from the window-seat opposite. There is also the noise of cars on the busy street outside. To my left glasses clink and far behind me a door is slammed – but even though the sound at a nearby table of a suitcase being shut is very similar to that of the door, I can distinguish between the two and also estimate that the one sound is about three metres away and the other ten.

The ear's capacity to transcend is not therefore linked with incapacity to make distinctions or the obliteration of transitions. As we have seen in various contexts, it differentiates more meticulously and precisely than our other senses. We can therefore assume that even when the ear transcends it does not stop making distinctions, in other words it does not bring together realms that are unconnected but builds bridges where necessary in order to open up connections and transitions, making us aware of the possibilities involved.

The idea of 'going beyond' need not always signify transcendence; it can also entail something similar to crossing a river. The ear shows us crossing-places so that we can get from one bank to the other. It shows them to us precisely where our other senses believe that there are insurmountable barriers. If our ear did not constantly offer us crossing-places – transitions and possibilities of transcendence – we would really live in a walled-in world, enclosed by actual material barriers that can be seen, felt, and grasped. Mechanistic and rational thinking exists in such a world – or, more precisely, since such a world does not exist, that way of thinking has attempted to create it and banish us there. By viewing things in that way, such thinking has made the world smaller, reducing it to what can be seen, felt, and measured. It did not accept the crossing-places indicated by the ear. The new thinking, however, makes use of these crossing-places.

4

THINKING THROUGH THE EAR

Suite on Essentials

'Thought is a *Fair* Hearing.'
Martin Heidegger

I
TWO THEMES

Two themes are prominent in this book:

1. To hear = To be.
2. All is One.

Both concepts are interrelated. Being is only Oneness. A human being who listens hears and understands that. Just remember: When we sleep, we close our eyes and mouth. Feelings are switched (almost) off. But our ears remain open.

Our ears have even been opened before we are born. The ear is more important than the other senses in the stage before birth.

Consciousness. Within a few weeks of impregnation the embryo develops its ears. The child in the womb hears its mother's heartbeat and later also the sounds of the world outside – which signifies that before a human being can perceive 'the world' with any other sense, he or she hears it.

The situation is similar at the other 'end' of our existence. Modern research into dying has often pointed to the fact that hearing is in the great majority of cases the last human sense to be switched off. When seeing, smelling, tasting, feeling, and speaking have long atrophied, we can still hear.

So we can hear before we enter this world, throughout our lives, and even in the hour of death when all our other senses fail us, which demonstrates that hearing is a state of being unmatched by any of the other senses. Isn't that the real reason why we can never shut our ears so long as we are alive? Because to hear is to be?

II
DUOS ON THE SECOND THEME

'He who sees oneness everywhere has surmounted illusion and sorrow.'
Upanishads

Sluch is Slovak for hearing, and *bluch* means deaf. *Kan* is Bengali for ear, and *kala* deaf. In Tibetan *kolto* signifies deaf, but in Bontok *koling* stands for the ear. In all of the world's languages contrasting phenomena sound almost the same. Whoever has a *mouth* cannot be *mute*, and yet the two are linguistically related – and even more closely in German with *Stimme/stumm*. We believe that someone who can see cannot be blind, but in dozens of languages there is hardly any differentiation, and in English and German *blink* is very close to *blind*.

In Italian *senso* signifies meaning whereas *senza* from the same root means without. Language thus appears to indicate that no great difference is involved whether something is meaningful or meaningless.

The world's languages abound with related words indicating both abundance and its opposite. The Greek *holos* becomes *whole* or *hole* in English, *hohl* (hollow) or *voll* and *viel* (full and plenty) in German, and *kol* (whole) in Hebrew. Such derivates extend in all conceivable directions. *Garr*, for instance, is Arabic for a full moon, but *gar* means a measure of capacity. In Bengali *Chand* is the moon, and *shunna* hollow.

Calda in Italian stems from the same root as *cold* but means exactly the opposite – *hot* (in French *chaud*). *Ciel* in French points to the heavens, but the corresponding English word *cellar* leads downwards.

One would think that striving upwards and thrusting downwards would be carefully distinguished in language, and yet the words involved overlap. *Valley* in English is related to the German *Wall* (embankment, rampart), and the German *Höhle* (cave) to *hole* and *hill*. In Latin one word, *altus*, means both high and low. Even heaven and hell are ultimately related. It might seem that someone who enters *hell* can hardly be *holy*, but language links the two.

Our moral consciousness says that good is the opposite of evil, but in the world's languages moral categories are as turbulently confused as in reality. The root *bad* must originally have meant both good and bad since *good's* comparative *better* appears to be a worse form of *bad*ness, intensified by its superlative *best*. The Middle High German word *baß* (an exact equivalent of the English *bad*) was also used to signify good, and provided the basis for the comparative *besser* (*better*). When Lao Tse writes 'He who says good at the same time says bad,' that must be taken literally.

The word *good* evokes *God*, but here too language indicates that God and the Devil are one, thus according with many mystics and esoteric schools. *Devil* and *divine* are interrelated, extending into *dieu* and *diable* in French, *deva* in Sanskrit, *Teufel* (Devil in German), *Zeus* in Greek, and so on.

The Greek *logos* in the New Testament, the Divine Word that was in the beginning, in German becomes *Lüge*, which is also related to the English *lie*. That is not just 'chance', and the connection between 'word' and 'lie' is present in many other languages – including *Quallu* and *Lulla* in the Amerindian language of Quechua, and *Njalme* and *Gjela* in Samoyed.

Even the words for opposed primal elements in antiquity – fire and water – often come from the same root. The English word *burn* means destroy by fire and can also refer to a small stream, related in that context to the Old Norse word for a 'spring'.

What is big cannot be small – and yet many languages indicate the contrary. In Thai, for instance, *leg* is small and *laag* big.

Palaeo-linguist Richard Fester has shown that almost every word initially – and particularly at that moment of human development – contained its opposite within itself. Scarcely anyone is aware of that – but it is so strikingly obvious that one must ask oneself: Why does no one notice? Because we don't listen?

If we listened, we would hear that language is telling us: What you think are irreconcilable opposites are fundamentally the same. The person you think your *foe* could also be your *friend* – another pair of opposites which were once one.

'Upwards, downwards, the Way is one and the same' according to Heraclitus. 'As Above, so Below' (Hermes Trismegistos) is primal wisdom among many cultures. Early archaic man must still have known that. That is why he used the same word to express opposites, at most distinguished by inflection, accentuation, or a change of vowel or consonant.

Linguistics has shown that language reflects reality. What kind of reality does it thereby show us? Only one answer is imaginable. There are only minimal differences between what we believe to be irreconcilable and antagonistic. That is reality. Splitting up and separating the world into polarities is make-believe, illusion, *Maya*. All is one. If we were to listen, we would hear that. The coin may have two sides but it is a single coin. That is why it only has a single sound.

But the coin has that sound because it has two sides. We cannot have oneness without wholeness, without the antipodes: without God and the Devil, good and evil, life and death, love and hate, joy and suffering. Anyone who does not recognise that represses the antipode in the unconscious where – as C. G. Jung has shown – it 'proliferates', causing even greater trouble. Anyone who focuses exclusively on the 'good' aspect of things sees only half the picture and lacks wholeness. That is also a political statement.

When we recognise ourselves as being what we are, when we see the universe as what it is, when we give ourselves and it a *fair hearing*, we will comprehend oneness and wholeness. *Uni-verse* means turned towards oneness. What appears to us as multiplicity is 'adornment' – and the Greek word *kosmos* means just that. The two words – *Uni-verse* and *kosmos* – complement one another, together signifying wholeness adorned with diversity, 'oneness amid multiplicity', and what Hegel termed 'the Absolute'.

Perhaps some readers may have observed themselves as they read just now about the primal oneness of words and their surmounting of apparent contradictions. Why do we read, why do we hear, such ideas with such great inner satisfaction?

All happiness involves achieving oneness. In such moments we experience language becoming one, reflecting our potential unity and wholeness. Opposites unite. Isn't that rather like watching lovers embrace affectionately? Are we in such moments voyeurs of language? Are we seeing unity? Are we observing the attainment of oneness?

III
FUGA CANONICA

'If you would stop clinging to contrary concepts, illusion would cease of its own accord.'

Huang-Po

If we made greater use of hearing in our thinking, if we listened more intensively to language and to how similar polar words sound, we would perceive oneness much more often and polarities much less frequently – and we would become aware of unity in diversity. Polarised thinking takes the shortest possible route from cause to effect. It is eye-thinking, which always means that it over-simplifies, offering a one-dimensional interpretation of Leibniz's 'Nihil est sine ratio' (Nothing is without Reason).

Much of our scientific thinking is one-dimensional. Until recently scientists devoted almost all of their attention to the way in which our behavioural patterns are conditioned by society and environment. Now, all of a sudden, they are once again discovering the importance of heredity, which they too used to think significant before they became so preoccupied with social variables. They have thus been constantly swinging, for 150 years now, between the two poles of 'environment' and 'heredity', and do not notice that those are just different aspects of the same thing. They will not grasp the truth until they at long last start comprehending the poles as simplifying abstractions, only applying very superficially to what actually occurs.

We increasingly frequently encounter problems that cannot be solved by resorting to the traditional way of thinking in polarities. Such thinking has achieved what it could achieve for us. We now enter areas where it obstructs rather than facilitates results – in research into cancer and Aids, in the problems involved in huge increases in city traffic, in the proliferation of urban areas and bureaucracies, in the cost-explosion in health services, in unemployment and computerisation, and in the death of forests, rivers, lakes, and seas (where the wheel comes full circle with regard to the impact of mono-causal scientific thinking).

We will only move forward when we learn to comprehend as two sides of the same coin, as oneness, what we have hitherto divided into opposites. There already exist scientific disciplines that show us how to proceed: cybernetics with its feedback control systems, biology with its new systemic concepts, and, above all of course, physics ever since the start of the twentieth century. 'Common sense' may still think it absurd to view a physical process as simultaneously a wave and a particle, but that is no difficulty for physicists any longer. When will we learn from that? And what can we learn from that? Certainly that our traditional ideas about the incompatibility of wave and particle must be an illusion so that the phenomena themselves (at least as we conceive them) must be an illusion. In reality they constitute oneness and wholeness.

We are starting to understand that the same is true of all the other polarities into which our one-dimensional causal thinking has dissected the world.

IV
HERACLITUS'S GRAND CADENZA

A celebrated saying by Heraclitus runs: 'Hidden Harmony is mightier than what is revealed.' The great contrast with which Heraclitus is concerned becomes apparent when one carefully examines the two adjectives employed. In the Greek original they are both visual words with the former negating the latter: *phanerós* and *aphanés* – on the one hand visible to all eyes, radiant, and revealed, and, on the other, unmanifest, invisible, hidden.

We must, however, also investigate the exact meaning of the word Heraclitus uses to compare the two kinds of harmony. In the original Greek his aphorism consists of only four words:

Armonía aphanés phanerós kreísson.

Truly a sentence whose meaning and literary elegance have confronted entire generations of classical scholars with considerable problems! The word *kreísson* with which the saying culminates means: stronger, mightier, more tremendous, more excellent, more outstanding, more useful, better, happier, superior, victorious, and, ultimately, Master. All that is involved when Heraclitus compares manifest, radiant harmony, visible to everyone, with what is hidden and invisible. One could translate the aphorism completely correctly as: 'The hidden harmony triumphs over what is manifest,' which might well have come from the Tao Te Ching.

No matter how one may translate Heraclitus, it becomes apparent here that the harmony which the eye can see is not so 'mighty' as that which cannot be seen. The comparative *kreísson* implies that visible, 'revealed' harmony may be tremendous, mighty, outstanding, and useful, but the hidden harmony manifests those qualities to an even greater extent.

V
RONDO INTENSIVO

We hear Heraclitus. We hear the Upanishads. We hear Jesus Christ. We hear the Buddha. And we observe that if we really listen to them, what they said unfolds like a blossom out of the bud. We take in what they said much more intensely if we hear it. That intensity does not just derive from Heraclitus, who stands here for many others. It is the result of hearing, which becomes, which is, its own intensity, its comparative and its superlative. It relates to the way in which we perceive and take in. Reading, thinking, loving, living, feeling, seeing, smelling, and tasting all become more intense, multi-layered, and rich when we hear more and more attentively than before.

That is beautifully expressed in a rondo-like poem by Kurt Wolff, that endearing patron of the German Expressionists.

> Whosoever has ears,
> hear.
> Whosoever has eyes,
> hear and see.
> Whosoever has hands,
> hear and see and do.
> Whosoever has feet,
> hear and see and do and go.
> Whosoever has a mouth,
> hear and see and do and go and speak.
>
> And be silent
> and be silent
> and be silent
>
> and speak.

As we said, listening brings about intensity. The greatest intensity – as experienced in love – is that of becoming one. The question 'Who hears what?' may be important but it remains superficial. It is an eye question. The person who sees stands there and looks somewhere or other, beaming out his gaze. Seeing is not possible without separating into subject and object. Someone listening, however, takes in, dissolving separation. Hearing disperses 'isolation'.

VI
MOZARTEAN VARIATION

With Heraclitus, seeing and hearing flow together to become inner seeing and inner hearing. There exists a letter by Mozart where he explains that for him a composition is already 'there' as a whole before he has written it down: '. . . even though it may be a long work, I see it again in my mind at a single glance as if it were a beautiful picture or an attractive human being, and in my imagination hear the notes sounding simultaneously rather than in succession as must later be the case. That is a great treat!' Mozart referred to seeing everything at a single glance and to hearing everything simultaneously. Heidegger writes that 'Such ways of seeing and hearing become one. They are one and the same thing.'

But they only become one if hearing is 'real hearing', hearing with the *Third Ear*. Like seeing with the *Third Eye*. As Heidegger says: 'Thinking should catch sight of what can be heard. Thinking is a fair hearing that catches a glimpse,' throwing light on what has been heard.

VII
FINALE WITH T. S. ELIOT

Outer hearing is bound to the unfolding of a piece of music in time, but inner hearing which, like Mozart, hears everything simultaneously is independent of perception through our sense organs. Modern physics and neurology have shown that those organs are a screen (as around a lamp) rather than a medium through which the world enters us. They screen us from the world, only admitting and tolerating what serves evolution and what we need to survive. Our organs – and particularly the eye – protect us by filtering out reality in the same way as a camera filter excludes colour impressions and light intensities unsuitable for the film being used.

Inner hearing and inner seeing, however, perceive everything simultaneously. They are independent of the dimensions of space and time. Nowhere is that more convincingly and beautifully expressed than in T. S. Eliot's *Four Quartets*.

> Words move, music moves
> Only in time; but that which is only living
> Can only die. Words, after speech, reach
> Into the silence. Only by the form, the pattern,
> Can words or music reach
> The stillness, as a Chinese jar still
> Moves perpetually in its stillness.
> Not the stillness of the violin, while the note lasts,
> Not that only, but the co-existence,
> Or say that the end precedes the beginning,
> And the end and the beginning were always there
> Before the beginning and after the end.
> And all is always now . . .

5

ANALOGIES LEAD FURTHER
THAN LOGIC

Harmonic thinking entails thinking in analogies. When I say 'The
World is Sound,' I am establishing an analogy – between the world
and sound. That analogy at first still seems very vague. But the more
I look into it, the more precise it becomes. Finally it is clear that the
world *is* sound.

Investigation can proceed in various ways: intellectually through
precise thinking; by way of feeling; through experiencing; and by
meditation. 'Thinking' in analogies requires those different levels of
realisation. Logical thinking only needs the intellectual level, which
is one-dimensional. Analogical 'thinking' is multi-dimensional,
which is why I put the word thinking in inverted commas.

Logic is an element within reason. Both love straight lines. That is
why they are a favourite playground for the eye person. The straight
line has an impelling and simplifying quality. *Ana*-logic is linked
with the ear. It moves, cautiously and carefully, along curves and
spirals – like the spirals in the human ear. Human thinking was
originally founded on analogies – and analogical 'thinking' is still
more flexible, creative, revolutionary, intuitive, free, spontaneous,
and less rigid, fixed, and violent than logical thought.

Early human beings discovered the world in the same way as a
baby does – tentatively moving from the known to the unknown by
way of associations. They compared what was already known and
investigated whatever new object came into view. This development
of analogies became all the more creative as the familiar was convincingly discovered where it was not – or scarcely – to be expected.

Science assumes that early peoples used the mammalian brain's
limbic system much more than is the case today. It is thought that
dreams originate in the limbic system.

Dreams entail establishing connections between the known and the
unknown. We thereby set up far-reaching bridges, so bold that our
waking consciousness often doesn't want to set foot on them and
even experienced psychologists have difficulty in understanding and
interpreting – which in fact only the dreamer can do since the interpretation is not 'correct' until the person concerned suddenly grasps
what the dream is saying.

Language and writing, humanity's greatest achievements, developed analogically rather than logically – as people today would probably assume. The new science of palaeo-linguistics has shown that early human beings had only very few words. They characterised things immediately to hand – and particularly aspects of the human body: breast, head, vagina, penis, etc. Analogies were established between those parts of the body and more remote objects – for instance, between the female breast and a hill-top, the milk spurting out of the breast and a fountain, the vagina and a cave, valley, or hole, between the moon's aureole and the area around the tribal home, between the river and the sound it makes, the penis and a tower (or man himself), the vagina and a vessel, the arm and the branch of a tree, the back and a mountain ridge, the tongue and a promontory, the head and a knoll or headland, between birth and the 'hole' through which it takes place, the mouth and a river estuary. That is why so many of those words derive in many languages from the same linguistic root. Richard Fester, the great palaeo-linguist, has demonstrated this in detail – in hundreds of languages from across the world.

The 'sexualisation of language', which linguists time and again discover to their great astonishment, developed analogically. The sexual being is an *ana*-logician par excellence. What he or she experiences in love expands by way of associative comparisons to take in the world.

Conversely, logic endangers – and often enough kills off – sexuality, eroticism, and love.

Hundreds of thousands of years later, writing developed in similar fashion to language – first the cuneiform script where the eye is analogically depicted as an arrow, and then the Sumerian, Egyptian, and Chinese written forms. In Chinese script a mouth and a bird still signify 'song', a woman in a house 'peace', and the sun and moon together 'light'.

Analogical thinking has shaped humanity's great symbols: the cross as a meeting of the vertical and horizontal, the transcending and the concretising, transfixing the suffering human being; the triangle symbolising the three phases of the moon and the female sex; the circle as a metaphor of the universe and oneness; the arrow as a sign of aggression, fertilisation, and masculinity; three lines as an expression of the Trinity (and also of the lunar phases); three crosses as symbolising intensified suffering surmounted in the Trinity (which also signifies femininity).

Many of these symbols are still employed today, and even though we often cannot understand them in rational terms any longer, they nevertheless still touch and affect us. They are deeply imprinted on our soul as archetypal 'letters'. Human beings today, who think predominantly logically and functionally, are no longer capable of inventing similar signs whose power will exert an impact over millennia. Their incompetence with symbols becomes apparent in the visual language employed for signs at airports and railway stations, international congresses or Olympic Games, which are supposed to be comprehensible to everyone.

Thinking in analogies is important for us today, but the rational human being does not want to accept that. The great scientific discoveries – from Kepler's planetary laws and Newton's comprehension of gravity by way of the nineteenth-century harnessing of electricity to Max Planck's quantum theory – were analogical rather than logical. The very first discovery with which the history of Western science began also involved analogy. Pythagoras is said to have passed a smithy where he heard different lengths of iron producing different notes, which served as the basis for his harmonic experiments and the idea of the harmony of the spheres. Niels Bohr's model of the atom came into being in similar fashion almost 3,000 years later by way of comparing planetary system and microcosmos.

It is only a small step from there to the most mighty of all analogies: the ancient esoteric wisdom of 'as without, so within', and the mystical knowledge, found in all cultures, that God is in you and you in God.

It now becomes clear that any analogy stands for all the others. Each is contained in all. In the same way as DNA, the genetic code, is contained in the I Ching, the Chinese Book of Wisdom.

The I Ching is mankind's earliest book – or at least one of the earliest. DNA is a 'book' too – the book of our genetic heritage. It consists of four bases (adenine, cytosine, guanine, and thymine) which are arranged in groups of three. So there are $4^3 = 64$ triplets. One could call them the words of the DNA book. To be 'spoken' the 64 'words' require $2 \times 3 \times 64 = 384$ syllables (with the 2 standing for the DNA's two helical chains, and the 3 for the basic pattern of triplets). The 64 hexagrams of the I Ching are also formed from 384 lines (= 'syllables').

So the numbers 64 and 384 are fundamental to both the I Ching and DNA. It is inconceivable – and also logically impossible – that this should be a matter of 'chance'. It contradicts any mathematical probability of coincidence. The universe isn't as yet old enough for that. And there are many more parallels between the I Ching and DNA – as German scientist Martin Schönberger has demonstrated in dozens of calculations, tables, and graphs.

Books, words, syllables, and letters could not have been invented if DNA were not a 'book' consisting of those very elements. Researchers into genetics also refer to 'words', 'syllables', and 'letters'.

The analogy between DNA and the book is perhaps the most momentous and creative within humanity's evolution – and also makes clear that analogies can start exerting an impact even before people become conscious of them. They 'occur' – as was said at the start of this chapter – multi-dimensionally: on various levels of possible human experience, both conscious and unconscious.

If the book is a symbol of human thought and creativity, and if the 'primordial book of life' is the DNA molecule which cells have to 'read' so that we human beings may develop, then it really becomes clear that: Each analogy contains every other – as is also the case with God Indra's pearls and with Bootstrap physics where the information comprehended in an electron is contained in all of the universe's electrons.

Logic cannot grasp that, but analogy can. Analogy is more comprehensive and penetrates deeper. Is that the reason why the great enlightened ones – Jesus, Buddha, Mahavir, the Zen sages, the great Sufis, shamans – mostly spoke in analogies? 'Parable' is only another word for 'analogy'. That is the only way of understanding the parables in the New Testament, and all the other allegories in humanity's spiritual traditions. In every single one is concealed all the rest – is ultimately concealed the Divine Spirit itself, the *Brahman*.

It thus becomes absolutely clear that nowhere is spirit, consciousness, or the human being more creative than in the realm of *analogic*. Paul Feyerabend's harsh criticism of today's scientific thinking essentially concerns the fact that such activity is merely logical and causally oriented, thereby blocking access to the creative possibilities of analogy. The logician cannot understand paradoxes and absurdities, which is why he is inclined to dispute and deny them – and yet every individual has experienced, dozens of times, that the world, and our lives, are full of them. The process of analogical thinking particularly excels, however, in surmounting paradoxical and absurd hindrances to thought.

In recent years science has gradually been opening itself up again to deliberately analogical association – as we become suspicious of the mechanistic age's exclusively logical and causal orientation. It seems that many of the recent discoveries made by the new sciences involve the predominance of analogies rather than logic – and perhaps also the fact that people are at long last regarding both possibilities as being of equal standing and making sovereign use of them. In the same way we are also gradually learning to deploy both hemispheres of the brain. In most people the 'logical brain' is on the left and the analogically thinking brain on the right.

It is possible that this new consciousness of the potential of analogical 'thinking' also derives from the process that led to harmonic 'thought'. Fundamental harmonic research establishes analogies between cosmic relationships and symmetry in crystals, musical intervals, the forms of leaves and flowers, architectural proportions in masterpieces ranging from Chartres to the Taj Mahal, frequency readings in meteorological fluctuations, etc. It finally becomes apparent that the chain is unending – what German philosopher Peter Sloterijk calls an 'ontological sound', a 'general formula' for knowledge necessary for our survival. The world is a single whole. Everything is linked with everything else. The world 'sounds'. It is a 'chord'.

The imagination and freedom necessary for feeling, experiencing, and living through – rather than merely knowing – this are more likely to be associated with an *ana*-logical process of perception than with logical thinking.

Logic aims at security.
The *ana*-logician has the courage to embark on risk and adventure.
Logic is goal-orientated and passes judgement.
Analogy ponders and establishes relationships.
The logician sees.
The *ana*-logician listens.

6

LISTENING WORDS

'Man behaves as if he were the maker and master of language but
language remains the mistress of mankind.'

Martin Heidegger

I

THE 'ABSOLUTELY SUPERFLUOUS ABUNDANCE
OF LANGUAGE'

Language confirms that our ear is assimilative, receptive, passive,
and feminine whereas our eye is emanative, aggressive, active, and
masculine. For passive activities there are fewer words than for
active. Such words as: *hear, listen, eavesdrop* . . . If we want to go
beyond that we must visualise the process of hearing by resorting to
such expressions as 'to prick up one's ears', 'hang on someone's
words', etc.

We accord visual perception very many more linguistic possibilities whose significance is far more than linguistic: *see, scrutinise,
overlook, contemplate, see through, observe, eye, inspect, stare,
gape, gawk, goggle, glare, peer, blink, wink, look, sight, behold,
oversee, notice, perceive, espy, squint, examine, glimpse, behold,
discern, mark, note, notice, regard, view, witness, envisage*, and,
revealingly, *catch sight of*.

A completely different picture is produced if we examine language
in terms of the *outcome* of the many seeing words – and also of the
few words describing the activity of hearing. Such examination
confirms that the eye can go wrong much more frequently than the
ear. Many expressions concerned with the possibility of illusion and
error come from the visual sphere: *overlook, appearance, semblance, imaginary* (from the Latin *imago* = picture), *mirage, appari-
tion, obscure, myopic, blind spot*, etc.

The eye's liability to illusion becomes absolutely clear if we bear
in mind that there is a hole of considerable size in the retina. We
should therefore see a blank circular black spot at the centre of
everything we perceive with the eye. But we don't. We don't see that
there is blackness and emptiness at the centre of everything. As
Rupert Sheldrake, the English biologist, says: 'We don't see that we
don't see.'

Our eye scans surfaces. Seeing basically entails a ray of perception which scans surfaces. I have been looking for an hour at the sheet of paper on which I write these ideas, but I cannot penetrate even a fraction of a millimetre beneath its surface. The eye glimpses surfaces and is attached to them, always remaining superficial (= on the surface). The ear penetrates deep into the realms it investigates through hearing.

The number of words describing what is experienced through listening is therefore almost endless. Some verbs are listed here. The reader should note the subtle and precise differences involved, and the accuracy the ear demands of language in its delineation of what has been heard. Such accuracy and subtlety derive from the ear itself. The reader should – for a moment – demand that of himself or herself by pausing at each of the following words and attempting to allow the sound described to resound within. It may take quite a while to 'read' this but that will provide a training in sensitivity of hearing and – beyond that – of our inner ear. Here are some of the words:

Babble, bang, bark, bawl, bellow, bicker, blare, blather, bleat, bleep, blubber, bluster, boo, boom, bray, bubble, burp, buzz;

cackle, carol, caterwaul, caw, chatter, cheep, chide, chime, chuckle, clang, clank, clap, clatter, click, clink, cluck, coo, crack, crackle, crash, creak, croak, crow, crunch, cuss;

dribble, drip, drivel, drone, drool;

echo, explode;

fizz, flap, flop, flutter;

gasp, gargle, giggle, grate, grind, groan, growl, grumble, grunt, gurgle;

hiss, honk, hoot, howl, huff, hum;

jabber, jibe, jingle, jubilate;

knock;

lisp, low;

moan, mumble, mutter;

nag, natter, neigh;

ooze;

pant, patter, peal, plop, pound, prate, prattle, puff, purr;

quack, quarrel;

rap, rasp, rattle, rejoice, ring, roar, rumble, rustle;

scrape, scratch, scream, screech, shriek, shuffle, sigh, sizzle, slam, slap, slosh, slump, smack, smash, snap, snarl, sneer, sneeze, sniff, snigger, snivel, snore, snort, sob, spit, splash, splutter, squeak, squeal, stamp, strum, stutter, suck, swish;

throb, thump, thunder, tick, tingle, toll, tootle, tremble, trickle, trill, twang, tweet, twitter;

wail, warble, wheeze, whimper, whine, whinny, whir, whisper, whistle, whoop;

yap, yell, yelp, yodel;

zip.

The fact that many of those words are vernacular or only now becoming part of written language is revealing. This shows that simple people are more expressive and creative in their interpretation of acoustic impressions than members of the 'upper' classes, who also constitute the majority of the dominant eye people. Hegel was also such a 'Lord of the Eye', so it is not surprising that he thought all these listening words constituted an 'absolutely superfluous abundance of language'.

Experts in information theory have discovered that there exists a relationship between the number of words we dispose of in a specific sphere and the wealth of differentiation, meticulousness, and attentiveness possible within that area. Language confirms what we have established elsewhere – that the ear is more precise than the eye. The eye can compensate for that deficiency by utilising thousands of expressions to describe and circumscribe what it sees. That, however, remains compensatory, an attempt at making up for the ear's precision as expressed in each instance in a single word. The difference becomes particularly striking if one compares the exactitude of all those verbs and all the inaccuracies with which the eye has to contend in depicting colour. (See Chapter 1.)

Let us summarise before we proceed further. In everything that the eye actively undertakes, it is superior to the ear, which ultimately can only hear, listen, and take in. But with regard to everything that the ear can take in, it surpasses the eye many times over in both receptivity and the amount of activity involved. The fact that this finding – backed with the greatest possible degree of precision by the words presented above – arouses surprise reveals Western man's fixation on activity. Even a few active possibilities still seem (!) more profitable to him than what is by now a vast abundance of receptive potential – even though nature shows him the contrary day in day out, whether it be in technology where, for instance, a radio receiver can pick up hundreds of programmes whilst a transmitter, although usually considerably more elaborately constructed, normally beams only a single programme; or in biology where the female in any species is capable of receiving very much more energy and generative power than a male can offer. (Earlier chapters dealt with the female nature of the ear's form and functioning, as well as the masculinity of the eye.)

II
JIMI HENDRIX
THE VEIL OF THE TEMPLE WAS RENT IN TWAIN

We experience many of the words I have just listed as being *onomatopoeic*. Their sound is imitative of the noise or action designated. Our ears hear language imitating what is represented by the word involved. The expression *onomatopoeic* is in fact frequently imprecisely applied. The relationship between the sound of a *rattle* – and what I say here applies to many of the words above – and the verb *rattle* seems virtually inevitable. The rattle *rattles*. In our opinion the verb *rattle* exactly catches the sound a rattle makes. If that were true though, then the word should be the same in German and French since babies in those countries play with the same kind of rattles as young children in English-speaking nations. In fact the verb *rattle* is *klappern* in German and *cliqueter* in French.

German and French people also believe that their *rattle* word is *onomatopoeic*, viewing the relationship between the sound described and the sound of the word itself as inevitable. That means that different people – even if they come from nations and cultures so closely related as the German, French, and English – hear the same sound, the same noise, differently.

That applies to epochs as well as peoples – as can be seen even more clearly in the case of music by, for instance, comparing how Bach's music originally sounded (as reconstructed on many worthy gramophone recordings) with modern performances. 'The veil of the temple was rent in twain.' Bach wanted his listeners to really hear that in his St Matthew Passion – and his contemporaries did experience that too, most forcefully. Even when the celebrated passage was played on the instruments of Bach's time with their considerably reduced volume, great delicacy and subtlety, and subdued power and brilliance. To experience the rending of the veil of the temple to anything like the same extent today, we need more modern instruments – *high fidelity* with much greater presence and volume. That would not even be enough for many young people. They would want something like the violent wailings, slashings, and poundings of a Jimi Hendrix guitar improvisation. For them only then would the veil the bourgeoisie have hung before the mystery be rent.

So it becomes apparent that people from different nations and different times hear differently. They also see differently. And taste and smell differently. That, however, is particularly revealing. Specialists in media, advertising, and public relations know that the same TV *spot*, and even the same picture in a commercial, is seen and comprehended differently in, say, Scotland, and California. Highly paid advertising experts have carried out detailed surveys in the USA revealing that specific TV images affect New England viewers differently to people in New Mexico or Louisiana. Art scholars have also for generations carried out careful research into why, for instance, Italian painting of the *Quattrocentro* was founded on a visual consciousness almost diametrically opposed to that of German art during the same period.

National and regional differences in taste have, of course, long been exhaustively investigated by the food, perfume, and toiletry industries. No such comparable data exists in the sphere of auditory perceptions, despite the fact that such perceptions are obviously much more richly differentiated, much more divergent, than those of the eye, tongue, or nose.

So if one compares the different *onomatopoeic* expressions in various (and particularly related) languages, which are all so similar and yet significantly divergent, it must be asked whether the diversity of ways in which human beings are accustomed to hear may have led to the diversity of languages.

The fact that listening habits really do shape languages becomes apparent in dialects. The same words are used for the most part, perhaps minimally varied, but the actual speech sounds so different that it could be another language. So it is not just a question of the words employed. Australian English sounds very different to what can be heard back in England. Few words have actually been changed and there are not all that many different ones, but the speech-melody is certainly dissimilar.

Speech-melody is shaped by the way in which those speaking a language hear themselves. They want, as it were, to rediscover their own inner 'melody' in the way they speak – and in their fellows.

Language developed later than listening. It was only with dialect that there got under way a process of differentiation which ultimately led to different languages. What was originally only a dialect became a language. The cleavage into various languages might also have resulted from the fact that listening became differentiated at a very early stage into a variety of ways of hearing.

All that – and the other phenomena covered in this chapter – should be investigated. Ear-sensitive experts and researchers will be kept busy for generations. Fortunately a start has at long last been made in America even though not as yet in Europe. That would certainly have happened long ago if visual phenomena had been at issue.

We will only make up for neglect of our ears – and the resultant and now scarcely bearable 'pollution' of our environment by noise – if we devote as much care, and of course money, to investigating acoustic phenomena as to researching optical problems.

7

LANDSCAPES OF THE EAR

A Summer Experience

World literature abounds in descriptions of landscapes, presenting what the writer *saw*. Such depictions ignore and omit what can be heard and yielded to. Here I attempt the opposite, playing down visual impressions – and thereby experiencing the abundance of what can be heard. The ears 'see' the landscape. The eyes – for the most part closed – participate in that listening, asking other, greater authors: How about letting your senses 'eavesdrop' more often?

The setting: The Crane Prairie Lake in Oregon's Cascade Mountains, 1,700 metres above sea-level. I am lying on a bed of pine needles by the water.

Time: August 1984, a hot summer day, 35° Celsius, intolerable in the valley with its busy Highway 97 from which I have escaped.

Towering above me as my eyes blink into the brightness of the summer sky there are three pine trees against a backdrop of brilliant blue. Not a single cloud. Now and then a bird follows its course. Closer at hand, flies flitting past, dragonflies dancing, mosquitoes circling. Not much for the eyes.

But I hear: Silence. It is the silence which I hear first of all. Like a weight that I can grasp. A heavy, smooth weight. My ears feel it as if they were groping fingers. I observe that the weight feels good. I think: You haven't heard such silence for a long time.

I occupy myself with: Silence. It is alive. A drop of silence. My ears penetrate it. I am inside it. The drop becomes a universe. A cosmos that begins to resound.

This is the cosmos. First of all, the lake. A rhythmic gurgling. A deep sound – bubbling somewhat – and two higher notes: splashing and sploshing. Triple time, as if the lake were dancing a waltz. This isn't a joyous dance. Rather listless, self-forgetful, leisurely. Hanging onto someone's neck. Whose neck? – I wonder. Summer's burning, short, bull-like neck.

The deep gurgling sounds like a tired tom-tom. The two higher notes are wooden, like a ballophone, the West African xylophone. A lake playing tom-tom and ballophone?

Then the first dragonfly makes itself felt. I hear it before I can actually see it. The whirring of its rotating wings. The primordial helicopter. Still more functional than any made by man. More dragonflies follow and I discover: there are many different dragonfly sounds. Higher notes, whirrings fast and slow, and dark dronings. And all possible gradations in between. A scale performed by dragonflies. It is long before I am aware of that since it is only seldom that a dragonfly comes buzzing by.

Other insects appear more frequently. They circle above my face as if assessing me as a possible victim. But none settles on me. So they reject me. I rarely hear them approach. All of a sudden they are there. Where the curve of their flight comes closest to my ears, the deepest tone is to be heard. It rapidly slides up the scale again as the insect flies away. A mosquito glissando. Sometimes with a slightly whining quality to it.

The flies are producing the most varied sounds. For instance, a dark drone with a high-pitched component. As if there were a flute concealed in it, gently intoned, whilst the deep sound is strong and self-contained, like the fly itself. It is black. As if a tiny, intensely luminous object had been placed inside a dark box.

Once again it is only after a while that I notice: there are many different 'shades' of fly-sounds. Nearly all produce the dark drone – also of course in numerous variations – but one kind of fly, which tends to circle slowly, conceals an oboe rather than a flute in its sound; maybe the Arab version of an oboe, the *zoukra*, the instrument of the great caravans. That used to be played by the rider leading the camels when they approached an oasis or entered a town.

Yet another kind of fly makes a truly goatlike bleating sound with a nasal undertone. I wonder: Why haven't I listened to insects more attentively ever before? Why do we tend not to hear their sounds? Is it because they might remind us that nearly all animal and human sounds are already present in insects *in nuce*? That means, in view of the extraordinary antiquity of most types of insects, between 100 and 200 million years before we, the hominides and our ancestors, ever began to develop all these sounds! Did the insects show us how to do it with their genes teaching our genes?

Suddenly an insect settles in my ear. Its approach is as swift as an arrow. I can't see that but I hear it – the arrow and its flight. A moment later I can feel the insect as well even though it isn't moving. I know it's there. It tickles a little. I don't chase it away. The insect is sitting in my ear, and after a while I hear: Though it doesn't buzz around it is emitting a very faint sound. The hint of a chirp. A higher potency of the humming noise with which it approached. Its homoeopathic dilution. A sophisticated car in neutral.

The tickling increases. I move my head, disturbing the insect. In the fraction of a second before it takes off I can feel and hear the process of acceleration. Potentiality becomes reality. The hint of a chirp now becomes a loud buzzing presence bordering on a roar (since all this is happening inside my ear). The insect leaves my inner ear as if a plane were leaving its hangar, powerfully intensifying the sound again until it reaches the pitch which a moment previously had only been a scarcely audible chirping.

Sometimes polyphony develops: the murmuring and droning of many insects giving urgent voice to high-pitched, wildly whistling sounds, like animated human chatter emerging from a dark corridor. But then – even outdoing those voices – a mosquito like a muted trumpet. Like Miles Davis. Piercing. Striking. A flash of lightning for the ear.

The lower the sun sinks, the more sumptuous the concert becomes. From double-bassoon to piccolo, each instrument glissandos into the next. Duos, trios, quartets, chamber ensembles.

The air had been perfectly still for about two hours. Then there is a sudden single gust of wind. Only this one to start with. I can hear it before feeling it on my skin. It rustles through the pine trees, commencing with high frequencies, hitting needle after needle as if they were a keyboard. When the breeze has touched them all – millions of pine needles – it shouts with joy. A shout drifting through the air. Are the pines shouting? For joy? Is it because – for a moment – they have been released from the humming heat?

After a while the second gust. This time there is a roar intermingled with the rustle. Increasing like a crescendo. Not allowing space for the decrescendo because the third gust is already there . . . Then a fourth. Each is itself, entirely itself: a gust of wind with a particular personality. Not to be mistaken for any other. Leisurely, quiet. Leaping, stumbling. Grabbing, tolerating no protest. Dancing. Strutting. Rushing. Rumbling. Whispering. Crackling. A whole family: men, women, children of wind. As if the trees were their toys. Or their instruments? Both require: playing. The pine trees as organ pipes. The wind as their organist. Sometimes it blows one pipe, sometimes another. It plays a concerto with their registers – until it has activated them all. *Con organum plenum*.

However: My ears must penetrate beyond. I had concentrated on the pines and failed to hear something else. There are reeds too. A narrow strip by the lake. Rustling. Slapping. Clapping. Clattering. Wailing. Clacking. Creaking. Rasping. And there's always the sound 'Ah'. Amazing how much 'Ah' can express: surprise, questioning, pleasure, pain, encouragement, confirmation, displeasure. Yes! The reeds are saying all that. Variations on the sound 'Ah'.

It's a long time since I closed my eyes. So as to hear better. After all, there's not much to be seen.

The reeds question the lake. The lake's triple time has changed. Surely quite a while ago, but there's been so much happening that I haven't yet got round to mentioning it. The water isn't waltzing any longer – isn't doing the sluggish, nonchalant waltz it had been dancing for so long: the pulse underlying everything I have tried to describe.

The water's rhythmic pattern expands. Now I can count up to five before it repeats itself. The gurgling incoming swell approaches to a count of three and recedes to a count of two: a quintuple rhythm not to be found in music. The stress is exactly in the middle: on the third beat. In music five beats to the bar usually involve triple and duple time – or the other way round. First comes the duple and then the triple time. The watery 'Five in a bar' of my lake in Oregon consists of two duple times separated by a sombre thud in between. No resemblance to 'Take Five' by Dave Brubeck and Paul Desmond, the piece which helped so many people learn to hear 'Fives'.

A long time has passed since the first of the trees towering above me up into the sky started creaking as it bowed under the force of the wind and then returned to a vertical position. A rusty, creaking noise. An elderly gentleman who insists that he is right. Whenever there are two or three creaks in succession, I think he wants to proclaim: Didn't I say so! Other trees join in. Do they all say the same? Rebuffing or even rebuking the others? Don't they like one another? Or does it only sound as if they don't?

I open my eyes. I suppose because I instinctively feel: Where there is so much to be heard, there ought to be equally much to see. But I am mistaken. I see: Just a few slightly bent tree-tops swaying gently, their branches extending the way the wind is blowing, the trunks just as vertical as ever. Hardly anything has changed – for the eye. Immeasurably much since the breeze got under way – for the ear. That shows how much earlier the perceptive powers of our auditory sense come into operation! How much more would have to happen before the eye had something noteworthy to perceive! As an ear person I have heard since the first four or five gusts of wind that the world is different now. As an eye person I observe that the world is the same. Again I marvel: how much more sensitive is the ear.

I close my eyes once again since I thereby miss hardly anything. At least I lose less than I gain by doing so: More intensive listening. Is it possible to conceive the contrary? Blocking my ears so that I can see better?

I wish the rush of wind would become fiercer, attaining the strength of a hurricane. All four organs in some majestic cathedral playing at the same time. I lay down on my bed of pine needles during the midday heat. Now I sense: the wind heralds the evening. I wish it would bring clouds. And it would start raining. I imagine the sound of raindrops. I would feel them on my skin as if I were a drum onto which a heavenly hand drops something very light – just heavy enough for my 'hide' to respond.

I imagine all that might be heard if there were rain, but then I'm glad it doesn't rain. It would be hopeless trying to describe the abundance of sounds. There would be a swooshing and swooshing and swooshingswooshingwooshingswooshingswooshingswoosh-ingswooshing. It would hardly be possible to say anything else. One wouldn't have anywhere near the two or three dozen swooshing words whose sonic counterpart the rain has at its disposal. The Eskimos have nine different words for 'white' since most of what they see is white. Would the peoples living at the time of the Flood – when, so scholars tell us, the rain must have continued for generations – have had a richer vocabulary for the sounds of rain? Why has so little of that come down to us? Is it because we don't listen?

I hear somebody calling my name. And at that moment I hear: Myself. Without feeling for them I can hear: My pulse throbbing, my heart beating, my temple vibrating, the blood rushing through my veins – the primordial stream and the primal *Nada*, the mini-model for all the rivers of the earth. I hear all that as clearly as previously the lake and insects, the wind, trees, and reeds – and believe I hear it for longer and more intensively than ever before. But my name is called again and again, ever more insistently. Only after some time do I feel free to answer.

I am asked: 'How did you spend your afternoon?' Me: 'I listened.' Question: 'Nothing else? Wasn't there anything to look at?' Me: 'A blue sky and three pines.' The friend who has come to fetch me (I am reducing our conversation to the essentials): 'Poor you. You must have been bored.' Me: 'No way. It was great.' She: 'I always said you were crazy.' I tell myself: you would have gone crazy with boredom if you hadn't spent those five hours listening. What you heard made it a fulfilled afternoon.

Hardly anything seen but lived most intensely.

8

EARS THAT DO NOT HEAR

On Noise

'Silence is man's centre . . . Today silence is malfunctioning noise.'
Max Picard

I
NOISE IS ACOUSTIC GARBAGE

The fact that it has mainly been eye-orientated human beings who permit, who *make*, the noise which fills every corner of our towns and cities cannot just be fortuitous. People orientated towards hearing would never have allowed that to happen. They wouldn't have been able to put up with it. They *can't* tolerate it.

Noise is garbage perceptible to the ear. It is noise, and not the refuse and other rubbish tipped on the dumps spreading like the plague around towns and villages, that constitutes our civilisation's greatest problem in this sphere. 'Visible' garbage is taken away by refuse trucks, but 'audible' garbage remains – as if the auditory dimension wanted to take its revenge for centuries of suppression, discrimination, insult, and injury. If people still able to listen don't take their revenge, the auditory dimension will.

II
SILENCE AS A HIGHER POTENCY OF SOUND

The opposite of light is darkness. But the opposite of sound is not silence, which is an intensification of sound. Poets speak of the roaring of silence, of silence as an organ. 'Nothing in the universe' – says Meister Eckhart – 'is so like God as silence.' If the world is sound, and if God is more than His creation, then He is silence.

Silence is wrongly viewed if it is felt to be the opposite of sound. The opposite of sound is noise. Anyone who does not want to listen must at least hear noise.

III
NOISE MAKES YOU ILL

In our civilisation we can feel noise in our bodies. And not just close to airport flight paths: in every large town or city; on or near any motorway; at any busy crossroad; at work. As early as 1976 over a third of all vocational ailments were caused by noise. Noise is thus the most dangerous cause of illness in the world of work. It is not just 'us' who feel that: our organs do too, and react by becoming ill.

The death rate among people living around Los Angeles' international airport is about 20 per cent higher than in the rest of the city. There are also 31 per cent more psychiatric cases and 14 per cent more liver diseases. Children already suffer from high blood pressure, and have greater difficulty than their peers elsewhere in coping with mathematics, solving simple problems, or even doing jigsaws.

American acousticians estimate that the noise level in most cities increases by between ½ and 1 decibel per year – a terrifying figure as will become apparent in a few pages.

IV
'MOUNTAINS OF NOISE'

'One day man will have to combat noise as he once combated cholera and the plague.'

Robert Koch

Silence hardly exists any longer. Even in the country the air is filled with the noise of lawn-mowers, saws, harvesters, and many other machines farmers now consider indispensable. Wherever people live, they hear their neighbours' radios, TV sets, and record and cassette players as well as their own. Modern architects and implementers of building regulations have failed here as in most other spheres. They are not interested in insulation and sound-absorbent materials – even though such materials and technical possibilities exist.

No household equipment – not even the oil-fired central heating and refrigerator, and certainly not the washing machine and dryer – functions noiselessly. Even the simplest juice extractor, mincer, corn mill, bread-cutter, mixer, ventilator, vacuum cleaner, dish-washer, spin drier, or waste disposal unit is noisier than technologically necessary today. Designers and engineers display admirable inventiveness with regard to form and colour. They are concerned about how and where such equipment can be used and stored, but are thoughtless and careless about the noise it makes.

Millions of Americans – and increasing numbers of Europeans – are surrounded, day and night, by the gentle humming of their air-conditioning. That is the 'keynote' on which their lives are based. Just as Indian music is founded on the drone of the Tampura. The difference is that the drone is 'right' – harmonically, physiologically, musically, and physically – whereas the air conditioning's 'humming' is totally arbitrary. In 99 per cent of all cases it clashes with and neutralises organic sounds and vibrations since, no matter how quiet it may be, it is certainly louder than them. (See section VI, 'Harmonic Pollution', in Chapter 9.)

Large libraries are among the quietest of public areas. Many of them are islands of tranquillity amid all the rushing to and fro of a university or city. But now there already exist the first libraries – in California, South Africa, and Japan – *constantly* 'fed' with music. There are even schools where all lessons are accompanied by a centrally regulated background of Soft Rock.

For many years I worked for a large radio network. One might have expected that its architects, who have non-terminable contracts, would have been sensitive to the problems involved in radio, but they incorporated air-conditioning with its 'eigentone' in the recording and broadcasting studios. Those architects maintained – and I swear they told me this – that 'It couldn't be heard.' But you only needed to turn up the microphone and the 'eigentone' was 'there', leaving its acoustic mark on almost everything produced. Anyone who didn't want to have that – producers of radio plays, chamber music, and literary programmes – had first to telephone around the place so as to track down a member of the technical staff who then – usually reluctantly – switched off the air-conditioning in the building. I don't know of any better example of contemporary architects' deafness and total lack of auditory sensitivity. What will become of our auditory culture – or rather lack of culture – if even an extensive radio network lacks building experts who can actually hear?

The German word 'eigenton' has been taken over in acoustics, and is used in American, French, and English publications. Every room has its 'eigentone', its own sound, even when there is no air-conditioning. This is the outcome of sound-waves being reflected by opposite walls, and is to be found where the resonance between sung and reflected sound is heard most readily. That can be ascertained by singing various notes in the room concerned. Much has been written about the psychological and physiological problems associated with this 'eigenton', but the overwhelming majority of modern architects cannot be prevailed upon to take them into account. It nevertheless goes without saying that extreme care is lavished on the 'eigenfarbe' (the inherent colour) of the materials employed.

That epitomises the situation. Careful attention is devoted to whatever is visible, but the 'auditory spheres' of our environment and everyday surroundings are neglected. They are 'left to chance'. Town-planners, architects, clients, and construction companies ignore them, thereby demonstrating a heedlessness of the ear, the most sensitive of our organs, they would never dream of inflicting on the eye. Even the most elementary of measures providing protection against noise are forgotten – or at most established later as with the ugly walls between a motorway and a new settlement, even though much better solutions could easily have been found with a little application of auditory forethought.

Just one other example – but hundreds would have been possible. For some years now, hardly any more rubbish has been dumped in, or sewage channelled into, Alpine lakes in Switzerland, North Italy, Austria, and Bavaria, but high-powered speedboats are still allowed to roar around. Their engine noise is magnified many times over by the surrounding mountains, so that strollers and walkers, bathers and seekers of rest and recreation, along the promenades of the Lago di Como or in the beach cafés of Lago Maggiore can no longer hear themselves talking. Anyone who speaks about that to spa directors, heads of tourist offices, or simply the people who live there quickly realises that they think this 'acoustic garbage' unavoidable and have come to terms with it, despite having fought successfully against visible, material pollution.

One of the worst sources of noise in our environment is the motor car. Here too technologies that could protect us from the worst have long been developed – including sound-capsules insulating the motor. Motoring organisations believe it possible to transform all cars into whispering wraiths and – even more important – considerably quieten lorries, the greatest source of noise, but most manufacturers think it unnecessary to apply such technologies. According to the German Automobile Club, 'Anyone who hears such a cotton-wool-packed lorry would be surprised by how quietly it can purr.'

The greatest noise occurs when people drive without showing consideration for others. A single driver who suddenly whips up his motor to 4,000 revs per minute makes 'as much noise as thirty-two other drivers satisfied with only 2,000 revs'.

Most motor-cyclists are even more inconsiderate though sound-dampening technologies have long been available. According to a BMW dealer, 'We simply wouldn't be able to sell motor-bikes if they were silenced.' If noise is acoustic pollution of the environment, young people's 'Super-Screamers' can be seen as machines continually spewing out 'muck'. If that were visible 'muck', the police would intervene.

We lead existences that are 'sound-blind'. It's inconceivable though that we should be 'light-deaf'. The real reason for the often no longer bearable increase in noise in our everyday surroundings is that no one is bothered about it. As if mayors, town councils, policemen, town-planners, and local authorities were deaf.

Noise will continue to grow. There will be 'mountains of noise' – they in fact exist already – as there would be mounds of kitchen waste before our doors if it weren't cleared away. We will only master noise – and the resultant edginess, illness, and desperation – if we devote as much love and attention to our ears as to our eyes. If we fail to do so, noise will drown us like a wave of stinking filth.

V
'ROCK AROUND THE CLOCK'

The more we penetrate into the world of listening and the ear, the more things make sense. A diabolical logic is entailed in the fact that musicians – and in general people who work and live surrounded by music – are on the way to becoming deaf. The hearing of what should be the most acoustically sensitive professional group is most at risk in a civilisation where hypertrophied seeing rules. It is not workers in steel-mills, or road-workers using pneumatic hammers, or airport mechanics constantly exposed to the roar of aircraft taking off, who are most endangered. They have taken seriously the hypertrophy of the visual. They've stopped listening. They wear ear-muffs and also stick cotton-wool into their ears, like Odysseus's comrades in former times. Musicians, however, cannot work with ear-muffs and cotton-wool in their ears.

The upper permissible noise limit in factories is 85 decibels, but people who work in discos and in studios where Rock and Punk are recorded are exposed to 100 or more dB. When experts surveyed discos, they found that even the 'quietest' was too loud at 100 dB. Others attained 110 or even 120 decibels.

It should not be thought that 110 dB is 'only' 10 more than 100. The decibel is a complex logarithmic unit of measure formed from the quotient of the squares of two similar physical magnitudes. Once a specific level of loudness has been attained, the dB curve mounts sharply – much more so than when a plane takes off. A reading of 86 dB is already 66 per cent more for the human ear than 80 dB. Volume roughly doubles between 100 and 110 dB. A disco featuring rock at 100 dB may be loud, but another with music at 110 dB is twice as loud. The terrible din of a steel-works is four times 'quieter' than a top disco. For many people disco decibels are way beyond the 'pain threshold'.

Some 33 per cent of students entering the University of Tennessee in 1981 were unable to hear very high notes. A year later the figure was 60 per cent. Professor David Lipscumb commented: 'Young people's hearing is often twice as old as their actual age.' A German specialist adds: 'Today senescence begins earlier in the ear than in any other organ.'

As recently as 1968 the Swiss Federation for the Hard of Hearing estimated that between 50,000 and 100,000 of the youngsters entering military service had defective hearing. By the beginning of the eighties their number was up to 300,000. A Swiss newspaper concluded: 'It is possible that more and more young Swiss, men and women, will have to exchange their Walkman headphones for a hearing aid before they reach pensionable age.'

The Swedish navy blames sailors' poor hearing for Soviet submarines having so often penetrated protected waters off Stockholm. Youngsters are no longer capable of operating sound-detectors adequately. 'They listen to too much Rock music', says their commanding officer. 'Twenty years ago – before discos existed – we had no problems in manning the detectors.'

VI
GREATER VOLUME, MORE OUT OF TUNE

The ears of people who produce rock records are most under attack. I know what I'm talking about after having spent quite a bit of my life in a studio. Maybe I did 'only' produce jazz records – 250 or so – but the sound engineers and staff who work there have got used to the volume reached in rock music. Of the six or seven people in the studio during recording or mixing there is usually at least one whose hearing has already suffered damage. The person whose hearing is worst determines the volume level – which means that anyone who works in a studio cannot avoid being exposed to a high level of decibels. One *must* also listen at that level in order to discover even the subtleties concealed in loud music.

An investigation carried out by Zürich University in 1984 revealed that the hearing of 70 per cent of the disc-jockeys and hard rock musicians examined was 'considerably reduced'.

Many studio musicians and engineers are condemned to chasing around in circles. On the one hand they have to listen to excessive volumes, but – as René Chocholle points out in his investigations into 'Qualitative Hearing' – sounds only take on 'a specifically tonal character when their intensity is neither too high . . . nor too low'.

Excessive volume is detrimental to both musicality and exact tuning. Fritz Winckel established in experiments that 'accuracy of tuning declines as volume increases . . . A crescendo from (just) 50 decibels to 80 – the normal increase from *piano* to *forte* – when the note C_0 is played on a flute already produces a 6 per cent degeneration in tuning.' Both Chocholle and Winckel have shown that there exists a marvellously 'correct' physiological relationship between volume and tuning. Musicians can tune their instruments most accurately when keeping within low to middle ranges of sound. It is as if nature is no longer so concerned about precise tuning in spheres outside the volume 'pleasant' for our ears. Beyond that obvious connection there is also a more profound link between those three categories of: what is 'pleasant', 'tuned', and moderate in volume. Plato wrote that 'The essence of the beautiful and the good lies . . . in right proportions.' As if a middle-range volume with its particular 'tunability' and 'rightness' provided the psycho-physical listening landscape man can most pleasurably explore. If man is the 'measure of all things', the degrees of volume allowing particularly precise and appropriate tuning must also be those where he feels at home.

VII
ALARM AND AGGRESSION

Just a few years ago specialists assumed that the ear was indifferent to whether it heard loud music or a pneumatic hammer. What counted was the decibel volume. By now it is known that a frequently repeated sound is less dangerous than continual sound. Para-doxical though it may seem, a pneumatic hammer pounding away at the street every few seconds does less damage to hearing than loud music listened to for a long period without interruption.

As soon as volume exceeds 80 dB, blood pressure also rises. The stomach and intestine operate more slowly, the pupils become larger, and the skin gets paler – no matter whether the noise is found pleasant or disruptive, or is not even consciously perceived . . . Unconsciously we always react to noise like Stone Age beings. At that time a loud noise almost always signified danger.

That is therefore pre-programmed, and when millions of young people hear excessively loud music they register: danger. They become *alarmed*. That word comes from the Italian *Alarm*, which in turn leads to *all'arme*, a call to arms. When we hear noise, we are constantly – but unconsciously – 'called to arms'. We become *alarmed*. Is that one reason – alongside television and everything else – for concentrated aggression among people today? Does our music 'attune' us to aggressiveness?

Many young people believe the opposite, maintaining that loud music shuts them off from modern society's aggressiveness and gives them 'peace'. Hardly any of them realise that the 'Sounds' they think 'theirs' correspond exactly to the society (and its noise) they wish to keep at a distance. A survey has shown that 29 per cent of young people go to discos frequently, and even more (around 40 per cent) expose themselves to bombardment at home. Many are addicted to their Walkman. They lie back and let music 'pour into their ears' via headphones as if 'boozing' – for an average of 24 hours a week at around 100 decibels. That's 'wild' and 'crazy' – according to them. They say that everyday reality wouldn't be bearable without their daily 'shot of music'. Music as a means of intoxication, as *dope*. Like the intoxication of their speeding motor-cycles, 'Super-Screamers', which also generate noise. They are *sound junkies*. Decibel power becomes theirs. Like the horse-power of their Yamahas – and Yamaha manufactures both speed and sound machines. They talk about 'Full Power', and it is uncertain whether they are referring to their Sounds, motor-cycles, or simply to – power. Those are their means of gaining the power they otherwise lack.

VIII
ENAMOURED OF EXPLOSIONS

A connection exists between noise and machines. Especially between noise and machines whose performance is based on explosions – in that chain which started with the internal combustion engine and ends, one way or the other, with the atomic bomb. What all these 'machines' have in common – different though they may be – is the imbalance between energy and output. That becomes most apparent in what we first think of as a 'motor' – the internal combustion and diesel engines in our cars where a substantial amount of the energy expended and released is blown out of the exhaust, fouling the air and poisoning the countryside. The car is a symbol of the affluent society. It is wasteful. One of the products of that process of squandering is acoustic garbage: noise.

Many people – and not just the young – are still enthusiastic about cars. They think themselves up-to-date, but the car is in fact an antiquated form of locomotion. It does not accord with our knowledge – let alone our state of consciousness – at the end of the twentieth century. It belongs to the nineteenth century as a product of that era's mechanistic view of the world. Nothing essential about the car has been changed since then. There have only been improvements – in an endless chain still used by industry as a means of continually making profits.

Writers of Science Fiction in fact know more about tomorrow's world than most scientists, and help devise the future since it is after all our ideas that create the world. Futurologists, technologists, cyberneticists, physicists, and town-planners have also participated in development of a vision of a means of transport that glides silently through our cities, wasting almost no resources. They refer to the model supplied by nature (on which we otherwise so willingly base our activities): the smooth movement of blood corpuscles in our veins or of insects in bee-hives, termitaria, or ant-hills where the population is far more dense than in human cities but there are scarcely any collisions – and certainly not any squandering and noise. They have shown that throughout this century technicians and engineers have been fixated on the idea of the automobile, and that industry, politicians, banks, and top managers have been virtually obsessed by what provided a sure means of accumulating and maximising ever more capital. Intellect, strength, energy, and money were no longer free – were not meant to be free – to develop other models opened up by the potential of electronics, remote-controlled sources of power, and solar energy. Industrial lobbies and the electricity industry have influenced universities and politicians against investing larger sums of money and contemporary humanity's full intellectual potential in research and development of alternative models for energy and transportation. Money continued – and continues – to be primarily available for 'explosive' technologies.

Twentieth-century man is neurotically fixated on explosions. Neuroses receive expression in aggression. Aggressiveness demands weapons. It is not just by chance that this fixation culminates in the atomic bomb, which is not explicable except as a fixation. The aggressivity of the atomic bomb is that of the optically hypertrophied human being, constantly indulging in self-deception about himself and the world. (See Chapter 1.)

We race along some highway, take a break somewhere, and notice at the roadside, just a few yards away from the roar of the traffic, a blade of grass which has forced its way through the asphalt. We can feel the road vibrating as big lorries thunder past, but it takes years before the resultant wear and tear make repairs necessary. And then we see this blade of grass which has found its way in the course of a single spring – without any thundering and explosions, any lethal fumes or noise. What has gone wrong with our senses, with our way of perceiving the world, that no one notices where the greater power is to be found?

IX
NOISE = POWER!

Fixation on explosions also entails fixation on noise. Young people racing through the streets on their BMWs, Hondas, and Yamahas and the people who shake their heads over that are agreed: the more noise, the more *power*. They cannot imagine – and if they could, they wouldn't like the idea – that there exist energy-models producing little or no noise. They need noise as 'proof' that energy is there. The 'proof' is almost more important than the energy itself.

An American manufacturer of electrical equipment developed a silent vacuum cleaner, but housewives didn't buy it. They believed that if it didn't make a noise it wasn't vacuuming properly.

Fixation on noise and explosions also has sexual overtones. Women are also fascinated by *power*. They too need noise as 'proof', and often as 'the thing itself'. Girls, sitting behind their boyfriends on motor-bikes, feel – more intensively than their mates – why what they *experience* is so good. For them sex lasts for hours and often an entire day, starting when they mount the bike and stopping when they climb off – as another logarithmic curve that mounts and mounts and mounts.

X
PIANISTIC POTENTIAL: 17 TO 19 TONS

The connection between sound and noise, on the one hand, and power and strength on the other is not just speculation. That relationship is not a modern development. It is deeply rooted in every form of sound-production. We make our voice louder, we shout at someone, if we want to make our power and strength felt – and we ourselves must summon up greater energy for that.

The history of many musical instruments makes clear that power is concealed in sound. The strings in an old single-manual Baroque harpsichord exert a pressure of 500 kg, and in a dual-manual instrument 800 kg. The comparable figure for a modern concert grand is between 17 and 19 tons! That is the power over which a pianist disposes, potentially present in every note he plays!

In the sixties when young players of electric instruments didn't know so much about electronics, *Melody Maker*, the English rock and pop paper, reported every few months that someone had been killed because his guitar was wrongly connected. The 'electrifying' energy we think we feel through listening to a record by Jimi Hendrix was really 'there' as physical energy when Hendrix played this music. It is still there wherever electric instruments are played.

XI
CHECKING SERVICE FOR BODY AND SOUL

Significantly, machine civilisation didn't develop in Italy or Spain, countries which were initially on a higher spiritual, cultural, and intellectual level. It developed North of the Alps where repression of bodily narcissism was strictest. The first country to be mechanised was puritanical Britain. And body-hostile immigrants from England and Holland – rather than from elsewhere in Europe – contributed most towards determined, rapid, and successful establishment of America's machine civilisation.

We ourselves – our body, our soul, our consciousness, and our unconscious – constitute the model for what we make of the world. A 'feedback control system' exists between ourselves and the world. By interpreting nature mechanistically, man feels himself to be a machine. By feeling that, he makes himself into a machine. People go to doctors, who now operate with machines rather than curative knowledge and healing powers, and they consult analysts so as to be 'repaired' and become capable of 'functioning' in society, or in their marriage or at work. Like machines being declared 'roadworthy' by some Checking Service for Body and Soul.

The neuroses that are a human 'waste product' are analogous to the noise which is machines' 'spin-off'. Machines would not be able to produce noise if we did not bear 'noise' within ourselves. The explosions of technology – and certainly also of bombs – parallel the explosions within our souls and minds.

9

THE WORLD IS SOUND

'Assuming that an absolutely correct and complete explanation of music, accounting for all the details, were to be conceptualised . . . that would also immediately be a satisfactory . . . explanation of the world – in other words, true philosophy.'

Arthur Schopenhauer

I
THE WAY OF HARMONICS

The world is sound. We find music everywhere: in planetary orbits, pulsars, genes, oxygen atoms, crystals, leaf forms, etc. This chapter is concerned with such phenomena. Once again only a selection from the available material can be presented. Almost everything in the macro- and micro-cosmos and in our terrestrial world obeys the laws of harmonics, so a book about all that would be encyclopaedic in extent.

Heisenberg viewed reflection on the harmonic thinking developed by Pythagoras as being 'one of the strongest impulses within human science'. He believed that the development of knowledge has 'confirmed Pythagoreans' belief to an inconceivable degree'.

I am concerned with what we hear since my experience – as I have time and again demonstrated – is that both inner and outer hearing, which cannot be separated, change consciousness to a greater extent than anything else in our eye-orientated age. That is why facts about harmonics are necessary.

Harmonics is a Way involving whole numbers. We find it in the overtone series and in intervallic proportions, in Lambdoma's law, electron spins, planetary orbits, and all the other phenomena considered in this book and its predecessor. It is, however, necessary to realise that rhythm is also a 'whole number phenomenon'. Rhythms that we can dance to and feel with our bodies are fractions of whole numbers. As with the overtone scale: the lower the numerical relationship, the greater the 'consonance'. What in the overtone scale is the octave's 1:2 relationship becomes the 1:2 metre of the march among rhythms.

Demonstration of the relationship between our heart (which at rest beats around sixty times a minute) and our pulse rate which is twice as fast (120 times a minute) will throw light on the sliding scale involved in the intermingling of rhythms and sounds. 120:60 is 2:1, which can be perceived as a simple duple rhythm as found in marches. If each of those two pulsations becomes ever faster, at some point they change from a beat into a ringing, but the two notes thus produced maintain the ratio of 2:1, thereby forming an octave. We thus see that sounds are rhythms which are so fast that they can no longer be registered as such. Or rhythms can be seen as sounds that vibrate so slowly that they can no longer be heard in that way.

II
THE MIRACLE OF THE OCTAVE

'Octavus sanctos omnes docet esse beatos.'

'The Octave teaches all Saints to be Blessed' runs the motto heading this section, which is to be found on one of the mysterious columns in the abbey church of Cluny in France. In no other ratio do the musical and the universal, the material and the spiritual, and the artistic and the mathematical come together so marvellously.

When men and women sing together, they sing in octaves more frequently than in any other interval. When cell-division occurs in DNA, the mitosis selects precisely the place where the octave is 'established' as if the cell were a string. By dividing exactly in two, it creates an octave. As Dane Rudhyar has written: 'The first octave . . . symbolises the sexual love of male and female as it reflects the divine love of Shiva and Shakti.'

Plato's account of the ancient idea that the male and the female body are nothing but separated halves, and that the whole, complete human being will only come into existence with reunification, is *also* a Pythagorean concept. Separation – the division into two – entails the downward octave, and reunification (doubling) the upward octave. Love is thus a process of initiating octaves.

The octave vibrates twice as fast or half as fast, but is nevertheless the same note. It splits oneness into two parts, and the outcome is the same again. It is something 'completely different', many Hertz above or below the keynote, but when a woman sings a melody an octave above what a man is singing, she is still singing the same melody. We use the same names for notes an octave apart. The octave is the most convincing symbol of oneness to be found in nature – and it is omnipresent.

The octave is also the first note in the harmonic series – and also its largest interval (1:2). The next is the fifth (2:3), followed by the fourth (3:4), the major sixth (3:5), etc. The intervals become ever smaller. They finally become so small – starting in the seventh octave – that the ear can hardly hear any difference. For Ptolemy and the Greeks the last musically meaningful interval entailed the ratio 45:46, an enharmonic quarter tone.

The harmonic series thus begins with the octave as a symbol of oneness, and then it leads on again to unity. At its beginning and its 'end' are oneness. I put the word 'end' in inverted commas because the harmonic series is infinite whereas for our ears 'oneness' (now also qualified) begins much earlier, soon after the seventh octave.

The octave is the only aspect of our tonal system that is not tempered. The ear may measure all intervals with astonishing accuracy but none more accurately than the octave. Even someone 'unmusical' can do that.

The Devil has always been viewed as the destroyer of oneness. That defines him. The interval that does so most strikingly is the tritone. It divides the octave into two parts. Is that why the ancients called it the *diabolus in musica*?

The octave provides the 'seed' for polyphony – *still* the same yet marking the start of differentiation. For Pythagoreans the word *harmonia* at first signified octave.

The octave is the 'most complete' of the whole-number relationships underlying the harmonic series, and overwhelmingly abundant and recognisable everywhere in nature – defying all statistical probability. That becomes clear in electron and proton spins whose rotation is in octaves. 'Rotation can be parallel or anti-parallel to the orbit.' In the former case scientists speak of plus-spin, and in the latter of minus-spin. The octave leaps upwards or downwards.

With the octave there begins what physicist Paul Gohlke summarised as follows: 'If Max Planck was right in saying that all impact on the world can only be a whole-number intensification of the least impact . . . then the whole number is of unique significance with regard to perceiving that kind of world. The laws regulating whole numbers must be world laws.'

III

THE EARTHLY TRIAD: DAY, YEAR, AND
MOON TONES

Music is inconceivable without transposition by octaves. When a child imitates a melody its father has sung, in the overwhelming majority of cases this is transposed upwards by octaves. If a man wants to sing a melody written for a piccolo, he will usually transpose it downwards by complete octaves. Of course he could transpose the melody into another key, but experience shows that simple people particularly try to avoid that because they feel it gives the tune 'another character'. A great deal has been written by musicologists about the 'character' of different keys: the 'radiant G major', the 'sturdy C major', the 'spiritual D minor', etc. The reasons for such diversity have still not been convincingly explained. Scholars maintain that it is all a matter of ratios, which are exactly the same in every key thanks to tempered tuning. Do we also sense in the process of transposition the original ('correct') tuning, and do our ears compensate for the 'wrong' (tempered) transposition from one key to another, resulting in 'right' distances between notes? That by the way would be particularly convincing evidence in favour of our ears' capacity both to measure with mathematical exactitude and to evaluate intuitively and spiritually – a capacity that, as we have seen, the eye cannot match. Our ears would thus have the fascinating ability to, as it were, evade tempered 'mis-tuning' and basically once again overturn the possibility of modulating from key to key for which tempering was introduced in the eighteenth century. The ear may accept that possibility and, as we know from our musical experience, gladly acquiesce in it, but only up to a certain point. It 'scrutinises' tempering in every single case.

This makes all the more clear that anyone who wants to transpose accurately must proceed by octaves. No more accurate procedure is conceivable. It is *a priori* immanent in all music.

Hans Cousto, the Swiss scholar, has applied this procedure so as to make audible the music of the spheres. The heavenly bodies can thus be heard – 'each with their own tones . . . The likeness corresponds homophonically to the original, and the keys are the same, displaced by octaves.'

Planetary frequencies are based on orbiting times: 24 hours for the earth, 224 days for Venus, 4,332 days for Jupiter, etc. Rotations entail vibrations. In order to move from planetary vibrations to those of our earthly music one must 'octavise' between 26 and 50 times – depending on the planet's distance from the sun. Our solar system thus covers a range of exactly ten octaves, exactly paralleling – in another of those miraculous surprises – our ear. Is that so that the 'inner ear' can 'hear' the planets?

If you want to reach the visual sphere, you must pass through another forty or so octaves. Pluto is then a deep blue and Neptune somewhat darker still. Uranus is a bright orange and Jupiter's red is even more luminous than Saturn's resplendent Prussian blue. Mars and Mercury are also blue while our Earth is an orange-red and Venus somewhat more yellow.

I don't want to bore my readers with mathematics but 'octavising' – doubling or halving a frequency – is so simple that anyone can do it. The ratio between time (still with reference to the Cousto method) and frequency is:

$$\text{Frequency} = \frac{1}{\text{Time}}$$

The frequency produced by the earth's orbit around the sun (365 ¼ days) is thus calculated by dividing 1 by 365 ¼. To make that frequency audible I must double it – i.e. octavise it – until I reach the sphere of tonal vibrations perceptible to our ears. As Cousto says: 'Apart from establishing reciprocal values and multiplication with the number 2, no kind of mathematical knowledge is needed for calculation of a metre, a note, and a colour analogous to an astronomical period.' This is the most precise and most plausible of the many procedures discovered since Pythagoras for making audible the sounds made by planets – the 'harmony of the spheres'. One says of a child repeating a tune its father has just sung that this is 'the same melody again' – just one or two octaves higher. The 'primordial tones' of the Earth, Sun, Moon, etc., made audible by the Cousto method are also 'the same tones again' rendered accessible to our hearing.

Let us take as a starting-point the most important frequency for life on this planet – the earthly day of 24 hours (or to be precise: 23 hours, 56 minutes, and 4 seconds = 86,164 seconds). We unconsciously sense how this permeates our existence in a multitude of ways. Our meals and eating habits, our working hours and leisure time, are based on that. So too is the way flowers bloom and birds sing. Almost everything in our daily life 'dances' to that tune. It is wonderful to see that happening in concretely mathematical (and musical) terms as well as feeling it to be the case. In order to discover the frequency (vibrations expressed in Hertz) of the median earth-day, I must calculate the reciprocal value of 86,164 seconds. That amounts to 0.000,001,160,576 Hz, which is obviously way below audibility, which starts at around 16 Hz. But if I transpose that upwards by just 24 octaves, I can hear it and get a G of 194.71 Hz – and it is unimportant in this case which concert pitch I use: the old English of 432 Hz, the Parisian of 435 Hz, or today's of 440 Hz. The G is so central here that it is always produced.

It is the G that indicates the treble clef, and is thus of crucial importance for our key system as the fifth note from C and the fundamental interval for most processes of tuning. The French term is *sol* – and it is strange how that word relates to both heavenly bodies: *sol* (= Earth in terms of soil) and *soleil* (= sun). The French word for singing scales is *solfier*, which may relate to both sun and earth. The name *sol* was in fact chosen 'unconsciously'. It goes back to the Gregorian Johannine hymn *Ut queant laxis* from which Guido of Arezzo, a Benedictine monk, derived the names of notes in the eleventh century. In the fifth bar of this hymn the G occurs on the first syllable (*sol*) of the words *solve polluti*. It occurs there 'by chance', but it is similar to the kind of 'chance' whereby the Ancient Greeks' Attic foot was precisely derived from the diameter of the earth's equator without the people who devised this unit of measurement ever having had a chance of calculating the equator.

The impatient reader may long have been wondering what colour the earth-day is. In order to move from the G to the visual sphere (limited to a single octave) we must pass through another forty octaves. In the 65th octave we attain a frequency of 427 billion Hertz, referred to by physicists as 702 nanometres, which produces a luminous orange-red. For almost three thousand years – and perhaps longer – that has been the colour worn by Sannyasins, both Hindu and Buddhist monks and their successors today. If we pass through just one more octave we attain precisely the resonance of DNA (deoxyribonucleic acid). This vehicle of human heredity thus vibrates in the 66th octave of the earth-day. Orange-red resonates in conjunction with DNA at a distance of a single octave, which is the most direct and most powerfully effective of all harmonic relations. It oscillates in the note G, which is of central significance in our music as the dominant to the tonic of C major, vibrating in relationship to the frequency of the earth-day.

Of course the Earth also has a 'year tone' as well as a 'day tone'. That can be calculated on the basis of the 'tropic' year which lasts 365.2422 days: 525,948 minutes and 46 seconds – or precisely

31,556,926 seconds. That is an especially important frequency for life on this planet – alongside the daily and monthly cycles. If we transpose it upwards – simply 'making it higher', the most natural thing in the world in any music-making – we reach the audible sphere after 32 octaves, attaining a frequency of 136.102 Hz, which is just below the C sharp on the chromatic scale (based on the old Parisian concert-pitch).

In the case of the earth-day the G with its central significance for our musical system establishes a striking relationship to the corresponding cosmic vibration. Virtually no relationship exists, however, with regard to the 'year tone'. Its existence in Indian music is thus all the more remarkable. The fundamental note, *Sa* or *Sadja*, corresponds exactly to the 'year tone' – and there has not been any change for thousands of years. In India the Master teaches his pupil (often a father his son) this tone (136 Hz) with an intensity far beyond anything experienced in similar situations in the West. The young musician must play or sing this note for years until it has become securely established as a vibrating part of his self. Never again can he be mistaken about pitch. Anyone who has worked with Indian musicians knows how seriously they take that.

Sa, the 'year tone' serving as the basis for Indian instruments, has been known since ancient times as the 'Father of the other notes'. This tone, which can also be called the Earth-related Sun tone, is not only the foundation of all Indian music; it serves too as the preferred basis for tuning bells (including temple bells) and gongs – in Tibet and Indonesia as well as in India. *Sa* has also been the note most frequently used since antiquity for the primal word and sacred mantra OM.

At her institute in Denver, Colorado, Dorothy Retallack, the American biologist, played different kinds of music to various plants in a number of hot-houses. The plants 'loved' Indian music most of all, followed by Johann Sebastian Bach. In their effort to reach the source of this music, they lay almost horizontally, forming angles of up to 60 degrees so as to twine around the loudspeakers. They 'hated' rock music. When that was played they grew away from the loudspeakers, and if it went on for a long time they died.

At first I assumed that this phenomenon was linked with the kind of music involved – and that certainly continues to be correct. In the meantime, however, it is clear that attention must also be directed towards the fact that Indian music is 'organically and cosmically correctly tuned' to *Sa*, the 'Father of notes', the sun tone and its long-established relationship over millions of years with everything that exists on this planet. Plants have grown and trees have developed their age-rings to this sun tone since time immemorial, but rock music is tuned to a higher concert-pitch (440 Hz, and often even more), lacking any cosmic or biological legitimisation, and selected only for the sake of greater instrumental brilliance.

Young scientists working together with Hans Cousto in Munich have induced geraniums to bloom in winter by holding a tuning-fork producing the sun tone near the flower pots for just a few minutes a day until the sound died away.

There is also the month or Moon tone, the third most important frequency for existence on our planet. We can base our investigation on various 'months' – synodic, sidereal, solar, etc. The most 'obvious' to humanity is the synodic month which is the period of time between two equivalent lunar phases – i.e. from full moon to full moon, or from new moon to new moon. This lasts 29 days, 12 hours, 44 minutes, and 2.8 seconds. That amounts to 42,524.047 minutes or 2,551,442.8 seconds. The reciprocal value of that number entails a frequency of $3.919,351 \times 10^{-7}$ Hz. We have to transpose by 30 octaves in order to reach median audibility at 420.837 Hz. Today that is a G sharp, which is not a very important note in our music. The relationship between the Moon and today's music is not therefore very strong. Things were different during the Baroque era and Early Classical period, which resonated with the Moon. Mozart's tuning-fork, for instance, vibrated at 421.6 Hz, Handel's at 422.5 Hz, and Bach's (according to the Sophia organ in Dresden) at 415.5 Hz, while concert-pitch was 422 Hz in Berlin at mid-eighteenth century and 423 Hz at Paris in 1810.

Only after 1820 did the rise in concert-pitch get under way – for the superficial reason of producing a more brilliant impact – so that Western music increasingly left the Moon's sphere of resonance, which ancient astrological traditions view as being particularly 'responsible' for art and artists. In the nineteenth century it was mainly French musicians who pushed standard pitch ever higher so that their music sounded 'more brilliant', thereby getting ever further away from the cosmic relationship – and today the great American symphony orchestras do the same.

Astonishingly, if we add forty octaves to the moon tone, it attains the Sannyasin colour of orange (corresponding to a wavelength of 648 nanometres) in the seventieth octave of the synodic month.

We can utilise that method to discover the frequencies – and thus the notes – of all the planets by way of a simple transposition of octaves. We then get a D for Mercury, an A for Venus, a D for

Mars, an F sharp for Jupiter, a D for Saturn, a G sharp for Uranus, an A for Neptune, and a C sharp for Pluto – based on the old Parisian concert-pitch of 435 Hz.

We can establish an abundance of highly interesting harmonic relationships between year, Earth, Moon, and the various planetary tones. Both the individual heavenly bodies and their inter-relationships 'sound forth' in a multi-levelled network of great musical richness.

IV

THE HARMONY OF THE SPHERES FROM
PYTHAGORAS TO KEPLER

Kepler's choice of a fundamental tone for his 'Planetary Music' was still arbitrary, despite being based on profound wisdom nourished by Pythagorean tradition. In the meantime it is, however, clear that every planetary tone, inclusive of the fundamental note, results from the process of octavising – which signifies (as Kepler already knew) that any human being's horoscope can be transformed into audible music. The circle initiated by Pythagoras is thereby completed.

What is probably the oldest Pythagorean planetary harmonics derives from Nikomachos of Gerasa, a Neo-Pythagorean in the second century AD. That is a model based on two tetrachords (or fourths). The Moon was the nearest (lowest) and Saturn the most distant (highest) heavenly body. In between were Venus, Mercury, the Sun, Mars, and Jupiter – whereby the first and second levels were each separated by a whole-tone from the surrounding levels while there was a semitone between Mercury and the Sun. Those intervals were repeated in the second tetrachord. The planets were thus attributed with the following notes:

Saturn	E
Jupiter	F
Mars	G
Sun	A
Mercury	B
Venus	C_o
Moon	D_o

– in accordance with contemporary Greek tuning of the cithara where the strings were vertical with the deepest nearest the player's head and the highest furthest away. Greek melodies descended, striving towards the lowest note.

That model was constantly refined and varied. Pliny the Elder (AD 23/24–79) thus developed a nine-part scheme where the Earth preceded the Moon and the fixed stars followed Saturn – a model extending through six whole-tones which was taken over, changed, and further developed by the Church Fathers in the Christian era. The world was viewed as 'God's musical instrument' (Censorinus, third century AD), and the seven planets as analogous to the seven-stringed lyre. The purpose and meaning of the music of the spheres was to provide an eternal hymn of praise from Sun, Moon, and stars in honour of God. Beyond the planetary orbits the exultant choirs of the heavenly hosts sing before God's throne. In the later Middle Ages music-making made planetary sounds superfluous so that they were forgotten – until Kepler, the German Pythagoras *redivivus*, rediscovered them. In his *Mysterium Cosmographicum*, an early work, he wrote:

> I search for traces of Thy Spirit out in the universe, gaze in ecstasy upon the splendour of the mighty edifice of Heaven, that elaborate work and miracle of Thy Omnipotence, regard how Thou hast created the five-fold orbits of the planets, and in their midst the Sun, donor of life and light; contemplate the law regulating the course of the stars, how the Moon changes and what labours it fulfils, and how Thou scatterest millions of stars upon the Heavens.

Kepler worked with great precision and irrefutable mathematical logicality in his discovery of the seven 'primordial harmonies' – Octave, Fifth, Fourth, Major Sixth, Major Third, Minor Third, and Minor Sixth – measuring the angular velocities of planetary movement at the extremes of their ellipses (the perihelion nearest the sun, and the aphelion furthest away). Hans Schavernoch concludes: 'The harmony of the spheres is thus heard directly by way of the sun, and humanity derives spiritual delight from experiencing this concord' – as did Kepler and, earlier still, Pythagoras and his followers, who viewed earthly music as having resulted from the fact that human beings unconsciously reflect cosmic music:

> The movements of the heavens are therefore nothing other than unceasing polyphony . . . a music that moves by way of dissonance and tension, syncopations and cadenzas, towards pre-determined sextuple constellations, thereby establishing distinctive specifica within the immeasurable course of time. It is therefore no longer

surprising that humanity, imitator of the Creator, finally discovered the art of polyphonic song which was unknown to the Ancients. Humanity wanted to capture the ongoing duration of world-time in a creative multi-voiced symphony lasting just a brief part of an hour, enjoying a taste of the Divine Creator's pleasure in His works so far as that is possible in the bliss engendered by this music in imitation of God. (Johannes Kepler)

V

SCIENTIFIC CONFIRMATION

Only we who are alive today can judge the rightness of the idea of the harmony of the spheres. Only now can that be scientifically and precisely assessed. The long chain extending from Pythagoras by way of Plato, Cicero, Philo of Alexandria, and all the rest down to Kepler, and from him to Hans Kayser, Rudolf Haase, and Cousto in our time, produced two harmonically based calculations of distances between the planets so accurate that they might have been made by modern science itself.

Johann Daniel Titius, a German scientist (1729–1796), discovered a regularity in the medial-positions between the six planets known at that time which led Johann Elert Bode (1747–1826), director of the Berlin observatory, to assume the existence of a planet beyond Saturn. That was discovered just a few years later and named Uranus. The Titius–Bode school of thought also postulated a heavenly body between Mars and Jupiter, and the tiny Ceres was detected there in 1801. In the meantime around 1700 such mini-planets, known as asteroids, have been discovered, occupying the median-position between Mars and Jupiter calculated by the German scientists. Many astronomers are of the opinion that they constitute the ruins of a larger planet which circled on precisely the orbit discovered by Titius and Bode.

The Titius–Bode theory was the logical outcome of ideas first developed by Pythagoras and ever further refined over the centuries. Taking the distance between the Sun and the Earth as 1, that formula produced distances of 0.4 to Mercury (compared to the true distance of 0.39), 0.7 to Venus (0.72), 1.6 to Mars (1.52), etc., thus achieving astonishing precision. The only deviations worthy of mention are with Neptune and Pluto, neither of which were known at that time, but they in fact confirm the procedure since the calculation relating to the former (38.8) actually applies to the latter (39.46).

E. Zederbauer achieved similarly amazing results in 1917. Convinced of the rightness of Pythagorean ideas, he based his work on a right-angled isosceles triangle whose harmonic proportions had been known to the Greeks. Following Hellenistic pupils of Pythagoras, on the sides of the triangle he established squares whose corners touched the circumference of a circle. He thereby ascertained distances even more accurately than Titius and Bode – with minimal deviations of between 0.01 and 0.46, which could be disregarded since only mean distances were required.

The main reason, however, why these divergences could be ignored is that the cosmos only operates in terms of discrepancies. Carl Gustav Carus, the great doctor and philosopher of science (1789–1869), stated that 'Pure law can never receive absolutely clear-cut expression in nature or else the appearance would be the law itself.' Rudolf Haase refers to Theodor Lipps' basic aesthetic principle whereby in art and music 'minimal deviations from exact proportions are necessary so that the latter seem particularly beautiful and attractive.'

Such concepts are universally valid – throughout the cosmos. They receive convincing confirmation in the existence of what are called 'spheres of compensatory hearing', which have been known since the Baroque era and constitute a crucial element in the tempered tuning system. Anyone who hears an out-of-tune piano experiences how that works. After a while one no longer notices that the instrument is off-tune. The ear provides precise 'compensation' so that one hears the 'intended' frequency.

If 'spheres of compensatory hearing' (of up to 48 per cent of a semitone) exist, then they must certainly also exist in nature. It would be absurd to demand greater accuracy of nature than of music, which after all reflects the proportions of nature. On the other hand, we cannot expect of music accuracies which do not exist in nature – and are also undesirable since this is a question of spiritual qualities, and the soul needs 'room to manoeuvre'. The very fact of 'divergences' is therefore a confirmation of the harmonic character of the universe. Such 'deviations' are not only to be found in the planetary system. They also occur in the proportions of leaves and bodies, and also, of course, in the microcosm. In fact everywhere in nature.

It is also revealing that Titius and Bode, on the one hand, and Zederbauer, on the other, approached this question in completely different ways – the former arithmetically and the latter geometrically. They were, however, convinced of the Pythagorean idea of a harmonious planetary system, of the symmetry and balance of its proportions, and of the law of integrality. They verified all those hypotheses more convincingly than was to have been expected in terms of the premisses of positivistic science.

VI
HARMONIC POLLUTION

We have seen that Indian music and European compositions during the Baroque and Early Classical periods in many respects resonated in harmony with the earth-day, earth-month, and earth-year. That congruence where cosmic and earthly music come together no longer exists in Western music today.

We must become fully aware of the fact that the music enveloping us daily – from radio and television, on record-players and cassettes, and in supermarkets and hotel foyers – is not in harmony with the vibrations of the cosmos. There are other disharmonious frequencies too. The 60 Hz (50 Hz in Europe) of the power supply system in which we are trapped are omnipresent as if they really were a 'net', never releasing us in our homes and on our streets. That does not involve any kind of cosmic (or even biological) connection. It thus contradicts and frustrates cosmic and biological vibrations.

We could intensify – to an unimaginable degree – the 'good' vibrations in harmony with nature and the cosmos if only the electricity in our homes, permeating our existence so constantly, powerfully, and measurably, were related by octaves to an important cosmic vibration.

Radar waves, power cables, micro-waves from ovens and other technical equipment, fluorescent tubes, X-rays, and ultra-sound also contribute to pollution of the natural vibratory fields surrounding us. Ultra-sound is still used for diagnostic purposes even though disturbing discoveries have been made – for instance at the University of Illinois Institute of Preventive Medicine – about the resultant destruction of DNA cells, delayed maturation, and even the possible development of cancer.

The electromagnetic waves of radio and television in a great diversity of wave-bands also envelop us daily – just like electricity. Telecommunications experts even talk of 'chaos and confusion', which is now increasingly compounded by satellite and cable network frequencies.

Attention was drawn in the last chapter to pollution of the natural vibratory field by air-conditioning. It is as if modern man had 'cocooned' himself in a network of unnatural technical oscillations, radiation, and frequencies so that the organic vibrations of this planet and the cosmos cannot reach him – as if he unconsciously wanted to escape their power and impact.

VII
COSMIC ASPECTS OF ARCHITECTURE

Marius Schneider drew attention to the mysterious relationship between great architecture and the proportions of both our earthly music and the cosmos. It has long been assumed that the ancient Egyptians 'knew' about those proportions, partly consciously and partly unconsciously. They had (as John Michell shows in his book *City of Revelation*) three units for measuring length: the *remen* (37.1 cm), *cube* (52.4 cm), and megalithic *yard* (82.9 cm). If one calculates the time that light takes to speed through any of those units of measurement, the answer involves figures closely related to the earth's rotation or the globe's orbit around the sun. The *remen* thereby accords with the day-tone G, the *cube* to the year-tone C sharp, and the megalithic *yard* to F, the tone of the Platonic year. In each case the answer is found by octavising the frequency.

Today many experts are of the opinion that 'the pyramid of Cheops entails symbolic depiction of the earth's dimensions to a scale of 1:43,200' (Cousto). The figure 43,200 is half the number of seconds in an average solar day as well as being a twentieth of the sun's diameter in miles and the former English concert-pitch of 432 Hz multiplied by a hundred.

It is also exciting to compare the dimensions of the pyramid of Cheops with those of Chartres Cathedral – both highpoints in the architecture of the two cultures. The circumference of the Cheops pyramid amounts to 231.92 m. Divide that by ten and you get 23.192 m, which is exactly, to the millimetre, the length of one of the sides of the celebrated quadratic ground-plan at Chartres. The area covered by Cheops is thus a hundred times greater than this ground-plan.

The Chartres 'Elle' is 0.738 m – to the millimetre a two-hundredth part of the height of the pyramid (147.6 m) or a two-thousandth part of the sun's gravitational length (1476.6 m).

The height of the Cheops pyramid also corresponds exactly to the Equator's diameter (12,756 km) divided by the 86,400 seconds of the median solar day, so that even that measurement is to be found in Chartres Cathedral.

Cosmic relationships are present in many of humanity's great sacred buildings. It is possible that architects knew from the start about cosmic dimensions and made them the foundation for their plans and buildings; or it is also conceivable that many master-builders were unconsciously – and thus all the more convincingly – at one with the universe in what they did. It may now be taken as established that the great architects of the Middle Ages did not operate as 'unconsciously' as people assumed just a few years ago, following now superseded ideas about the 'Dark Ages'. Many medieval plans of cathedrals and churches contain depictions of the Sun, the Moon, and the planets in the skies above the building, and it is hardly likely that the architects merely drew these heavenly bodies as ornamentation.

If we transpose the dimensions of an artistically important building into music, the outcome is always that the sounds thus produced are convincingly harmonious.

Paul Brunton, jazz musician Paul Horn, and many others have reported on the wonderful experiences they had when meditating in the burial chamber in the pyramid of Cheops. Millions of Christians have had similar experiences in the great monuments of European sacred architecture. Do we think architectural masterpieces – such as the Taj Mahal in North India, Borobudur in Java, the Banyon at Angkor Wat, Miyajima near Hiroshima, or Chartres and the pyramid of Cheops – so marvellous precisely because they are at one with the cosmos? Because they are – in the highest sense of the word – 'attuned'? And because we too become 'at one' with cosmic dimensions when we collect our thoughts, pray, and meditate in these buildings?

VIII
HARMONIC ARCHITECTURE TO MAN'S MEASURE

Great architecture – and especially sacred buildings – are 'rightly aligned' in three respects:

1. By being harmonically 'correct', i.e. according with the proportions of the harmonic series in forming octaves, fourths, fifths, and thirds. Such architecture is 'frozen music'.
2. By being based on cosmic dimensions – as I showed in the preceding section with regard to Chartres and the pyramid of Cheops.
3. By according with the forms and proportions of the human body. As Vitruvius stated: 'A temple lacks symmetry, proportion, and rational form if its elements are not related to one another as the limbs of a well-shaped human being.'

Almost all the units of measure in ancient architecture are based on the human body: the ell (length of the forearm from the elbow to the tip of the middle finger), the span (width of the extended hand from thumb to little finger), the hand's-breadth, the foot, the pace, and the cord (distance between the finger-tips of the outstretched arms), etc. The Ancient Greeks also knew such measurements. Their smallest dimension, the *daktylos* (= fingers-width) was a quarter of the *palaiste* (= hand's width) – four of which were contained in the *pous* (foot) and six in the *pechys* (= ell). The Romans had the *palmae* (hand's width), *pollices* (thumb's width), *digiti* (finger's width), etc.

What is decisive, however, is the fact that possibilities 1, 2, and 3 merely signify different ways or methods whereby architects attained 'harmony' in their buildings. Possibility 1 is all-embracing since the human body and the cosmos are also harmonically structured.

Paul von Naredi-Rainer, the Austrian art historian, has demonstrated immanent harmonic, human, and cosmic proportions within the Western architecture he knows so well. The temple of Athena at Paestum is thus an immense architectural embodiment of harmonic relationships. The axial dimensions (40 × 96) of the temple can, for instance, be derived from what for Pythagoreans were the sacred numbers of the tetraktys.

Renaissance architects devoted even more conscious attention to harmonic aspects. Leon Battista Alberti (1404–1472) urged in his highly influential tract *De Re Aedificatorio Libri Decem* (printed in 1485) that 'the entire law of [architectural] relations should be derived . . . from musicians who are best acquainted with such proportions'. He too was concerned with the 1, 2, 3, and 4 of the tetraktys, and with the intervals – viewed as consonants – of the octave (1:2), fifth (2:3), fourth (3:4), twelfth (1:3), double octave (1:4), and whole-tone (8:9).

In his celebrated painting 'The School of Athens' (1509/10), Raphael 'incorporated' both forms of the tetraktys – 1, 2, 3, 4, and 6, 8, 9, 12 – as Pythagoreans' great secret.

Alberti warned the man in charge of construction of his Tempio Malatestiano at Rimini not to change the dimensions and proportions of the pillars in any way, disrupting 'all the music' ('tutta quella musica'). Naredi-Rainer shows that the building's arcade-like façade consists of a succession of octave-relationships while the areal proportions accord with the ratios of the twelfth (octave + fifth). Filippo Brunelleschi (1377–1446) demonstrated possibly even greater harmonic subtlety in his work on Florence's cathedral whose dome was largely constructed in accordance with the Fibonacci series. That series of numbers was devised by a medieval mathematician, Leonardo da Pisa (c. 1180–1240) known as Fibonacci. It is said to have been an answer to Emperor Friedrich II's question about how many pairs of rabbits would be produced from a single couple in the course of a year if every new pair also gave birth to another couple every second month. The numbers of rabbit couples born monthly resulted in the numerical series, 1, 1, 2, 3, 5, 8, 13, 21, 34, 55, 89, 144, etc. Every link in the chain is the sum of the two previous numbers. The Fibonacci series is a manifestation of sixths, but is also a wonderful expression of ancient harmonic wisdom: 'Uniformity is the origin of all proportions.' If we remove a rectangle from a Fibonacci series (e.g. 13 × 8), and then a square from that, and so on for as long as possible, two squares of the same size will remain. Even such a complicated sequence as the Fibonacci series thus leads directly by way of the octave-ratio (1:2) to equality and unity (1:1). The 'one', unity, is the supportive 'foundation' of this series, and the source from which it emanates.

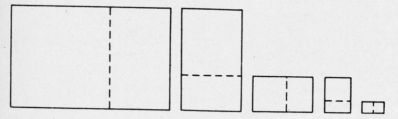

Guillaume Dufay (c. 1400–1474) from the Netherlands was probably the most important musician of his age. For the inauguration of Florence's cathedral of Santa Maria del Fiore on 25 March 1436, he composed a festive motet related to the Fibonacci series involved in the dimensions of the dome. The architects had thus based their work on musical ratios, and then the musicians composed in accordance with architecture founded on musical proportions!

At the end of the previous section I mentioned the spiritual experiences undergone by Paul Horn, Paul Brunton, and many others in the vault of the Taj Mahal, the grave chambers of the pyramids, and similar sacred buildings. It must now be asked what is experienced today by millions of people in modern architecture's 'machines for living' which lack structured relationships. It has been demonstrated that great old buildings focus thought, resulting in centring and concentration – but what ideas will be sparked off in the consciousness of people learning in today's schools and universities, usually so arbitrary and inorganic in their proportions?

IX
VISUALISATION OF HIDDEN HARMONY

Some readers may remember the Chladni sound figures many of us encountered in physics lessons at school. Grains of sand and particles of dust strewn haphazardly on a sheet of glass assume the most beautiful symmetrical shapes amazingly quickly when a violin bow is used against the glass. Anthroposophist Hans Jenny has utilised a similar procedure for making 'visible' in the truest sense of the word the great music of the West. The trill in the 59th bar of the first movement of Mozart's 'Jupiter' symphony thus becomes a cosmic galactic system whose impressive radiance manifests Heraclitus' 'hidden harmony' throughout.

Jenny has shown that the patterns he obtains through the 'visualisation' of great music exactly correspond to nature's own preferred forms – in the development of fleecy clouds and the formation of sand dunes, in the shells of mussels and snails, in the structures of sea- and lake-beds caused by the movements of water, in foam, in ostrich and peacock feathers, in snake skins and skeletons, in coral shapes and seed-capsules, and in blossom and leaves. He has brought out two illustrated books entitled *Cymatics*, offering a fascinating demonstration of the 'musicalisation' and 'harmonicalisation' of the world. One literally sees what George Leonard so succinctly expressed: 'Before we make music, music makes us . . . Music's deep structure is identical with the deep structure of all things.'

Jenny's discoveries cannot be dismissed as the work of an outsider. In a 1958 lecture marking the 100th anniversary of the birth of Max Planck, Werner Heisenberg compared the symmetry within the equations of Planck's quantum theory to the 'elaborate ornamentation in Arab mosques': 'Mathematical structure – i.e. rational numerical relationships as the source of harmony – was certainly one of the most momentous discoveries in the history of humanity . . . Mathematical relationships were therefore also the source of the Beautiful . . . The entire programme of today's precision sciences was thus basically anticipated by Pythagoras.'

X
IN THE BEGINNING WAS SOUND

Chladni's sound figures do not only exist in the two-dimensionality of area. They are also to be found in one- and three-dimensionality. We can fill a vessel with liquid, add a scattering of particles of the same specific weight, and then make the container vibrate by applying integral oscillations. We can thus observe how the particles cluster to form symmetrical shapes and patterns. If we then freeze the entire apparatus, crystals seem to appear. The impression is of having observed a process of crystallisation. The next question is: Did crystals develop in that way? Did enormously powerful integral harmonic vibrations bring about crystalline order among atoms? We shall see (in the chapter on 'Audible and Inaudible Sound') that sound is not dependent on whether we hear it or not. It is defined by integral vibrations – thereby distinguishing itself from the many other possible non-integral vibrations that remain 'oscillations' and cannot be called 'sound'.

We now need only persist in such questioning. If sound can set off such processes of crystallisation, is it not probable that sound also created all the other patterns in nature – everything that we find 'beautiful' in leaves and flowers, shells and cochlea, skins and hides, bodies and fruits, sand and stones, the air and the water, molecular structures such as the DNA double-helix, and galactic spirals . . .?

The 'mathematical relationships' Heisenberg called the source of the Beautiful are an abstraction. If one wants to make the expression 'mathematical relationships' more concrete, the word 'sound' offers itself. So is sound the source of the Beautiful? As we shall see, chaos does not exist and is merely a degree of order and harmony which our senses cannot (yet) perceive. Is sound therefore the source of everything created?

Is the primordial 'Big Bang' sound? Are we coming closer by way of scientific premisses to the view of myths, legends, and spiritual traditions in almost all of the world's cultures that God created the world through 'Sound'? Is it also being demonstrated here that the old myths are true?

Does the idea of a primordial boom, an enormously noisy 'Big Bang', perhaps merely reflect modern man's fixation on noise and explosions? Many modern cosmologers believe that in the beginning was a bang. Not Logos, Spirit, or Word – but a bang! Scientists believe that they can still hear dim reverberations in their highly sensitive equipment. They can measure – across billions of light-years and the ever-growing cosmos – the enfeebled echo of a vast explosion with which the universe began. The first people to hear this echo were two American communications engineers, Arno A. Penzias and Robert Wilson, in 1965. They thought it was 'interference' affecting their radio equipment. Physicist Robert H. Dicke identified that as the 'background noise' he had already calculated and predicted.

Paramahamsa Muktananda, the important Indian researcher into Kundalini energy, asks: 'Why must that have been an explosion reverberating there?' And he ensures his question is not misunderstood by continuing: 'Why do people like explosions so much?'

Cosmologists and physicists hear the echo of a sound that – according to their calculations – must have occurred between 12 and 15 billion years ago. Many peoples' myths and creation stories also maintain that the universe began with a mighty primordial sound – the Primordial Word!

Cosmologists are certainly right to think that they are hearing an echo and a reverberation – a 'background emanation'; but it could also be that 'resonance' which Jakob Böhme, the seventeenth-century Silesian mystic, believed to be the distant reflection of the Primordial Word and Primordial Sound. Why, however, the echo of an explosion? Do not researchers say a great deal more about themselves there than about the universe?

Critical examination of modern science has shown that scientific theories may also be 'myths' – which can often not be proved but are completely plausible for those who devised them. The same is true of all myths. The history of creation presented in the Upanishads is plausible too. The theory of the 'Big Bang' could thus be seen as a plausible modern myth, commensurate with contemporary consciousness in the same way as the story of the creation told in Genesis was appropriate to the consciousness of the second millennium BC.

Paul Feyerabend has shown that myth's decisive characteristic is its reflection of the society in which it arises and flourishes. The concept of the primordial bang truly reflects contemporary society with its love of explosions.

It is possible that even the central idea within the mechanistic and materialistic age now coming to an end was a myth – the idea of matter to which the age owes its characterisation. Has anyone ever seen matter? We can see wood or iron, sunrays and moonbeams – but matter? So is matter a myth? And no longer even a plausible myth since nothing remains of it in the concepts of the New Physics except for space and a united field.

The foundation of the materialistic view of the world – the most antagonistic to myth that has ever existed – could be the very thing that its adherents thought superseded for ever: a myth itself!

Back to science. Itzhak Bentov, a Czech-born American technician and physicist, speaks of 'a great sound which contains all the possible frequencies . . . creating an infinite number of interference patterns of *potential* beings and event matrices'. Such creation is a continuous process. The reverberating sound resounds in the flexible and extended 'subjective space-time' of the creative act (or of the Creator of the universe). 'But to us simple mortals, who would be watching the action somehow from a distance, all this would occur suddenly because we spend most of our conscious time in objective time-space. Therefore, while the Creator can take His time to contemplate, design, and construct His universe at leisure, to us it would appear in a big bang. Suddenly the whole thing would be just there.'

It could be our filtering, limited consciousness with its miscomprehension of space and time that reduces Jakob Böhme's divine 'resonance', Indian tradition's primal *Nada*, the eternal primordial sound of the Sufis, the *Logos* of the Gospel according to St. John, the voice of the Creator moving over the waters in Genesis, and Sikhs' *Naam* to a bang, an explosion lasting only a fraction of a second – because this consciousness is incapable of perceiving 'the whole'.

And now I must return to the primal image of all these vibratory patterns become visible – to the Chladni sound figures. The violin bow strokes the sheet of glass which starts to vibrate – and the sand scattered on the glass forms symmetrical patterns. Where do these patterns develop? The answer must be: Where the glass is not vibrating. The grains of sand 'take refuge' on the few parts of the glass free of vibration – where they are distributed, forming patterns and shapes. Physics makes a distinction between vibrating and standing waves. It is the standing wave, the point of repose, that becomes visible, not the vibration or movement.

That finding can, however, be generally applied since, as we have seen, the Chladni sound figures reveal a primal form of behaviour affecting matter (both visible and invisible) and the cosmos. It also applies, for instance, to a vibrating string, or to the air column in a wind instrument. The sounds 'sit' where the wave is standing. The formative impulse is provided by stillness and silence, not by movement.

As Lao Tse might have said: Immobility is stronger than movement, silence more powerful than sound.

10
TOTAL LISTENING
The Implications of Holomovement

'All things are created out of nothingness. Their true origin is thus the void.'

Meister Eckhart

I
LISTEN TO THE WORLD!

'Total listening . . . To listen to it all . . .' Those words are the culmination of a conversation about physics' new world-view of *holomovement* between David Bohm, Einstein's pupil and a celebrated atomic physicist working in England, and Renée Weber, Professor of Philosophy at Rutgers University. Let us try and trace what led to such a declaration, so uncharacteristic of theoretical physics.

The New Physics got under way with the quantum theory Max

Planck put forward in 1900 and Einstein's two theories of relativity (1905 and 1916). Both Einstein and Planck were unsure about their own discoveries. To start with they thought it important that such discoveries should be integrated in the old Cartesian world-view with its classic concepts of matter and causality. They believed something was wrong if their new theories clashed with what had underpinned physics since Descartes, Bacon, and Galileo. Einstein's expedient – and it wasn't more than that – of 'curved space' entailed a desperate attempt at incorporating the consequences of relativity into Euclidian concepts of space.

Einstein's touching idea was that we should assume that space is curved. It would then at least fit in to some extent with the concept that worked so marvellously for our fathers and grandfathers. Space would then remain as it was – except for now being 'curved'.

The decisive turning-point came later – most obviously in 1927 with Werner Heisenberg's theory of indeterminacy. 'The natural laws we express mathematically in the quantum theory are no longer concerned with elementary particles as such. They involve our knowledge of and way of observing those particles. The question of whether they "per se" exist in space and time can no longer be put in this form.' The conservative Einstein then immediately warned the 26-year-old Heisenberg: 'What quantities are observable should not be our choice, but should be given, should be indicated to us by the theory.'

In the meantime it is quite clear that we determine dimensions. We are present and involved in all happenings in the micro-world. The classical situation of observer and observed – with the former behind a glass wall, a microscope, or other equipment with its dials, watching what is happening – suddenly no longer existed. The observer and the observed are illusions. We participate when we observe. American physicist John A. Wheeler has said: 'The vital act is the act of participation. "Participator" is the incontrovertible new concept given by quantum mechanics. It strikes down the term "observer" of classical theory.'

There have been many attempts to find new ways of seeing the world. Half a dozen exist by now, but, astonishingly, all these concepts, derived from a diversity of theoretical backgrounds, agree in their basic characteristics. Observers of this development were thus scarcely surprised when in the seventies David Bohm put forward his ideas on *holomovement*, perhaps the most systematic and internally consistent of the concepts thrown up by the New Physics so far. This innovatory *holomovement* fed on discoveries in two hitherto unrelated sciences, neurology and theoretical physics.

The discovery of laser beams in 1965 led to a new kind of photographic representation called a *hologram*. The name makes clear that the physicists who developed this kind of photography were immediately aware of the implications. The Greek word *hólos* means *whole*, so hologram entails a picture of the whole.

The 'images' in holographic laser-photography are three-dimensional, 'occupying' space. If you produce a full-length photograph of someone and then discard all but the head and shoulders so as to enlarge the face, the new picture will once again contain the entire person rather than just a blown-up head. In holography you cannot eliminate anything. The fact is that the information enabling reproduction of the face in the original photo *simultaneously* contains information about the totality of the human being. That totality is indivisible. Only the sharpness of focus diminishes. The *blur* becomes more obtrusive with every enlargement and attempt at observing detail with greater precision.

Anyone who works with holograms is directed back to the whole whenever he tries to separate off any partial aspect. This phenomenon makes it conclusively clear that the part and the whole are indivisible – contrary to what post-Cartesian science with its emphasis on segmentation and analysis had believed for three hundred years.

Discovery of the hologram had the impact of a stone dropped into the long-undisturbed pond of the sciences. The phenomenon also became apparent in other spheres: first in biology, and a couple of years later in neurology. Most strongly of all, of course, in particle physics, but also in cybernetics and information theory. In 1969 Karl Pribram, a Viennese-born neurologist teaching at Stanford University, announced that the hologram explained hitherto inexplicable brain processes, and was 'suitable as a model of what happens in the human brain'. As a neuro-surgeon, Pribram had spent thirty years searching (together with his teacher Karl Lashley) for the *engram*, the site and substance of memory. Lashley trained apes and other animals to make special use of memory and then operated on them to remove essential cerebral functions in the hope of discovering what parts of the brain stored up the information contained in memory. He came to the conclusion – confirmed by findings among human beings – that even though performance might be reduced through his intervention, it was impossible to eradicate what the animals had learned even when large portions of the brain were removed. Any further intervention would have brought about the animals' death.

When half of the neurons are removed by operation, that does not mean 50 per cent of memory is lost. Pribram and Lashley established that even when only 2 or 3 per cent of the nerve cells remain, the endowment of memory is virtually assured. Pribram thus views the brain as a hologram. Every single cell stores up the entire message. If I 'code' that sentence in accordance with the procedures of information theory, the 'steps' are as follows: Every cell contains the whole memory. Every cell contains the whole. Every cell *is* memory. Every cell *is* the whole. The whole is every cell. We must not, however, forget that the *blur* (in this case the 'imprecision' of memory) increases.

That neurological discovery and the development of laser-photography led David Bohm, trained in Einstein's conservative school, to coin the term *holomovement*. The word *hologram* alone implies something static and immovable, but the world is constantly in motion.

Bohm explains that *holomovement* combines a Greek and a Latin word. One could also say *holoflux*. The totality is in motion. Everything flows. A hologram, like a photograph, is only, as it were, a fixed image of a single process of movement – an abstraction of the entire movement, of the whole.

Bohm takes two realities – the 'enfolding' and the 'unfolding' – as his starting-point. The enfolded order is paramount. Bohm also calls it 'real', meaning a reality that is 'more real' than what we see with our eyes. That leads to an almost Platonic view of the world with, on the one hand, the realm of Ideas, and, on the other, that of the visible, 'material', and graspable.

The *holomovement* takes place within an 'implicate order', which can both 'enfold' and 'unfold' as an ordering, shaping, creative force. As an 'unfolding order' it is 'manifest', i.e. perceivable with our senses; whilst as 'enfoldment' it is 'non-manifest'. This order 'constitutes' the whole and keeps it ceaselessly in motion.

David Bohm does not offer his model as a theoretical concept. He created it as a physicist, not as a philosopher. He and his colleagues have calculated all the consequences and implications. When Renée Weber asked him whether the mathematics for this already exists, Bohm answered: 'Oh yes. It's being used all the time.' Many quantum physicists believe that mathematically *holomovement* functions better than all comparable models.

For David Bohm the new world-view – which I don't want to describe in detail here since that has been done in many recent publications – can be comprehended through Total Listening. No longer through seeing – as in Classical Physics' world-view – but through listening as this chapter intends to demonstrate.

First, however, mention should be made of the highly interesting and revealing human constellation where this view of the world was developed. Never before has there been anything comparable in the modern world. Both Karl Pribram, the Viennese-born neurologist and successful neuro-surgeon, and David Bohm, the American nuclear physicist well-versed in the West's humanistic tradition, have a spiritual advisor and friend. Bohm was close to Krishnamurti, the Indian wise man who coined the term 'Total Listening', and Pribram time and again refers – even in scientific publications – to Swami Muktananda, the venerable master of Kundalini energy, as 'my guru'. One is almost reminded of the monk-researchers in medieval monasteries, Islamic mathematicians, and Sufi chemists, who also received 'spiritual guidance', and would have thought inconceivable the idea of pursuing their scientific work without such 'assistance'. The same is true of Pribram and Bohm. Is a new image, a vision, of both science and the scientist coming into view here – something new that is at the same time very old? The 'alienated', 'separated', 'non-participating', and constantly 'self-abstracted' scientist would then have been just a transient intermezzo, lasting from Descartes and Newton (who helped shape this kind of scientist even though as someone who *also* pursued alchemy he was not such himself) to the middle of our own century.

II
THE INTERCONNECTEDNESS OF EVERYTHING

'The entire universe is thy eye.
The entire universe is thy source of light.
The entire universe is within thy source of light.
In the entire universe there is no one
Who is not thyself.'
Ch'an-sha Ching-ts'en, ninth-century Chinese Zen Master

Jack Sarfati, one of the American physicists involved in the development of new concepts of the world, raises the question: 'Can all particles be one particle?'

Physicists John A. Wheeler and Richard P. Feynman had already taken as their initial assumption the existence of just one electron in the universe, containing all the other electrons – like Indra's pearl which incorporates all the pearls in the world and is at the same time contained within each of those pearls.

Bohm coined the term 'undivided wholeness'. 'A quantum multi-body system cannot really be divided into parts existing independently of one another . . . We must reject the classical idea of the world's reducibility.'

And elsewhere: 'The attempt to live in accordance with the view that the parts to which we reduce the world really are separated from one another is essentially responsible for the increase in the many extremely threatening crises facing us today. That way of life has blessed us with pollution of the environment, destruction of natural balance, over-population, and worldwide economic and political chaos.'

Physicists also talk about magic. For instance, John A. Wheeler from Princeton University: 'There may be no such thing as "the glittering central mechanism of the universe" . . . Not machinery but magic may be the better description of the treasure that is waiting.' Jack Sarfati compares science with a 'magical set of rules and attitudes' – similar to the concepts and ideas involved in an African medicine man's or Polynesian village shaman's understanding of the world. Such magic works for all of them, so they feel sure that it is 'correct'.

To that extent – and there alone – it is appropriate to employ the word magic. It is necessary to be aware that the traditional mechanistic view of the world is also pure magic, based as it is on a set of ideas and rules which can only be validated within that particular context – and which are mostly constructed to provide reciprocal confirmation by way of a kind of feedback.

In his studies of the foundations of mathematics, Kurt Gödel provides convincing demonstration that 'every system of knowledge contains meaningful tenets whose truth or falsity cannot be established if one remains completely within that system'. But that is exactly what both medicine men and academic scientists do. The fact that they reject everything from outside their system as 'tabu' (medicine man) or 'unscientific' (the academic) means that the ultimate truth of the theses underlying their view of the world can never be evaluated. All that is open to assessment is the functioning of the 'closed circle' within which experience confirms the world-view and vice versa. Viewed in that light, 'scientific' thinking is a pleonastic process keeping going by way of circular reasoning.

Of course one may also view as 'pure magic' what for David Bohm is the decisive significance of *holomovement*. Astonishingly, however, it is the same magic as shamans, medicine men, and spiritual human beings have taught since time immemorial: Everything is a single all-embracing system constantly in motion.

Bohm: 'We could probably identify the whole of nature on this planet if we could really understand just a single cell within a single human being.' Or Sarfati: 'A single electron could be enough for total recreation of the entire planet.'

All the world-views of the New Physics lead in that direction – including the Bootstrap Theory developed at Berkeley whereby nature cannot be reduced to its parts. If we none the less persist in that endeavour, our findings will be wrong. The bootstrappers say that 'Every particle consists of all particles.'

III
THE *DÉJÀ VU* OF CONSCIOUSNESS

'The world does not contain you.
You are the world.'

Angelus Silesius

The fact that all is one is ancient knowledge. Only individual human beings or individual civilisations could lose it. Humanity as a whole preserves it since humanity cannot lose what its genes know. That is why it is not absolutely necessary for the intellect to know. Red Indians, Zen masters and Sufis, Mexican magicians and African medicine men, Balinese village priests and Tibetan monks, and the shamans and healers within all cultures act on our behalf in preserving that knowledge. It is not, however, just saints, monks, gurus, and priests who do so. Every single person within such peoples – even the poorest and least educated – knows, feels, and lives that.

And now let us take a further step. We also 'know' that. Let us observe ourselves. The unbelieving astonishment we feel if bootstrappers or experts in holomovement tell us that 'All is one' is only superficial – as David Bohm says, just a 'ripple'. Beyond that we are awed by *déjà vu*. I am not introducing such an interpretation. Californian physicists employed those words when they were – yet again! – shocked by the conclusions to which their equations compelled them, and were surprised by the taken-for-granted way in which they established such ideas as if they had been 'there' right from the start. When asked where these ideas had been previously encountered, they hesitantly pointed towards themselves: our unconscious. 'All is one' is an 'archetype' recorded deep within ourselves.

They nevertheless refrain from mixing the two spheres. David Bohm has a spiritual master from India but says: 'I think it would be just as foolish for mystics to try and prove their case from physics as it would be for physicists to prove their case from mysticism.'

By now some people feel that the new discoveries in physics are a liberation – and there are similar developments in most sciences since our overview of the world is in process of becoming holistic. The blurred nature of the *déjà vu* reaction is the outcome of its long repression. We believed it unacceptable to think in that way. Science was thought to be antagonistic, having 'proved' that what one would have liked to think was 'wrong'.

We know from psychology what can happen if we repress something. We become neurotic, and many Westerners still have what could be called a 'mechanistic neurosis'. The better the Cartesian world-view functions, the worse the 'mechanisms' of our soul, concealed deep within ourselves, operate. The mechanists have strewn into our unconscious's 'transmission' the sand which might have blocked mechanical and materialistic functioning.

That sand is now being washed out. We no longer need repress anything. When we read David Bohm or John A. Wheeler – or Heisenberg and Niels Bohr – we have a sense of *déjà vu*. It is not important whether there is agreement between mysticism and physics. What matters is that *we* are in agreement.

We participate. When television shows the skeletal bodies of starving children in Ethiopia and huge sums of money are donated in just a few days, that happens because we feel that those children – remote from us as few other human creatures on this planet – are part of the whole to which we belong. When there is an accident on the other side of the motorway resulting in injuries and mutilations, our inability to calm down for long afterwards is the outcome of the existence within ourselves of an unconscious link with the people involved, albeit by now only an atrophied residue. We thus cry out as if we ourselves had been injured.

We constantly sense that things entail more – are more far-reaching and comprehensive – than rationalism wants us to believe. Why are we so attracted to gazing at the heavens when there is a full moon? Why do so many people feel inner unrest, creativity, and intensified sexuality even when unaware that the moon is again full – but are then satisfied by that explanation? Why do women respond to the phases of the moon in both the menstrual cycle and their moods? Why does science not investigate the signal concealed there when everyone can see and feel it?

If you observe people – and they might well be rationalists – gazing at the full moon, it is as if they were dreaming. A withdrawn, intoxicated expression appears on their faces. What are they dreaming about? What do they divine? Do they sense a relationship between the greater whole and themselves?

Many modern scientists have reluctantly become archaeologists of our unconscious. It is as if they were excavating 'fossils of our soul'; and when we look at what they have brought to the light of day, our response is *déjà vu*. The first such archaeologists were our century's great physicists. Einstein, Planck, Bohr, Schrödinger, Eddington, and others were quick to sense the spiritual secret behind their discoveries. We are now following in their tracks – and what we find, once we have shaken off the sand and dust of our 'mechanistic neurosis', looks like something very familiar. But where have we seen it? Or where did we hear it? Within ourselves? And of what does it remind us?

It was Gregory Bateson, analyst of the systemic nature of experience (in a sense the biological and anthropological equivalent of holomovement), who coined the classic statement: 'The map is not the territory.' Krishnamurti says: 'The description is not what is described.' The physicists have drawn maps for us. Now we are moving into the territory – and we see that we know it already. We ourselves are what is described. We scarcely need the maps any longer.

Our consciousness is changing even more than physics and the other sciences. As theologian Hans Küng says: 'The standard answer to the question: "Do you believe in God?" used to be, "Of course not, I'm a scientist"; but now it runs: "Of course, I'm a scientist." '

IV

PHYSICS CHANGES SOCIETY

'Consciousness is the means.
Consciousness is the key.
Consciousness is the objective.'

Satprem

Physics was always the key science. Even among the Pre-Socratics. Philosophy began with physical concepts. Such as: In the beginning was water. Or fire. Or 'Everything is in flux.'

Physics was also the key science in the world-view which predominated during the past three hundred years. If we call that world-view 'mechanistic' and 'materialistic', those two words make clear we also believed that biology, society, philosophy, and theology were determined by physics. After two centuries or so of great successes for physics' mechanistic world-view, in the nineteenth century it went on to exert enormous influence on the other sciences.

For biologists evolution functioned mechanistically. For medical scientists the human being became a chemical factory. Chemists viewed relationships between elements as if they were parts in a machine. Sociologists conceived of social systems as operating like clockwork. Theologians ousted myth from religion, which thus stopped being experience of God and became a 'science'. Freud established psychology on the basis of a mechanistic comprehension of the human soul – as if it were a steam-engine, and drives (rather than energies) were repressed.

Mechanistic and materialistic thinking finally became so all-pervasive that we also started feeling in those terms. We thought that we were objects whose task was to function – and that there was something wrong with us if we did not. When medical scientists solemnly affirmed that they had dissected the human body into a thousand parts without finding any trace of a 'soul', then that 'soul' was obviously not of importance. It was in fact possible for us to become 'mere objects' – and even (incomprehensibly!) be thankful if we were treated as such: 'object-ly'.

The old mechanistic thinking's insatiable urge to dissect the world into its constituent parts, miscomprehending the sum of these parts as the whole, also resulted in humanity and individuals being treated in the same way – as *bits* in terms of information theory. Man thus became a stranger to man so that ultimately even the individual was only *bits* and fragments. In the beginning were 'analysis', 'dissection', and separation, finally leading to estrangement, irresponsibility, chaos, violence, and destruction.

Bohm points out that the ultimate and inevitable outcome of all these endlessly many *bits* was the smashing of the atom. When people see such gigantic fragmentation within us all, they derive confirmation for the necessity of splitting into ever smaller units. Fragmentation is seen as being justified.

If, however, we recognise that the world is a living, open-ended, constantly changing system without any rigid, machine-like structures, that view must inevitably – as the mechanistic attitude before it – exert an influence on how people treat other human beings. 'If in the non-manifest world everything is interconnected and interpenetrated, and if we see that humanity is also a single system, a single extended living being, and if we know that matter is also one, then we living human beings must also be one . . . This new world-view can then bring about a much better civilisation' – a genuine civilisation!

Nobel prize-winner Eugene Wigner stresses: 'The being with a consciousness must have a different role in quantum mechanics than the inanimate measuring device.' We must remember that exactly the opposite prevailed until recently. Inanimate equipment played a much greater part than living consciousness in the mechanistic world-view.

When the new world-view is as much a matter of course – 'in the blood' – as its predecessor used to be, then every child will understand what is implied in bootstrap physics, holomovement, the complex theory of relativity, and even the principle of indeterminacy. My consciousness is response-ible. I must be responsive, answering the interconnectedness of the world. Physicists are now using the word 'responsibility' increasingly often – a word that previously scarcely existed in their vocabulary.

We have discovered that the old consciousness resulted in people feeling they were not responsible. We are not thinking utopianly but have already experienced – for three centuries – that physics' view of the world *also* entails morality. It conditioned and legitimated all of our hard-heartedness: the coldness of our functioning, the utilitarian nature of our relationships, and thus also lovelessness towards ourselves and others. Are we therefore justified in concluding that the world-view entailed in the new physics will involve morality – and that it will be a new kind of morality?

The previous world-view led – as we know – to a collapse of morality, particularly among those who were most closely involved: the scientists. Have we reason to expect, to hesitantly hope, that the new world-view will – in the future if not today or tomorrow – bring about a new kind of scientist who, because he is concerned with systems and the whole rather than parts and functions, realises that he too belongs to that system and is thus responsible to it?

Do we also have reason to assume that in this future world-view the scientist will be regarded as a model – and that such a new image will also shape the human ideal? Also that the new man will inevitably be permeated by a new consciousness just because he has a new view of the world?

Renée Weber concludes that 'Physics and ethics will become one . . .'

V
REVOLUTION NOW! THE PARADIGM SHIFT

Karl Pribram believes that we are in the midst of an epoch-making upheaval – a paradigm shift – affecting all the sciences.

John Battista of the University of California writes: 'It seems fairly clear that we are now in a process of paradigmatic shift in which all fields are being revised in light of these assumptions.' Such new discoveries include Gregory Bateson's systems theory in biology and anthropology, Emmet Leith's holography, Karl Pribram's neurological findings, and David Bohm's holomovement.

Fritjof Capra views the real crisis facing us as being one of perception: 'Our society, our universities, our corporations, our economy, our technology, and our politics are all still structured in accordance with the old Cartesian paradigm. We need change.'

The more recent sciences are, the easier it is for them to change. Cybernetics had the least difficulty of all. Information Theory did not have many problems either in suddenly accepting that it is meaningless to talk about information without taking the recipients into account. A fundamental law within contemporary Information Studies lays down that information is non-existent without consideration of the intended recipient. Heisenberg's principle of indeterminacy is thus applied to communications between people.

Biology has a more difficult time, but increasing numbers of biologists are conceding that the mechanisms of a reductionistically conceived evolution (adaptation, 'struggle for existence', survival of the fittest, 'chance' mutations, and selection – which all indisputably exist) are only part of the whole. They are not sufficient for a complete explanation of evolution.

Medicine and sociology are faced with even greater difficulties. Academic medicine was the last science to adapt to the mechanistic view of the world, and will possibly also be the last to break away from that. Sociology, the nineteenth-century child of mechanistic thinking, could be in danger of neutralising itself if its preconditions are no longer accepted by the majority of mankind.

Fritjof Capra offers a helpful thought there. He reminds us of what many have already almost forgotten: that classical reductionism with its analytical and mechanistic thinking really was wonderfully functional for specific situations and organisations, and explains our survival:

> When you must eat, it is important to learn to distinguish between minor details so as to find the right food. Today, however, we are faced by the opposite situation. Today for the first time it is the survival of the planet that is at stake, not just survival of an individual or even an individual species. That is the real reason for transformation of the paradigm. Evolution needs synthesis, the ecological perspective, and the holistic outlook so that life continues to be possible. That change from the old viewpoint, dividing up the world into ever smaller parts, towards a holistic attitude is biologically conditioned.

Morris Berman, mathematician and philosopher, also believes that the present breakdown of industrial society could be the way in which the planet seeks to avoid more extensive death.

We feel this transformation most clearly in the way in which individuals react. For centuries no one doubted that we must and could dominate nature. That was a standard conviction within Western civilisation – from the time of Descartes and Bacon onwards. Does anyone still seriously believe that to be the case? Morris Berman asks whether schoolchildren do not already giggle and adults look blank at the idea that we can master nature, the cosmos, and the universe.

When in 1967 Gregory Bateson drew attention to the fact that a purely functional rationality operating without regard for such phenomena as art, religion, dreams, or imagination must necessarily be pathogenic and destructive of life, that was considered revolutionary. But aren't a majority of discerning human beings by now convinced of the correctness of that view?

VI
SUMMA

'Total listening!'

Krishnamurti

Physics' new world-view amounts to the old Zen wisdom of 'the emptiness that is abundance'. David Bohm employs the equivalent concept in Indian spirituality, *sunyata*, translating it as 'emptiness and silence'. Philosopher Renée Weber then asked how that is to be 'grasped'. To which the answer was: 'To listen to it all.' To everything – the totality – nothing but listening!

Both Weber and Bohm refer to an idea Krishnamurti threw into the debate: *Total listening*. Renée Weber attempted to delimit: 'By that I suppose he meant total listening to that wholeness or void-plenum but not to the little surface things?' To which Bohm countered: 'Well, also to the surface. To listen to it all.' And continued: 'What interferes with listening . . . is that thought jumps in very fast with a word and all its associations, which then goes so fast that thought takes that to be direct perception.'

Bohm also thinks it necessary to delimit seeing. 'I think this is a familiar idea, namely to say that what we see immediately is really a very superficial affair. However, the positivist used to say that what we see immediately is all there is or all that counts, and that our ideas must simply correlate what we see immediately.'

Bohm, the atomic physicist, is absolutely sure that we can only experience the emptiness of abundance and the plenitude of the void – which are what is implied in holomovement – through *total listening*.

The argument comes full circle there. In the chapter 'We See Three Dimensions but How Many Do We Hear?' we discovered that our eyes cannot penetrate beyond the three dimensions of space whereas our ears have no problems with multi-dimensionality, and thus tend to perceive the world 'more correctly'.

We also saw that holography did more than any other discovery to promote the new holistic thinking. The relevant literature only makes passing mention of the fact that holography is 'lensless' photography – but that is decisive. The lens in cameras, telescopes, microscopes, glasses, and electron-optics is closely related to the human eye. For many people it symbolises the eye – *pars pro toto*. It therefore had to be renounced so that science could move beyond reductionist dissection and gain a holistic idea of the world according with reality. That idea of the world becomes graspable through hearing, through total hearing, which is much more effective than the seeing that previously prevailed in the old Newtonian physics.

11

AUDIBLE AND INAUDIBLE SOUND

'There are two fundamental cosmic truths: sound and non-sound.
The inner sound only receives manifestation in the outer sound.
This is therefore the way.'

The Upanishads

I
WHERE IS THE THIRD EAR?

Audibility and inaudibility merge on a sliding scale. Sounds that one species can hear are inaudible to others. Police dogs react to whistles which human beings cannot hear. Bats utilise ultra-sonic sounds, 20,000 to 100,000 Hz above the highest frequencies audible to man, for location purposes. The night-moths which developed during a later phase of evolution can hear in the realm between 40,000 and 80,000 Hertz – probably so as to protect themselves from greedy bats. The playing of whales and dolphins utilises sounds up to 50,000 Hz. Audible and electromagnetic vibrations come together in the sense apparatus of certain deep-sea fish. Biologists assume that these fish are listening in as if they were swimming radio-sets – which immediately gives rise to the question: Do other living creatures also listen in that way?

The word 'audible' delineates an area within which a sound exists for me – and in most cases one must qualify that by saying 'seems' to exist for me. The area in which the sound exists can, in physical terms, be completely different – usually much larger – to the place where I located 'audibility'.

Anahata and *ahata*, the unplayed and the played note, are two key concepts in Indian music. Both are equally important – and some schools even say that the unplayed is more crucial since it provides the foundation for what is actually played. The sounds which are played are symbols of the unplayed. Islamic wise men also call *anahata anhad*, which signifies unceasing and without end. 'This tone is called *anhad* or the unending since it has neither beginning nor end.' (Shah Niaz).

In the Indian tradition and particular schools of yoga there exists a practice involving blocking the ears with the thumbs so that one can better hear the unhearable. As musicologist Marius Schneider says: 'One then achieves inner hearing, listening to the sound of the ether present in the heart.'

We already know that 'inner listening' does not begin at some threshold. It gets under way where listening occurs: at the point in the cochlea where the logarithmic curve of hearing starts to rise.

Since time immemorial human beings have sensed the existence of a *third eye*, lying between and just above the eyebrows and making possible spiritual 'insight'. Perhaps people conceived such a visionary idea because they felt the incompleteness of our two seeing eyes and sensed there simply must be something taking them further. One reason why the unicorn is viewed as a mythical, holy beast is the presence of the horn where the third eye is located – like a symbol and its representation in the organic world.

The *third eye* is a myth – a necessary myth. The situation is different with regard to the ear. Transcendence, a going beyond, is implicit in the act of hearing, so our first and second ears already imply the existence of a third. There has never existed any myth of a third ear. No one needs it. The two ears we have already take us into the realm of the 'third'. They cannot function without transcending – whereas the eye operates independently of processes of transcendence. That is why a third eye is needed. The ear has its counterpart already.

Irony is at work in the title I chose for this book. We *have* a third ear. We only need know how to use it, and how to hear its messages.

II
LACK OF CLARITY ABOUT 'VIBRATIONS'

As we have seen, the world is sound. *Nada Brahma* means precisely that – and not that the world is vibration. To be more precise: in physical terms there are milliards of possible vibrations. But basic research on harmonics has shown that the cosmos, the universe, and nature have a tendency to select from those innumerable possibilities the few thousand that give rise to harmonic – which ultimately means musical – meaning: the integral proportions of the overtone series, the major and occasionally the minor scale, certain Gregorian and Indian scales, and the 1:2 polarity of the octave.

It is important to recall that those proportions, numerous though they may appear at first glance, are really only a minimal selection from the immense abundance of what can be subsumed under the concept 'vibration'. Such proportions were not merely selected by man for his music and art. Nature also chose them for planetary orbits, leaf and crystal shapes, ratios within the periodic table of elements, the forms of animal and human bodies, quantisation in the atomic nucleus, electron spins, the DNA relationships containing our genetic code, the messages communicated by pulsars milliards of light-years distant, the solar wind, earth magnetism, etc.

In other words: Not every number constitutes a tonal value, but every tonal value entails number. In the overwhelming majority of cases nature prefers numbers that at the same time constitute tonal values, i.e. it demonstrates preference for tonal values rather than numbers. It insists on – and consists of – sound.

The ratio involved in the universe's decision in favour of sonically meaningful proportions is 1:1 million – a ratio that cannot be interpreted as 'chance' even in terms of positivists' more than generous (and unscientific) interpretation of that concept.

Anyone who wants to use the word vibration in this context is guilty of imprecise thinking. That word is too fuzzy as a description of the vibrations that matter for the universe: sounds rather than any old 'vibration', and tonal values rather than numbers.

It is nowhere laid down that sounds must be audible. On the contrary, language has long also utilised the word for what is inaudible. The classic definition of the musical instrument – that it is there to make sounds audible – implies that sounds must already exist and only need to be made audible. Every musician reading a score hears the music contained in the notes. Many composers hear music sounding within themselves even before it is played for the first time. When they actually hear it, they encounter something they already know.

Every music-lover has had similar experiences. We hear certain melodies or pieces within ourselves even when they are not acoustically present or audible.

III
MUSIC OF THE SOLAR WIND AND
GEOMAGNETISM

Codes for the 'recovery' (Heidegger) of the hidden harmony, for transmission of the inaudible into audibility, are provided by

American scientists who have made accessible the sounds of both the micro- and the macro-cosmos. They followed procedures similar to the transposition by octaves described in Chapter 9. Physicists, astronomers, and biologists transposed cosmic and micro-cosmic ratios from spheres where they could not be heard to areas accessible to the human ear and the equipment used.

The DNA sequences made audible by David Deamer, a cell biologist at the University of California in Los Angeles, sound absolutely fascinating. The four nitrogenous bases for DNA – adenine, guanine, cytosine, and thymine – have been called the letters of the genetic alphabet, encoding all the biological character- istics of a living creature. If you listen to Deamer's cassettes, the DNA information seems more like the notes of a genetic melody. We can hear that melody *sung* by the biological qualities of the creature concerned.

Musicians have shown particular interest in the sounds resulting from friction between the solar wind and the earth's magnetic field. One needs to know that the huge natural nuclear reactor of the sun constantly throws out vast amounts of gases, heat, radiation, and particles into our planetary system. What are known as solar winds develop as a result of the decline in energy-level between the solar core and interplanetary space. They would penetrate right into the earth's atmosphere, endangering our existence, if we were not protected by the earth's magnetic field. Solar winds thus constantly buffet against the protective magnetic field, and vice versa. This activity is recorded on the '2kp index', which is measured every three hours at twenty places around the world and incorporated in a diagram that looks like musical notes. That is why physicists called it 'Bartels' musical diagram' (after German physicist Julius Bartels, b. 1899, who was the first scientist to investigate geomagnetism) right from the start, even before they became aware of the musical implications of such things, which has only occurred in recent years. A group of physicists at Princeton University, Columbia University's Computer Center, and in the Bell Telephone Laboratories, fed the Bartels' diagrams for 1961 into an IBM 360/91 computer to produce music that is now available on record.

One of the physicists involved calls what thus becomes audible 'the music the sun plays on the earth's magnetic field' – a music in which our planet and we ourselves are 'constantly bathed'. This is a moving, shimmering music, surging in a multitude of directions, whose underlying meditative mood is time and again disrupted by violent outbursts. In earlier times it was poets and mystics who produced such ecstatic declarations as 'The earth is bathed in music' or 'The sun beams music down onto the earth.' Nowadays physicists express such sentiments in order to provide an exact description of a state of affairs verified in their experiments and calculations: we are bathed in music.

IV
FROM SKINS TO ELECTRONICS

Anyone who has doubts about the electronic nature of such realisations of cosmic and micro-cosmic music should bear the following in mind. Numerical proportions are fed into computers and synthesisers to produce such music. Another word for proportion is interval, i.e. the relationship between two numbers. For instance 6:5 in the case of a minor third and 5:4 for a major third, 4:3 for a fourth, and 2:1 for an octave. A musician who employs modern computerised instruments is feeding them with intervals. But isn't that just what a violinist or pianist does too? He takes the numerical proportions – the intervals – from his sheet-music or score, making them audible by striking or bowing the corresponding notes.

Instrument originally meant a *mechanical implement* or *tool*. Any good dictionary will show that the word is much more frequently employed in technical than musical contexts. It is not just musicians who play instruments. Craftsmen work with instruments, and no technical process is possible without them. The hammer with which we knock in a nail is an instrument, fixing the nail in position.

Engineers need instruments in order to discover intervallic relationships. An aeroplane's cockpit is studded with instruments, and people talk about 'instrument flying' when there is no horizontal vision and the ground is out of sight. The tachometer in a car is also an instrument showing numerical relationships. The violin is an instrument in exactly the same way. It presents intervallic ratios to our ears. Here too we once again encounter the miraculous phenomenon of the ear with its ability to transform what is measurable (quantitive) into something that can be evaluated qualitatively.

The technical process used for realisation of the sounds of planetary orbits, genes, solar winds, etc., is the same as the method employed for making conventional music audible. Numerical proportions are 'fed' into an instrument so that they can be heard.

Anyone who dislikes the technical nature of such processes is subject to an illusion. Sounds are not *a priori* audible; they must be made audible. The piano and the organ are also highly complex pieces of equipment whose technical elaboration seemed just as perplexing at the time when they were invented and developed as today's computers producing music. For the people of the seventeenth century the organ was a mechanical and technical miracle – to an even greater degree, perhaps, than the synthesiser for youngsters today.

Music's 'social environment' starts with the fact that its 'means' – the instruments employed – accord with the state of civilisation involved. African music is largely played on drums and xylophones since the rain forest and its animals supply wood, skins, and hides. Africans knew how to make outstanding use of them at a very early date. When Bronze Age man learnt the art of metal-working, horns, tubas, and trumpets were immediately produced. For thousands of years now the closest of links has existed between constant improvements in metal-working techniques, the construction of brass instruments, and also the music played on such instruments.

The same is true of the development of string instruments. Their history – from animal hair and gut to metal and nylon strings – coincided with progressive refinement of our ability to manufacture thread, wire, cords, and other materials used for binding. New technical possibilities were often first developed and tried out by makers of musical instruments before they were used in handicrafts, industry, and technology. The Hammerklavier, for instance, is an 'appliance' whose mechanical complexity and sensitivity exceed everything that seemed possible in other spheres of eighteenth century mechanics.

Whatever workable materials were discovered – initially wood, stone, skins; and then from the Iron Age onwards iron, copper, tin, and bronze; and later glass – were immediately employed in the making of music. Musical 'utilisation' often preceded craft or technical uses.

As soon as electronics had been developed, man immediately set about trying out their possibilities for sound-production, new instruments in general, and construction of an ever-greater range of synthesisers and music-making computers. That was logical and nothing new in historical terms. Electronics offer 'material' – just as woods, skins, and hides used to; or later the wind in organ pipes, or mechanical pressure in the Hammerklavier or concert grand.

I deliberately employed the phrase 'trying out' since it indicates a 'playful' process. Playing music and playing with sounds and tones start earlier than we think – not just where music is made but at an earlier stage when instruments were invented, constructed, and developed since that couldn't happen unless people 'played' with the materials used. We have once again become aware of that – and I say 'once again' because such a view was a matter of course in the old musical cultures of the East, Africa, and the two Americas. Never before have so many new instruments been invented as today, and never before has there been such intensive playing on and with new instruments as since the sixties.

The prejudice directed against electronic instruments corresponds with people's distaste in Beethoven's time for the Hammerklavier because the harpsichord and spinet supposedly sounded so much 'purer' and 'nobler'. For us today – as can be discovered from thousands of record reviews in the relevant journals – the concert grand sounds 'purer' and 'nobler' than an electronic keyboard.

One should be aware how fatal it would be if no electronic instruments were manufactured. This would mean that for the first time in human history man had renounced putting a newly discovered technical possibility to musical use. That would entail capitulation of man's artistic urge to technology – which is exactly what those who don't like electronic sounds are doing. They are sacrificing their need for and understanding of art to the age in which they live.

All of our culture's musical appliances derive from Pythagoras's monochord. Pythagoreans didn't, however, know how to decide whether the monochord serves physics or the arts. They would not have been able to answer: both – as modern man does. They simply wouldn't have understood making any distinction between physics and music.

V

KEPLER : 'GIVE SPACE TO THE HEAVENS . . .'

'The instrument – That's you!'

Sun Ra

Once when I played tapes of pulsars, DNA genes, planetary orbits, solar winds, and geomagnetism at a seminar, a white-haired old gentleman stood up and said that he could hear such sounds without the help of electronics. He recounted how he and a group of young people had climbed Mont Ventoux in Southern France where they had meditated for a whole night beneath the starry heavens. And it was there that he had really heard in nature itself all the sounds I had just presented.

Similar stories are told of Tibetan wise men and Zen monks. Pythagoras left no doubt that he had really heard the harmony of the spheres. His pupils, Plato, and Pythagoreans up to the Hellenistic period were absolutely certain that he had heard what he taught. Iamblichos, for instance, wrote: 'Pythagoras directed his hearing and his spirit towards the sublime harmony of the world . . . by virtue of an ineffable and almost inconceivable divine capacity. That is why he heard and understood.'

We must also be quite clear about the fact that ultimately we ourselves are the instrument. All technical means are just tools for reminding us of what resounds deep within ourselves whether we are aware of that or not. Plato called that *anamnesis*, meaning memory of what is impressed on our souls right from the very beginning – from pre-earthly existences. Music is not even possible without that process of recognition, which also underlies any physical or physiological explanation. Without such memory music would be nothing but isolated and completely unconnected tone perceptions.

The instrument used is not of great significance. The same proportions, the same numerical relationships and intervals, sound out in the cosmos, in our genes, in our soul, and for that very reason also in our audible music. Audible music reflects the inaudible – no matter whether transmitted by violin or synthesiser.

Johannes Kepler: 'Give space to the heavens, and a true music will sound out.' That is just what the old gentleman experienced on Mont Ventoux. He gave space to the heavens within himself.

VI
THE DRIVE TOWARDS HARMONY

'The hidden harmony is mightier than what is revealed' (Heraclitus). The *drive* towards becoming 'manifest' is immanent within the hidden harmony. In group music therapy the following experiment is often conducted so as to help a group find its own identity. When the signal is given, every person present must immediately sing a note – without paying attention to what their neighbours are doing. Twenty or thirty people spontaneously 'belt out' (or that's how it usually sounds) 'their' notes, producing a discordant cluster of many different notes. The therapist initially laid down that everyone should hold 'their' note for as long as possible without being diverted from it – but after a minute or so (and sometimes even after 30 seconds) the many different notes endeavour to attain a single note. A variety of notes may still be maintained for a while, but they also tend to establish harmonious relationships. The cluster that was so painful to the ear cannot be upheld for long. It strives for harmony. It may initially be 'hidden' but it becomes apparent, or rather audible, within a relatively short time.

There is every reason to assume that this experiment is a paradigm. George Leonard has assembled examples. The hearts of patients lying alongside one another when being operated on start to beat in unison once the surgeon has exposed them. The brainwaves of people who understand one another – clergymen and their congregations, politicians and their audiences, and professors and their students – achieve 'resonance' remarkably quickly no matter how far apart they may initially have been. They soon oscillate together. Women 'synchronise' their periods – especially younger women who live together for quite a while. Dozens of technical appliances – such as TV sets – operate in accordance with the 'resonance principle'. Vibrations that are out of step with one another 'engage' and are suddenly 'in sync'.

The *drive* towards 'synchronicity' and harmony is elemental and universal so it becomes comprehensible that the 'hidden' harmony within ourselves provides us with the strength to find the 'hidden' harmony in the cosmos and universe. The more 'chaotic' and 'atonal' the cluster, the more quickly harmony develops. Disharmony is a springboard fostering the harmony within ourselves. Anyone aware of this primal drive within nature and the cosmos will 'take off' all the more quickly. And the aim of this book – like many similar books and sources of guidance suddenly appearing everywhere – is to create a consciousness which facilitates the drive towards harmony and thus towards peace, making us alert to the 'uncovering' of hidden harmony so that chaos, which is the chaos within ourselves, is not left in charge.

VII
LISTENING IS THE WAY

The transcendent nature of listening (see Chapter 3, 'The Ear Goes Beyond' – also with regard to the whole of this chapter) tells us that the audible and the inaudible are one. Some spiritually minded people are of the opinion that the unheard sounds are of unique importance. I can understand their viewpoint but it is nevertheless hardly less one-sided than that of rationalists who are only concerned with what is directly audible. As we have seen, the audible and the inaudible do not exclude one another. The flexible nature of transitions – differently located with regard to the great diversity of forms of perception involved – makes clear that it is not accurate to view them as opposites. *Listening is nothing but listening!* Listening takes me without a break from one realm to another, and is itself the vehicle for that. If I entrust myself to that 'vehicle', making attentive use of it without precipitate abandonment, I cannot but be transported from the audible to the inaudible – and of course back again.

The word 'vehicle' can be replaced by the word 'Way' – as in the Chinese *tao*, the Japanese *do*, and the quotation from the Upanishads heading this chapter. Listening is the Way. The Way is Listening.

12

WHY WOMEN HAVE HIGHER VOICES

The Pope died. His heart suddenly stopped. But one of his doctors
succeeded in getting it beating again. The Holy Father came back to
life. Cardinals and Bishops crowded around his bed – awaiting first-
hand information about the decisive question: Who is God? The Pope
opens his eyes and is immediately asked: What did you see? What does
God look like? The Holy Father, obviously much shaken, can only
stutter: 'She . . . is . . . Black.'

Californian Underground Joke
Summer 1984

I
MEN AND WOMEN HAVE TO SOUND DIFFERENT

This book is full of examples of how through listening we can gain
knowledge, make discoveries, and find connections inaccessible to
seeing. The more examples the better in order to convince Westerners,
brought up to glorify the eye, that they also possess another
wonderful sense organ whose elevation is long overdue.

Scientists believe that they investigate everything, but they
deceive themselves. They mainly examine what can be comprehended in visual terms. They neglect what can be heard, and even
the organ of hearing itself. Physiologist Wolf D. Keidel sums up:
'The functioning of the eyeball has become absolutely clear to science
. . . but that is in no way true of the inner ear.'

In a great variety of spheres, man and rationalistic science,
primarily interested in seeing, have devoted more far-reaching
research to optical phenomena and processes than to auditive. That
is also true of the basically obvious question of why women have
higher and men deeper voices. Or, approaching the issue from
another angle: Why do men generally speak at a pitch between 120
and 180 Hz while women are an octave higher? That question has
not been answered in all the writings by biologists, anthropologists,
psychologists, evolutionists, etc., that have come my way, which is
understandable since their theories and conceptual structures were
almost exclusively developed by men with little feeling for the

dimension of hearing. If a 'visual problem' had been involved, it would long have received exhaustive treatment. There exists, for instance, a vast amount of thoroughly researched material on why people living in northern zones have lighter skins and hair than southerners. And yet that issue only concerns certain peoples and 'races' whereas the question of why women have higher voices applies to everyone. Female voices are perceptibly higher in pitch among all peoples – including the inhabitants of India, Asia, Polynesia, Africa, and Australia. Women altos may be able to go a third or even a fifth below a male tenor, and a 'Heldentenor' may be able to go a fifth above a contralto, but such 'overlappings' change nothing about the fact that the average female register is considerably higher than the male equivalent. Interestingly, a tenor sounds 'deeper' to our ears when singing alongside an alto because he generates lower and the woman higher overtones. That is also true of speech.

Let us first devote attention to striking differences in our capacity for picking up high and low voices. That must entail some evolutionary function. It is certainly important that men and women sound different – as it is also important that they look different. When we are out walking and someone approaching is still too far away to be recognised, the first thing we know is whether that is a man or a woman. Perception of sex is more highly developed than other comparable capacities for recognition. We understand why that is important, but if it were merely a question of differentiating voices evolution could just as well have equipped men with high voices and women with low voices. In certain respects that seems just as plausible. The protective and soothing character of a deep bass voice accords more closely with primal motherhood in the early human tribes – as convincingly described by scholars – than a higher and possibly shriller soprano.

II
HIGH VOICES CARRY THE MELODY

So we perceive high and low sounds differently. But what does the difference entail? When we play a record by a symphony orchestra, we only register the deeper instruments – basses, celli, tubas, etc. – when they serve a soloistic function. Otherwise they merely contribute to the overall sound, providing warmth, sonority, and a background. Their solo passages can only be heard if the higher parts remain silent or are reduced in volume. The higher instruments play, the more easily they exert an impact. We hear the highest instruments – violins, flutes, trumpets – most clearly. Most people, exercising their right to generalisation, feel them to be the vehicles of the melody, the 'real' music. And no deep voice has to be omitted so that such melodies can be heard. Composers and arrangers of music do in fact give prominence to higher instruments as the carriers of what is perceived as 'melody'. They do not have any other possibility in an orchestral tutti. They have to accept the fact that high voices dominate there. If they want low voices to stand out, they have to keep the high ones silent – or at least at a very low volume. The impression is that the low instruments have to insist that the high ones hold back, or they will at most be heard in an accompanying function. A bass solo in jazz provides a good example. The accompanying pianist has to hold back, playing just a few notes or chords with lots of space in between. If he does more, he automatically becomes the solo and the bass the accompaniment.

I live in a little wine-making village on the slopes of the Black Forest. Very many song-birds are to be found there too. Their singing is most beautiful in the morning when they wake and in the evening just before sleeping. More important still, they all sing together at those times – at high, medium, and low pitches. And that provides confirmation of what has just been said. When many birds 'make music' together, we hear those with the highest voices most clearly.

Anyone who lives in a town and hears traffic noises instead of bird-song has the same experience. The highest sounds stand out from the general city noise-level.

The same can be observed in cafés and restaurants where women's voices are most likely to be apparent amid the general babble of conversation – because they have higher voices rather than because they talk more loudly (although they sometimes do that too as do men as well).

The Weber–Fechner law in physics confirms that observation and expresses it in a mathematical formula. Higher tones are more easily perceived than lower if the energy employed in the production of sounds is the same.

III
NATURAL DOMINANCE?

Obviously, as one can hear, high voices dominate. Low voices merely round off the sound, and in music they mainly fulfil a subservient function. As a listening human being I cannot shut my ears to the communicative function revealed in that finding. People must really have been excessively preoccupied with what could be seen to have been able to *overlook* that for generations.

In recent years scientists have discovered a wide range of evidence showing that early peoples made much more alert and attentive use of their ears in everyday existence than does twentieth-century man. They must therefore have understood – as a result of intensely personal experience – that nature can only have given women dominating voices because it wanted them to be dominant. Nature thus, right from the start, *attuned* humanity to female dominance, to what is known as matriarchy. Nothing is changed there even if some people argue that evolution intended high voices as compensation for women's other weaknesses. We shall see that such an objection cannot be sustained, but, even if it were true, nature's intention of signalling female superiority through a higher voice remains decisive.

I know that predominantly eye-orientated readers will respond with a smile. Even as a listener I write that with what is, I hope, a perceptible degree of irony. Nevertheless there can be no doubt about the correctness of this observation.

Early man accepted what evolution made apparent, and existed in a matriarchy for hundreds of thousands of years. In order to put that enormous epoch into perspective, it is good to realise that if the time humanity has spent on earth is depicted as a two-metre-long ruler, the matriarchy endured for 199.9 cm of that length whilst men have dominated for only a millimetre.

A higher voice is not merely more dominant and penetrating; it is also more differentiated over longer distances than the male voice. The idea that this was necessary because women look after children – and have to call them in from play – is patriarchal nonsense. Children do not wander so far away from their mothers – and especially not during the primal horde's early days on earth – that they are out of range of a deeper voice. In fact, a deep bass would be more plausible than a high soprano as a means of communication with children – just because of the contrast. After all, children themselves have high voices. If account is taken of conditions of existence among primal hordes in early times, then nature should have endowed men with higher voices since it was they who left their camps and caves to extend living-space, hunt, and struggle with enemies. High voices are more functional because they are more penetrating and alarming, and they are also capable of conveying warnings, even from great distances, of the approach of enemies or dangerous wild animals.

Evolution's reasons for making women's voices dominant must therefore have been all the more weighty – and the obvious intention was that women should dominate. If men want their voices to carry over long distances whilst remaining capable of differentiation, they must train them to reach the same heights as women. That is the origin of yodelling as found in the European Alps, the Himalayas, the Andes in South America, and in some Central African pygmy tribes. That means that in exceptional situations nature allows man a possibility of attaining the voice levels which signal dominance. Normally, however, nature intends the opposite. In the 'totality of human sound' the female voices direct what happens and maintain such dominance. The male voices 'serve', belonging to the 'lower' levels – in the same way as servants are said to be 'under' their masters. That is perhaps even the reason why we call high voices 'high' and low voices 'low'.

IV
ABOVE AND BELOW

High and low. In the beginning those were spatial terms, referring to mountains and valleys. But at a very early stage 'high' and 'low' must also have reflected social standing. Some elder – like Moses, Jesus, and generals and leaders everywhere in the world – stood on a mountain, hill, or elevated place, and spoke to 'his' people. Everyone could see who was 'above' and who 'below'.

For hundreds of thousands of years it was women who were 'on top', and spoke to their clan, tribe, or people from 'on high'. Their voice was therefore heard as being 'higher' in the original sense of the word. The men stood below. When they answered the women, their voice came from below – both spatially and in social terms. 'High' and 'low' therefore first applied to location, then to social status, and finally to what could be heard.

When today we hear a woman's voice as being 'higher', a

submerged trace of its higher status still lingers on in the process of hearing. René Chocholle, the French acoustician, established in tests that if the source of a sound is diffuse, most people instinctively locate the higher tone 'above'. If asked about the origin of a diffuse deeper sound, they indicate downwards. And yet men are generally taller than women. Might they have become so only in the course of development towards a patriarchy? That question is provoked by the huge, powerful bodies of women in the Stone Age sculpture found in the Andes, Mesopotamia, Africa, and southern Russia. Men were obviously viewed as being so unimportant that they were considered scarcely worthy of being the subject of sculpture. If men always were taller – which could be verified through fresh discoveries of ancient bones – then it becomes all the more clear that women's social and political position over hundreds of thousands of years has become a biological impulse. That is why we tend to locate high voices as coming from above and low voices from below – despite the fact that the source of a deep sound occupies a great deal more resonating space than a high sound.

V

HIGH DISTANCE AND LOW UNITY

Higher frequencies carry over greater distances as well as being clearer and more dominant. René Chocholle's experiments have also shown that a higher sound always seems to come from further away than an equally loud lower tone. Conversely, deeper sounds establish oneness. That is why all of the world's meditative music stresses low frequencies – and we even instinctively feel that a contradiction exists between very high music and the psychic process of 'becoming one'. Even relatively high instruments used for meditative music – such as the Shakuhachi flutes within traditional Japanese Zen – owe their fascination and expressiveness to great capacity for penetrating downwards, accompanied by the vibrations of a large number of low notes and undertones. No other human sound engenders such 'unity' as Tibetan monks' OM, descending into the lowest registers accessible to the human voice. Overtones establish (as I shall show in Chapter 13, 'Overtones Open the Door') our link with the cosmos, the furthest possible distance, but deep notes create the most direct connection with what is closest at hand – ourselves.

Viewed in social terms, no human singing entails greater distance than a coloratura soprano. A singer stands 'up there' on the stage, and the public looks upwards from a great distance, both outwardly and inwardly. Every note seems to say: Keep a respectful distance! Musicologist Kurt Blaukopf has shown that the West's great classical music – Mozart, Haydn, and Beethoven – would not have been possible without the patronage of absolutist courts, rulers, and princes, a patronage that puts an emphasis on high frequencies. Does it therefore imply that distance which the 'elevated' gentlemen who 'sponsored' the music demanded? Does musical distance reflect social distance?

We must then go further and ask: Why is that the case? Because for hundreds of thousands of years we were programmed to perceive the higher voice as the voice of the ruler from whom distance had to be maintained?

Low music, however, bridges distance – partly because we do not merely hear it but can also often feel its vibrations physically to a much greater extent than with higher sounds. A listener to deeper sounds stops being just a listener. He or she no longer maintains a respectful distance from the sound. The listener then himself or herself 'resounds' – which is of course *also* an outcome of the notes at the lower end of the frequency scale passing without a break from the audible to the realm of the palpable. We are no longer completely sure whether we are hearing or feeling. Is our body vibrating together with the sound? Are we not also a 'part' of that when our body resonates just like the wood, the metal, the skin, and strings of the instruments producing the notes? And yet that question is ultimately peripheral. It does not 'comprehend' the whole. It indicates a physical finding that represents, reflects, and symbolises something psychological, spiritual, and social.

Language once again makes clear that is so. It may not be able to measure frequencies but the ear can – and language answers the ear. Language characterises almost all 'powerful' unitary states and processes leading to oneness with the word 'deep'. We thus speak of being deeply in love, a deep sleep, a deep attachment, deep unity, deep belief, deep religiosity, deep rapture, deep spirituality, and deep meditation. We would view language as displaced if those substantives had been linked with the epithet 'high'. Even the adjective 'powerful' employed in that connection just now does not 'feel' right. 'Deep' is needed there too.

Even in what are generally viewed as negative experiences of oneness, the word 'deep' is also appropriate – as in deep suffering and deep grief. We only use such expressions when we were really 'deeply attached' to the people who evoke such feelings. The linguistic image of 'high suffering' does not exist.

As we said, language does not 'measure', and yet the word 'deep' is also mathematically 'right' – in a dual sense. On the one hand, it accords with the low sonic frequencies that express and often accompany such states musically, and, on the other, it characterises the frequency of the brainwaves we emit when experiencing 'deep sadness' or 'deep meditation', or are 'deeply' in love. We are then in what is known as an *alpha* state when our brain frequency is between 7 and 14 cycl/sec. In a 'normal' state when we transmit *beta* waves, that is considerably higher at between 15 and 51 cycl/sec – and our language would also employ the word 'high' to describe this state of being.

VI

HIGH MEANS : WATCH OUT!

The reader will realise that I am structuring this chapter in such a way that its findings extend ever further. In order to be able to continue doing that I need to ask the reader to recall the signals involved in warnings and exhortations to attention: door-bells and telephones; communications in offices, businesses, and factories – inclusive of those rare occasions when men shout; sirens when there is danger of catastrophe or war; and special sounds indicating the beginning, break, and end of school or the working-day. Wherever an acoustic signal announces danger or a need for attention or caution, insisting on immediate and unquestioning compliance, the preference is for higher 'female' frequencies. All that I have just written about such signals must also apply to women's voices at the time of the matriarchy – unwelcome though that conclusion may be!

The sergeant shouting at his squad on the barrack square instinctively pitches his voice higher so that it reaches the level used over millennia for giving commands. The objection that the sergeant only screams so as to be heard better does not go far enough. He is more easily heard just because the frequencies deriving from female levels of voice have over the course of time programmed us to 'listen' and 'pay attention'.

The 'warning' implied in higher frequencies also becomes clear from the fact that such frequencies are thought unpleasant very much more often than deeper tones. In the words of acoustician Fritz

Winckel: 'A critical threshold of unease is transgressed more quickly by high tones.' Almost everyone feels that if a shrill female voice is compared with a deep male voice. Many, many millennia of experience have led our genes to accept that a really high voice means 'Take care', 'Look out', 'Watch yourself', and 'Don't come near me'.

'Male' frequencies are more strongly intermingled in some of the signals deriving from relatively modern (male?) electronic technology – signals that go beyond merely simulating 'acoustic' sounds already possible in matriarchal times. It is as if men want to insist here on at long last making their 'sound', but things are against them. Even in such cases the higher frequency range is felt to dominate and carry further.

VII
THE RAGINGS OF THE GREAT MOTHER LINGER ON

'The hermaphrodite is the work of humanity.'

Théophile Gautier

The reader has picked up signals in this chapter – unconsciously to begin with, but from a certain point onwards with a mounting sense of unease. High frequencies make us become submissive, feel inferior and fearful of expressing antagonism, presume hysteria, keep well out of the way, expect opposition (palaeo-linguist Richard Fester has shown that the word 'No' derives from a female root in almost all of the world's languages), look upwards, adopt reverential attitudes, develop goose-flesh and shiver with cold, take flight – and dozens of similar reactions.

I certainly don't want to depict the women of the matriarchy as being nothing but sources of fear and terror – yet the cult of the Great Mother which existed at that time may provide an explanation. Researchers into myth assume that blood and cruelty played an important part in that cult.

Entire libraries are devoted to books about the matriarchy; and many relics have been collected and interpreted – even when so mutilated as to reveal virtually nothing. But none of the clever gentlemen who wrote all those books hit on the idea of seeking out audible relics. Such relics don't need to be excavated and cleaned up. We all hear them every day. The world of listening is older and more conservative, preserving in every single one of us, for a million years and more, what has long decayed in the visible world. The world of listening possesses just as many 'fossils' as its visual counterpart. One merely needs to use one's ears. And listen. And eavesdrop. And attend to language, to human tones and similar manifestations, and to our reactions.

That is simple – and the fact that scholars have done little or nothing in that sphere reveals their inner 'deafness' and the atrophy of their (and our) hearing.

What has nevertheless been found by the best listeners among scholars ready to hear within and by researchers into myths – Bachofen, Erich Neumann, Mircea Eliade, C.G. Jung, Berdyaev, and more recently Ken Wilber – is revealing enough: mountains of corpses in the matriarchy, sacrificed to the Great Mother whom the experts see as the 'dominant goddess' – a 'monster'.

Erich Neumann enumerates: 'The self-mutilation and suicide of Attis, Esmun, and Bata; Actaeon who . . . was torn to pieces . . . Aithon who burned in the fire of his own passion . . . Hippolytus who was dragged to death by his horses . . . The list extends for pages – and in each case the revenge of the "Great Mother" was the central factor.' Her cults must have been an epitome of terror.

Ken Wilber writes: 'One merely takes the whole corpus of what is called "Great Mother mythology" and subjects it to a type of statistical analysis as to the fate of the individuals who came into close contact with the Great Mother, as reported specifically and unequivocally in the myths themselves. What one finds is that the individuals involved with the Mother invariably came to a tragic end, invariably are killed or murdered, or commit suicide or are castrated – in general they are simply devoured by the Mother or one of her deputies.'

The Great Mother was present at graves and executions – up to the time of Jesus. By then everything had been covered up, but the decisive detail remained visible: the Mother at the cross.

Other evidence pointing to ancient Mother religions is still valid too. Mary was a 'virgin', and Christ was extolled as 'the lamb of God'. The lamb became the favourite 'substitute' for a human sacrifice as the Mother's bloody rituals gradually became 'more civilised' and living beings were no longer slaughtered without further ado.

The 'devouring', 'exterminating' power of the 'Great Mother' remained in people's consciousnesses until the Middle Ages. The Marian statues of the *Vierge ouvrante* constituted her strangest symbol within Catholicism. When the figure is closed, it presents the familiar image of the Virgin with the young Christ and the world-orb in her hand; but when open God the Father is revealed between her breasts, and the crucified Christ concealed deep within the uterus. The dove of the Holy Spirit is sometimes also represented. The 'Mother' was thus greater than them all, enfolding and containing after having devoured. It is not therefore surprising that the Church finally forbade such depictions.

Vierge ouvrante – open and closed (by an unknown Master).

No one shudders any longer when a clergyman offers the chalice with the blood of Christ and the wafer as the body of Christ. In that moment we still partake of human blood and human flesh as we did for hundreds of thousands of years in the 'Great Mother' cults. We have remained what Ken Wilber casually calls 'nothing but a "momma's boy" '.

We don't shudder when we drink the blood but we do obey fearfully and respectfully when something within listening-range approaches the Great Mother's high frequencies. Our ears preserve what our other senses have long forgotten. They 'hear' fossils, and 'divine' that things could turn out badly for us if we don't act accordingly.

Of course the Great Mother would not have that name if she were not also a sustaining, protecting, loving female force. She does not have to be viewed one-sidedly. What is important is that her exterminating, murderous, bloodthirsty aspects were strong enough to be preserved in our 'auditory memories' up to the present day – alongside her loving aspects. Both are often present at the same time. The deadly Durga of Indian mythology, demanding human sacrifice, can be viewed as an incarnation of the loving Shakti. The murderous Kali is simultaneously also the gentle maidenly Parvati and both are often Devi, the supreme goddess, who is the mother and yet – as Kali – drinks blood. Even the 999 arms of the Japanese goddess Kannon are not just for loving – as contemporaries think – but were originally also for crushing to death in the act of love.

Anthropologists and ethnologists time and again conclude that from a certain point onwards the matriarchy absolutely had to change into a patriarchy – in accordance with the laws of dialectics taught by Hegel. The patriarchy was not, however, the objective. It was a reaction, which has in turn worked through a development involving the inevitability of deformation and given rise to fresh reactions. Wilber: 'As the male once rescued consciousness from the chthonic matriarchate, the female might today help rescue consciousness – and her brother – from the patriarchate . . . The dragon we now must fight is simply the egoic structure itself . . .', is that 'male principle' to which Western civilisation and culture owe so much, but which by now is well on the way towards endangering and possibly even obliterating our very existence on this planet.

'We need today to develop intuition and alert but passive awareness, as we yesterday needed so desperately to develop assertive logic and active mentality . . . The patriarchy, the mental ego, which has served its necessary, useful, but intermediate function, will nevertheless soon prove, quite literally, to be the death of us all' – if we do not make fundamental changes. And by changes Wilber certainly does not mean a new thesis or antithesis -- and definitely not a new matriarchy – but rather a synthesis, which is the objective of dialectics: at long last the whole, androgynous, integral human being in which the male and the female come together to form a new unity where history (what a revealing word!) becomes both *his-story* and *her-story*.

VIII
WHY WOMEN WANT TO BE SEEN

What happened during the transition from a matriarchy to a patriarchy? As we have seen, for hundreds of thousands of years men listened to women – but then God drove Adam (and Eve!) out of paradise: 'Cursed is the ground . . . in sorrow shalt thou eat of it all the days of thy life. Thorns also and thistles shall it bring forth to thee.' And the reason for that was: 'Because thou hast hearkened unto the voice of thy wife . . .' (Genesis 3, 17).

The fact that women were no longer listened to was something new. The first woman in history to whom that happened was Cassandra. Troy would not have been destroyed, the destiny of Greece and even the whole of Asia Minor would have been different, and the dreadful self-perpetuating tragedy of the House of Atreus (Agamemnon, Clytaemnestra, Electra, and Orestes) would have been avoided *if* people had listened to Cassandra. She was the first of a long line of great women seers whose voices were ignored under the patriarchy. Women were, however, seen. They had to be seen. And they wanted to be seen. From that time onwards an increasing amount of time was devoted to making themselves beautiful, putting on eye-shadow and make-up, selecting and wearing beautiful clothing, attracting attention, and being in general eye-catching – as if the eye had supplanted the ear.

The society view used to be that 'The best woman remains silent,' and there's an old saying that one should wring the necks of girls who whistle and hens which crow. The Bible exhorts: 'Let your women keep silence in the churches.'

A woman was thus faced with a 'dilemma'. 'In order to be taken seriously and listened to, she had to talk like a man. If she does that, she is masculine and devalued as a woman.' (Senta Trömel-Plötz). Women talk less even if they are in public life – no matter what men may say to the contrary. Their contribution to debates in the world's parliaments does not even accord with a representation that is much too low anyway. And when they do speak, the level of noise in the chamber is noticeably higher than during men's speeches. The gentlemen simply do not listen. That is not intentional – they are not so impolite! – but results from their being inwardly programmed not to listen to the female voice.

They do nevertheless look at women. The inferiority of the visual sense becomes clearer here than anywhere else. No matter what women do to attract predominantly male attention, involving enormous expenditure which nourishes entire industries and determines shop-windows and the urban street-scene, they cannot make up for the 'minor fact' that they are no longer listened to. No visible effort has enabled them to compensate for that invisible 'auditory' defect. 'Thou shalt not hearken to the voice of thy wife,' which means – as every woman has experienced hundreds of times – that no matter what she does to please the eyes, this only affects symptoms, minimalia, stimuli, and pretty details. Anyone who is not listened to remains subordinate. The people who run TV know that best. When important news has to be transmitted, a male voice is more effective.

Perhaps the fact that women talking in their normal voices have not been listened to under patriarchy is one reason why they had to resort to high-pitched communications. That may be how the 'hysterical voice' developed. There are both genetic and social reasons for our negative programming with regard to female voices. The genetic factor is ancient, dating back to the matriarchy, but the social element is relatively new. It derives from the five or six thousand years of patriarchy, and cannot yet be part of our genetic code.

Men have simply been luckier. The pitch of the male voice does not set off a negative response. It evokes tranquillity, assurance, security, reliability, calm, and strength. It rarely becomes painful – except through excessive volume, which is the case with all frequencies inclusive of high 'female' frequencies. Even at its upper limit the male voice does not cause any feeling of unease. It simply 'silently' vanishes into the sphere of the no longer audible – unlike very high women's voices which cause pain before 'passing away'.

That positive image of the male voice dates from the time of the matriarchy when men had no possibility of taking on negative connotations. They had to be 'good' and do what was expected of them – in the same way as women had to be 'well-behaved' under the patriarchy. What was expected of men is today still concealed in the sound of their voices. .

So we must constantly weigh the situation, and constantly listen very carefully. Anyone who finds this presentation 'sexist' misunderstands it. The word 'sexist' is in any case unusable, is pure 'propaganda'. The women of the matriarchy were 'sexist' just as the men of the patriarchy certainly are. The word either applies to both sexes or to neither. The irony I have sometimes utilised here contributes more towards real and humane understanding of this problem than deployment of war-cries.

IX
FEMALE SOUNDS ARE OLDER

Human males only develop a deeper voice during puberty. Women are not alone in having high voices. Children do too. So long as children – and male children too – are dependent on their mothers, their voice frequencies accord with those of women.

Scientists agree that men were only tolerated on the periphery of the matriarchy's primal hordes. They had to remain 'outside' – outside of the home, cave, and communal fire. They had to 'serve' by dragging home the wild animals they killed – and in return they were from time to time allowed to spend a night with one of the women. Little has changed there in the patriarchy. Today men take flowers, chocolate, or jewellery so as to be able to stay the night.

When his voice broke, the young male left the 'inner circle'. What did he really leave? The vocal realm of the women and children who predominated in his surroundings – as if he were from then on 'separated' from them, which he really was in primal hordes' social systems.

Even today men instinctively raise their voices when they talk to babies and small children. Are they trying to re-establish themselves in the inner circle?

Men were only reluctantly and provisionally accepted in their own 'clan', so they developed an interest in roving far from home, discovering new things and finding partners elsewhere. Evolution thus conditioned man's urge to travel and his drive towards expansion.

Viewed biologically, human foetuses are all initially female. Our 'primordial nature' is feminine. The Y chromosome, which contains the masculine code, is the weaker and must constantly struggle for survival. Evolution has thus programmed man to struggle right from the start. The basic human code consists of two X chromosomes, i.e. two female chromosomes. The Y entails an alteration. It cannot survive on its own, and will die unless complemented by the female chromosome. The X chromosome is, however, capable of existing by itself.

Man was thus produced out of woman – and not the other way round as the Bible and similar patriarchally falsified myths of creation maintain.

The clitoris is not – as Freud made us believe – an atrophied and sorely missed penis. It is a vehicle of freedom and autonomy – the only human organ that solely and exclusively serves the gaining of pleasure. There is nothing comparable in the male body. All other human pleasure-centres fulfil an additional function which is their *raison d'être*. All those pleasure-centres teach us: delight is secondary. Only for the clitoris does pleasure come first.

If either of the two sexes is somewhat 'atrophied', then it is the man. The Y chromosome that engenders maleness looks like the mutilated, fragmented remnant of the female X chromosome. The male breast, still embellished with the nipples that a woman needs for feeding a baby, is of course 'atrophied' too since no longer needed. Man retained his nipples when he 'split off' from woman – and nowhere else in his body is this 'separation' so apparent. Even the pleasure they give him is only a fraction of what a woman can get from her breasts.

In the context of this book, this signifies that, viewed in evolutionary terms, the female voice is the older. It is the original 'human sound', and the deeper male voice derives from it.

It thus becomes conclusively apparent that it was evolution itself – and not just women – which wanted to keep men 'outside'. That explains why men were given an 'alien' sound from the time when they had to stay 'outside' – a sound immediately distinguishable from that made by the women and children belonging to the 'inner circle'. Almost as if evolution wanted to brand men in terms of the auditory sense, which was decisive for early humanity: Beware! Someone with a deep voice can only be allowed to enter under certain circumstances. He sounds 'different' to those who 'belong'.

Hardly any other word in the languages accessible to us betrays so much of man's outsider status as the English word *husband*, signifying someone who is *house-bound*. The word marks a triumph: at long last the man could move in; not just for a night – for ever. The word also reveals how he managed that. Among the Normans and Vikings the word was *husbond* – and *bonde* meant peasant, the man who *binds* the ears of corn. At no other period of human development was women's rule more absolute than at the time when cultivation was first being established – and they needed men to work for them. The word *husband* could never have come into being if it hadn't been something special, something new, something unique that had to be recorded in language: a man in the house! One is tempted to add – at last! The fact that *husband* is a compound word is also revealing. Something subsequent – formed later. In no way envisaged in the primal language, and something not present there. Something still to be established: the *house peasant*.

X
WOMEN CREATED LANGUAGE

Returning to the period before cultivation was established, the wild animals men hunted and dragged to their women were not needed – any more than today's gift of jewellery. The primal hordes lived amid abundance. Primordial humanity was black and lived in Africa. Food grew on trees and in the ground – and there was more than enough for the few people involved. Even in Europe it was much warmer than today. We need to realise – at long last – that the struggle for survival attributed to early peoples is a projection of a Protestant, capitalist, competitive society – just as Darwin's 'struggle for existence' was conceived at the very moment when the mutually exploitive representatives of Western civilisation were subjugating the earth, and everywhere sought biological, anthropological, and historical justification for their own misguided behaviour – and found it too.

For hundreds of thousands of years there was sufficient food. Meat was of minor importance. It was welcome but only as an additional treat – as can be seen from the anatomy of our teeth: twenty front and rear molars, eight incisors, but only four canines. Molars grind grain; incisors cut vegetables and fruit; and canines tear apart meat. So the legumes/vegetables/meat ratio is 20:8:4 (or 5:2:1). Only four out of 32 teeth for meat! Interestingly, there are more variants among canines than among the other teeth. Sometimes they are almost as blunt as the molars, which must mean that nature does not insist on them – or on meat.

Archaeological finds also reveal a great lack of utensils for dealing with meat. Meat really was something supplementary. So too therefore was the male activity of hunting. It was a 'hobby', a sport – ultimately so unimportant that anthropologist Doris F. Jonas could conclude: 'Examination of the entire panorama of human development back to the most distant past shows women's dominance within society becoming so great that it could not avoid giving rise to a male revolution.'

Not even hunters' most important attributes – virility: male virtue, strength, and courage – were masculine to begin with. Palaeo-linguist Richard Fester followed the word *virility* back to its roots where it everywhere signifies offspring – but in matriarchal times the line of descent was exclusively female (and only later became male). Only the female line of descent could claim *worth* –

another word related to *vir*. The femininity receives confirmation in the word *Virgo*, the Latin for virgin. Virility thus referred to female virtues until men usurped the word, and propagated views about praiseworthy aspects of their own sex.

Men were under-employed during the matriarchy – just like lonely suburban housewives today. Hunting was only a hobby so that was not enough. They therefore formed groups, clubs, associations, and communities. Women didn't have any time for such things. The gentlemen sat around and passed time together. The fact that they did that for hundreds of thousands of years meant that such behaviour became programmed. In Africa, in Polynesia, in Indonesia, among Red Indians, and among Westerners. It is always – or almost always – men who get together to form associations, societies, orders, gangs, gentlemen's clubs (which have no female equivalent), Rotary and Lions clubs, and much besides. Male choirs developed in that way too, allowing men's voices to be heard at last. Women were not in need of that. They did what was more enjoyable: singing together with men where they come across even more strongly. That is why there are so few women's choirs. Male choirs do nevertheless still dazzle with those dark, warm sounds which have fascinated listeners since antiquity: impressive, fear-inducing Islamic choirs; mysterious Indian choirs; homely German choirs; and faultless Japanese choirs.

The subordinate nature of male voices has always been a problem in choral literature: from early madrigals by way of Bach, the Classics and Romantics, up to the present day. Handel, for instance, deliberately tried to accentuate male voices more strongly. A good example is provided by the chorus 'He trusted in God' from the 'Messiah'. The men's voices can basically only be clearly heard when they sing by themselves: at the beginning when they introduce the fugal theme, and briefly each time they have a new fugal entry. As soon as the women join in, they dominate the music, and the men merely add weight.

That becomes even clearer in Schiller's celebrated 'Ode to Joy' in the last movement of Beethoven's Ninth Symphony. 'Be embraced, O millions. This kiss for the entire world' is sung by the men alone, just like a male choir. But when the women enter, the immediate impression is that they predominate, even though the men continue singing. The same happens a few bars later at the lines 'Brothers, beyond the canopy of stars there must dwell a loving Father'. When Beethoven wants the male voices to be heard as such, he must ensure that the women are silent. The men can, however, continue singing even if the women are to be heard as women. Women's voices are always the first to be heard.

What thus becomes audible in music is only an auditive print, an aural model of what also happens in society. Musical ensembles, groups, and choirs are social models become audible . . .

Only since the beginning of this century have women, inspired by early feminism, started forming their own groupings and – as people say today – 'organising' themselves. Male associations still serve as a model there since there is no better one. Anyone who has learnt something for several hundred thousand years should be sufficiently experienced!

Men were also seen as unimportant because the connection between procreation and birth was unknown – as it still is among such people as the original inhabitants of the Trobiand Islands. This link only became known during the transition from the Stone to the Bronze Age – which means that it remained a mystery for many hundred thousand years. The relationship between frequency of sex and rarity of a birth made it difficult to get behind what was involved. Even today many people – including the Dogon in West Africa with their highly developed social system studied and admired by ethnologists and psychologists from all over the world – believe that there exist two- or three-year pregnancies. In many Islamic countries pregnancies lasting several years are still provided for in law. People there are sure that the woman decides whether she wants a child. When she does, she will get one.

Even later, when the connection between the sexual act and pregnancy had been recognised, the distance between woman and man remained enormous for tens of thousands of years – to the disadvantage of the man. Richard Fester has shown that in every language *all* the words entailing domination come from female roots. All the emperors, princes, kings, maharajahs, pashas, and even samurai were originally women – as is linguistically revealed.

We can also see from the robes, habits, and gowns worn in any courtroom or church today that judges and priests were originally women. Men had to carry on wearing these women's clothes in order to retain credibility when they took over those 'jobs' from women. Cato was still aware of that, revealing why senators in ancient Rome wore togas (women's clothing): so that the 'people' – whose reactions were largely unconscious – might accept the senators' 'claim' to exercise the power which in fact they already possessed.

As early as last century, the celebrated French geographer, Elisée

Reclus (1830–1905) whose journeys and studies paved the way for so much of today's ethnological, anthropological, and sociological knowledge, wrote: 'Humanity owes to woman everything that has made it human. She was the creator of all the beginnings of civilisation.' A hundred years later Richard Fester's palaeo-linguistic research led him to conclude: 'Women were the beginning of the development of human society – and decisive for survival of the species. They created language – and thus the precondition for cultural development. They invented the first tools – and thereby laid the foundation stone for all further technology. They initiated religion and "churches".'

How ridiculous were older patriarchal researchers into language who maintained that men invented language while hunting! Richard Fester asks ironically: What for? So as to scare off wild animals? Lions, tigers, and wolves have developed perfect strategies for hunting and killing. Evolution didn't need language to make them more perfect. Only one of the primal words ascertained by Fester is male, another is neutral, and the rest are clearly female. Women created language thanks to the primal female impulse towards enriching love, making it more profound and abundant – very unlike the male drive which seeks the most direct and immediate means of gratification, and does not require language for that. Love was intended to become more differentiated with regard to children as well as to lovers and sexual partners. The phrase 'mother tongue' describes a personal experience that everyone still has. We still – like the first human beings – learn our first words, the words with which our ability to speak begins, from a woman: our mother.

XI
GIRLS TALK EARLIER AND SAY MORE

I am writing this by a mountain river. A young couple are making their way up the valley. The track is still blocked by snow so they are using the stream-bed. They are jumping – the young man leading – from ice floe to ice floe, and from rock to rock. Sometimes things don't quite work out. They misjudge the distance to a rock or the ice cracks beneath them. Then they are splashed and get wet. That happens to both the man and the young woman. The man simply carries on, but each time the woman slips, goes through the ice, or lands on a wobbly stone, she utters a little cry. In my opinion, such behaviour is relatively characteristic of her sex.

One can also observe couples coming out of a cinema. It is almost always the woman who first says something. Men have long maintained that women 'babble too much'. That is a patriarchal prejudice. It would be more objective to say that we all most frequently and pleasurably do what we are best at. Women 'can' talk. They are more skilful, quicker, more expressive, and more creative in that sphere. That is most apparent when they make love. Women's voices and the sounds uttered are much more active and intensifying than most men's contribution.

It is not just adult women who are more talented and gifted than men in the shaping of sounds. American behavioural researchers have also ascertained that baby girls react more strongly to aural stimuli and baby boys to visual stimuli – and mothers 'know' that. In the majority of the thousands of mother–child relationships observed, mothers made greater use of their voices and responded more to the gurgling and other noises emitted by newly born girls. With baby boys the mothers more frequently employed 'non-auditive' movements and colourful toys.

The fact that women very much more frequently punish children (and other people) verbally whilst men hit out points in the same direction. That too can be viewed as the outcome of woman's linguistic superiority at the time of the matriarchy – and of men's hundred-thousand-year-long experience of verbal inferiority and inability to express themselves, accompanied by a sense of being perhaps physically stronger. Women's experience has been diametrically opposite. They dominated and exerted power by way of language.

XII
THE PRIMAL HUMAN BEING – A LISTENER

Apes – and there too particularly females – have a richly differentiated sign language with hundreds of gestures and expressive movements used for communicating with one another. American zoologists have even succeeded in 'talking' directly to apes. Much attention has been devoted to the successes of Californian biologist Francine Patterson who spent five years teaching Koko, a female gorilla, 300 signs in the *Ameslan* deaf-and-dumb language, and even succeeded in motivating the animal to invent new signs of its own.

Another ape, Washoe, much depicted in illustrated magazines, even learnt to understand and employ metaphorical references. For instance he also applied the sign for 'dirt', learnt from the example of ape excrement, to a 'dirty' unpleasant character – which signifies that apes can think in analogies.

It seems as if men have retained primates' capacity to communicate by way of signs and gestures for longer than women. Doris and David Jonas point to the fact that today there still exist Red Indian tribes where 'tradition prescribes that men should only make limited use of language, and should communicate with one another by way of gestures'. And in another context: 'It is highly probable that early man made a virtue of his incompetence with language, especially as his main task, hunting, demanded complete silence . . . For women the thrust of selection was towards constantly improving manipulation of sounds whereas for men the pressure was towards improvement of orientation in space.'

All that remains to be perceived of that today are residues – of interest merely as a means of being able to understand ourselves better. Hundreds of thousands of years ago, woman's vocal and linguistic superiority was as important for the development of communication – and thus of civilisation and culture – as man's three-dimensional ability was for opening up new living space, and thus for humanity's spread across the earth.

Throughout the immeasurable period of the matriarchy the ear dominated – as had already been the case with the primates and animals as a whole. Researchers into evolution talk of the 'acoustic era' during the early stages of existence.

Jean Gebser, Marius Schneider, and others have carried out careful research and demonstrated that the primal human being was a listener. He or she lay or squatted in the hollows and dips of the great plains, listening intently to all the noises of the surrounding world, all those mysterious sounds thronging in from animal throats and the undulating woods, from the movements of grass and leaves, from the rustlings of snakes and reptiles, from caves and ravines, from winds and storms, from rain, hail, and thunder, from river and torrents. The Sanskrit word *Nada* (= sound) originally meant river. Sensing a river as sound must have been a matter of course for early human beings.

Evolution is served by our capacity to emulate what we hear. We can fill the silence that surrounds us – with words, laughter, tears, singing. Are we still aware how privileged the ear is? We cannot lighten the surrounding darkness since the 'source of light' is always outside ourselves. Perhaps that is the main reason why our visual faculty is so strongly outer-directed whilst our hearing takes us inwards. Hearing existed before speech, and thus inevitably also entailed inner listening.

The predominantly listening character of early human beings programmed and conditioned their need to create and refine language. It is highly probable that evolution fostered auditory abilities just so that language was created. It is possible that women were more responsive to that task since they were more concerned with processing the information heard and converting it into directives. That would also be another reason why women had to develop greater linguistic abilities. They absolutely had to make more careful and precise use of language so as to command obedience.

The fact that little attention has to date been directed towards such matters completes the picture. Scholarship is a male preserve. After everything we have said, it is clear that male scholars are not – or are only peripherally – interested in such things.

XIII
POLYPHONY AS A MODEL

To conclude these reflections on woman's vocal dominance and linguistic superiority, let us venture a little further, impelled by the ear and listening. Imagine a music in which the strongest element totally dominates in the simplest fashion. That would certainly be monody: a choir of many different voices – high and low, women and men – all singing the same melodic line in unison or an octave apart. What they are really doing is following the highest vocal line, which is what is felt to be the melody. The high women's voices thus dominate.

To that extent it is true that early music was monodic – long into the patriarchy. Music is conservative and reacts slowly. It only 'notices' social changes when they are long past.

Humanity had already long been immersed in the patriarchy when polyphonic music developed. And yet it came into being at exactly the right moment, just before the patriarchy set about its greatest expansion of power – the rise of Western rationalism, men's greatest triumph in the history of humanity. That was appropriate too since a considerable degree of rationality is needed for the production of well-organised polyphonic music. Maybe a many-voiced fugue or a toccata.

The logic is that the more independent the different voices within polyphonic music become, the more chances the deeper ones have of being heard as an autonomous 'male' viewpoint which does not just reproduce monody's separation – by octaves or fifths – from the 'female' line. No kind of fixed interval is involved since the choice is always open.

Adorno proclaimed that polyphonic music says 'We'. That – like much he said – may be true, but it is only a half-truth. The reality is that polyphony, where many different people make music together, is the only kind of music where the deep voices (at 'male pitches') can be heard as independent contributions. Otherwise even children have more chance of being heard than men.

Polyphonic music may say 'We', but it only does that in order to be able to say 'Lord and Master'. Its 'We' is predominantly male as a means whereby the weaker element assures itself of attention.

Man cannot, no matter how much he may try – and he certainly has tried – make his voice dominate. So if he wants to be heard he must strive for pluralism: for many different and contrasting voices, so that attention can also be paid to the lower, 'subordinate' parts.

The word *pluralism* indicates what I am driving at. If *everything* in the history of music is a model of society – and there exist enough competent investigations demonstrating that – then what we are talking about here is very much a model too. Democracy is a male invention. It had to be. There was no reason why women should have invented democracy. They had what they needed. And even when loss of their powers led them to call for democracy, they did so only hesitantly. Polyphony in music is what democracy is in politics: equality of rights between all 'voices' including those which are naturally 'subordinate'.

So my postulate is: polyphonic music as a model.

All of us, men and women, living in contemporary culture love polyphonic music. Not just fugues. New Orleans jazz and free jazz are also polyphonic. Good rock is too. What do we love there? The answer can only be: the equality of all the different voices we hear. In short: equality of rights.

And now let us sceptically assess what we hear in all the polyphonic music we love – from Bach's 'Art of Fugue' and Mozart's 'Magic Flute' to Coltrane's 'Ascension' and John McLaughlin's

Mahavishnu Orchestra. What do we hear first of all? Without any doubt – the high voices. We may hear all the others too – each (almost) equivalent in status – but the high voices certainly dominate. We could even weaken the treble line and strengthen the bass, setting a single piccolo against a dozen unison Wagner tubas, and we'll still hear the flute first.

Taken to its ultimate conclusion, polyphony, like monody, proclaims: 'Woman' – but it also says: 'We' and 'Lord and Master'!

13

OVERTONES OPEN THE DOOR

'Can we view overtones as a kind of universal mantra tuning the entire planet – as the real universal language?'

Roberto Laneri

I
MANY VOICES FROM A SINGLE THROAT

All of a sudden young people are singing overtones. Such vocal harmonics were virtually unknown in the Western world until very recently. Now there are thousands of overtone singers. The situation must have been similar in the seventeenth century when the technique of coloratura singing was developed, and within just a few years made its way into royal courts, theatres, and opera houses throughout Italy and then elsewhere in Europe. Today's fascination with vocal harmonics parallels that interest in a new way of singing. Seventeenth-century concert-goers were flabbergasted by the human capacity to sing in that fashion, and listeners today don't know what to make of the way in which a single throat seems to produce two independently moving melodies, or chords where the notes of the overtone series are superimposed. They don't want to believe what they hear, and think they're being taken for a ride. Some people even assume that concealed electronics, a tape machine backstage, must be at work, secretly providing the second – and third and fourth – voice.

For hundreds of years the noble and ancient art of overtone singing flourished in Tibet and North India, among the Siberian-Mongolian Tuwan tribe, in the Buddhist monasteries of Japan and China, and among a few talented Indian singers in the South American Andes. Rudimentary traces are sometimes to be heard in the disintegrating falsetto of flamenco singers, in the tumbling vocalisations employed by African pygmy tribes, and in increasingly rare Bulgarian and Romanian folksongs. It becomes strikingly apparent that vocal harmonics are almost always used in a spiritual context.

The young people who have suddenly started singing overtones in Europe and the USA are not, however, concerned with some exotic imitation. Most of them have little or no knowledge of Asiatic, African, or American Indian precursors. They sing articulated and well-controlled melodic phrases where every note reveals their Western origins.

A living culture of vocal harmonics now exists in Western Europe for the first time since the heyday of Gregorian Chant. Scholars point out that overtones were pursued – in a number of schools at least – much more consciously than in today's Gregorian singing. Overtones develop from vowels, and the protracted vowel-related melismata within ancient choral singing's melodic lines almost inevitably made the alert listener aware of vocal harmonics – with the architectural proportions of the church or cathedral also playing their part.

II
OVERTONES INFORM US ABOUT REALITY

Overtones are contained within whatever individual note is sounding as co-resonating higher tones whose oscillatory frequencies are very much greater than the frequency of the fundamental. In every note we produce on a percussion, wind, or string instrument, an entire scale vibrates: the overtone scale that contains all whole- and half-note intervals, initially widely separated and then becoming ever closer. The frequencies of oscillation and lengths of string involved are inversely related.

Let us imagine a string stretched over an instrument – most simply a monochord, used by Pythagoreans for their experiments over 2,500 years ago. Let's assume that the string is tuned to the note C. If we divide it exactly in the middle, the same note C is to be heard once again, but an octave higher. If we divide the string into three, we hear a note related to the previous ones: a G, the first 'other' note, separated from the C by the interval of a fifth. Children usually sing in parallel fifths when they start to harmonise.

When we divide the string by four, we repeat a previous action. We divide a half, and the outcome is once again a C, an octave higher. The interval between this C and the previously discovered G is a fourth. When we divide by five, we end up with the major third, then the minor third, etc. The intervals become ever smaller, and yet each note seems to open up a new world.

Everything is still in accord with the 'fundamental note', which we will continue to assume to be C. Stillness becomes sound – so irrevocably that this is confirmed by the next octave. Then the first opening occurs with the fifth, resulting from the third note in the series. Movement is still absent but is coming close – and is established with the next interval, the fourth. That could be said to 'awaken' the series – and the listener – to everything that follows. Firstly to the third, which immediately confronts us with a decision: major or minor? We decide in favour of a sex: major/male or minor/female. We sense the 'clarity' this decision brings – and also think of the associated 'clearing up' of the weather and resonances in many languages relating to consciousness and sexuality.

Only now can we become 'active', and we feel this activity when we hear the sixth note. Once again we are faced with the decision between major/masculine and minor/feminine, which excites us and urges us forward to the seventh, which we find strangely alien. No one likes remaining there. We sense we need a 'home' – and find it in the octave which we attain with a sense of relief, of inevitability – and even almost a feeling of happiness. And yet we set off again on the second octave, proceeding as previously: for the most part courageous because we tend to choose the major, but sometimes also inhibited and uncertain if we take the minor because some experience or other – probably unpleasant – holds us back from the greater step. It then turns out that the minor second is the very interval for forcing us onwards – to a greater extent than the major.

We now see – and this will be further corroborated later – that overtones are closely related to the reality in which we exist, to that reality which is the most important for every one of us: the reality of our feelings. Roberto Laneri, the outstanding Italian overtone singer and composer, says that 'Overtones inform us about reality.'

Harmonics, according to reference works, create tone-colour. The fact that a violin sounds different to a trumpet is the outcome of generating different overtone series. It isn't, however, only the tone-colour that is created by the overtones. They also 'make' the music itself. If music were to operate with 'pure' tones (with single-wave vibrations), musicians could slide up and down the tonal series without a break – similar to the way in which colour 'tones' merge almost imperceptibly across the entire spectrum. However, 'pure' tones practically never occur in the audible – as opposed to the visible – sphere. Harmonics accompany every note, and it is the interactions between the principal vibration and the overtones that make sliding smoothly down the scale – on, say, a monochord string – so difficult for us. We constantly home in on the points where harmonic intervals seem 'right' – and only at those points do we feel at ease. It is as if the auditory process 'insists' on this interval where it wants to stay. It doesn't want to perceive anything but the 'exact' interval. If it cannot avoid perceiving some – in most cases hardly audible – tones in between, it does so only superficially and with noticeable distaste, moving quickly on to reach the place where the 'correct' interval is 'established' – as if it were 'at home'.

The Sufis have marvellously captured the 'dwelling' of tones in specific places. The Arabic word *maqām* originally meant stopping-place or place of rest, but is also used in precisely that sense for the concept of 'musical notes' (i.e. where sounds come to a stop) – and additionally for the 'dwellings of the soul' on its way from birth in a physical body through the 'stations of the heart' to *maqām al-wisāl*, the 'station of Unification with God'.

So – to repeat myself but this is very important for everything that follows – there cannot be music without overtones! If they are absent, any sliding upwards or downwards – using some electronic source of sound since this wouldn't even be possible on a string – becomes an unmusical screeching, howling, and whistling where 'notes' are scarcely perceptible. Between 'tones' and 'overtones' there is constant *feedback*. The harmonics may be the outcome of a note being struck, but the fundamental would not have an impact as a note if the overtones failed to inform us of its character as such.

It becomes clear at this point that when we refer to the overtone series we are talking of an Idea. At times the third, seventh, ninth, and twelfth overtones may sound out, and at others the second, fifth, sixth, and eighth, etc. – depending on the colour-timbre produced by an instrument or singer. The complete overtone series is, however, never heard. It only exists as an Idea. Indian sages say that the universe would burst asunder if the complete series were to become audible.

The degree of difficulty Western musicians have with overtones must long have become apparent. They believe that the fundamental is almost all that counts, so it occupies virtually all their attention. They are of the opinion that the fundamental 'makes' the music with everything following on from that primary tone. Whether a melody is played on a harpsichord or piano may concern musicians to some extent, but ultimately they view it as the 'same' music. They are only marginally interested in the fact that the two instruments generate completely different series of harmonics.

Eastern musicians have other experiences with their instruments. For them the 'real' music derives from the overtones rather than the primary notes. As Indian music teachers tell their pupils: The music you make doesn't 'happen' in the notes you pluck or blow; it 'happens' in the overtones. That is why you must essentially listen to and work with them. The fundamentals are only a tool, an extension of the 'instrument' employed in this craft. In the view of Eastern musicians, anyone who remains at that level does not get beyond the (admittedly important) 'technical' aspects of music-making.

III
OVERTONES = *SUPERSOUNDS*

Roberto Laneri says: 'The first step is to hold a note for a long time and observe it. One takes the note and regards it as if under a microscope. A drop of water may not reveal much about itself at first glance, but when looked at more closely it contains the universe.' That is also true of overtones. Laneri: 'This is mainly a question of perception, of contemplation – not of taking action. The note is, as it were, illuminated from within.'

Michael Vetter, the best-known German teacher and singer of overtones, pursues the coming into being of such harmonics back to the process of speech: 'Without knowing it we speak in successions of chords.' In order to uncover that, Vetter says we must

> . . . slow down our tempo of speaking to such an extent that a single
> breath is scarcely enough for a word. We must therefore take time to
> really attend to what is happening in individual sounds and their
> transitions . . . for instance accompanying, millimetre by millimetre,
> the path taken by the tongue from i to u, which is more difficult than
> the hand describing a trajectory in the air feeling the slowness to the
> full.

All teachers of overtones refer to the slowness of this process, and to
the importance of listening and letting be. Vetter makes clear that
the important thing is to 'make music oneself', and yet 'basically
be nothing but a listener . . . never knowing whether I am hearing
what is actually taking place acoustically. Or does anticipatory
dreaming – or dream-like anticipation – mingle with a somewhat
sparse reality, which is nevertheless founded on overtones and thus
in turn makes no distinction between the audible and the inaudible
. . .? Time and again . . . under the spell of the question: Who is
really singing there?'

Time and again mention is made of: listening, perceiving, taking
one's time, being attentive, observing the inner aspects of what is
happening, allowing things to unfold without interfering, and being
conscious – in other words, factors that are also of importance in
meditation.

It's not just chance that almost all good teachers and singers of
overtones also meditate. Someone playing a piano reads a note in
the score and tries it out on the keys. The singer of vocal harmonics
listens to the note's constantly changing possibilities within himself
or herself. He or she must pursue an inner search in order to be able
to produce a note. Every time that is a new adventure, an
unrepeatable process. Perhaps that is why so many young people
are attracted towards singing overtones. You cannot simply 'come
on strong', 'strike out', and be sure that now this or that tone will
resound. You must be cautious and careful, listen inwardly and feel
what's happening there, and allow the overtones to come, assisting
them only with great circumspection. No strict relationship exists
between the fundamental and the overtones. There are many, many
possibilities. A friend of mine, who only recently started learning
singing vocal harmonics, believes: 'Overtone singing is a musical *I
Ching.*' The coins or the yarrow stalks fall differently every
time – and yet they always give a meaningful answer.

Overtone singing establishes a new sense of the body. The singer
must 'adjust the entire bodily system', become more sensitive, and
constantly be alert to inner activity. David Hykes, the American

overtone singer and choir director, points out that tones are made to rise – much more consciously than in other forms of singing – out of specific parts of the body: stomach, pelvis, abdomen, chest, throat, and head. In the head in particular there are various centres where the tones also develop in different ways. Experienced practitioners of vocal harmonics can thus develop intensified musical consciousness in the area of the hypophysis (the so-called 'third eye') or at the highest point of the cranium. The skull is seen as the primordial model for the cathedral dome where tones vibrate, move, and transform themselves, reverberating for long afterwards.

You thereby gain a different relationship to time, seeing through its illusory character. You think you've been singing overtones for ten minutes but two hours have passed.

Paul Horn, the jazz flautist and saxophonist from British Columbia, made a recording in the Taj Mahal near Agra in India – and later also in Egyptian pyramids – and was enthusiastic about the reverberation, which allowed the sound of his flute (and voice) to unfold like a blossom. It was as if the sound expanded above him like a cascading firework, and then slowly floated down as a thousand tiny light-particles. He only needed to be receptive and attentive, and then he could constantly absorb each tiny particle of time and light as a blessing, fusing it with the sound of his flute, and transforming it into renewed cascades of notes as if the music were happening with and through him rather than being made by him.

Huxley, Leary, and Castaneda – long preceded by medieval mystics – spoke of the 'Doors of Perception' through which we must step if we want to open up new areas of consciousness. The first 'door' for young Westerners in the fifties and sixties was *dope*: hashish, marihuana, LSD, etc. Today no one needs that any longer. They need breathing, *prana*, oxygen, meditation, contemplation. Those are the 'doors'. And overtones! That is the main reason why young people learn to sing in this way. They want to go through the 'doors'. Laneri: 'Using overtones as a vehicle you attain other dimensions.'

There exist infinitely many overtones because there exist endlessly many prime numbers. Every way into the realm of overtones is *also* a way into infinity. The overtone series never ceases. It continues for ever, and if you allow yourself to be carried along it will take you ever higher. That shouldn't only be comprehended metaphorically. It is also mathematically and physically true that an overtone series never comes to an end – to the extent that it is not limited by our range of hearing. The way begins as soon as one enters it – with the consciously and attentively heeded primary tone.

The more overtones sound out, the more 'resplendent' the music is. That is not poetic embellishment. René Chocholle, the French acoustician, uses it in a strictly scientific context to describe how 'numerous high overtones' can change music. In Roberto Laneri's words: 'Overtones light up music.' That is true both physically – because overtones really can make music brighter and more filled with light – and spiritually: because the infinite series of overtones leads us to higher and more luminous dimensions.

Laneri has fun in translating overtones as 'supersound' – a going beyond tones.

Anyone who enters upon the way of the overtones – as some inward journey like the *Tao* – moves in quanta. From whole number to whole number. From one harmonically meaningful tone to another. Omitting the many that lie between.

Max Planck developed the quantum theory by observing overtones on a monochord. Kepler discovered his planetary laws – particularly the third – through working with a monochord. Heisenberg says that insight into the law of harmonic relationships is 'one of the strongest impulses within human science'. Once again we see that overtones inform us about reality. They provided a man aware of harmonics with correct insight into the quantum character of reality at a time when academic science still thought nature does not proceed by leaps. It's hard to believe that people really credited that. That only shows the degree to which rationalistic and mechanistic thinking can lead us astray. And also demonstrates that we'll be rightly informed if we rely on the 'Way' of the overtones.

Tibetan Tantric sources indicate the enormous energy at work in overtone singing. Warnings are often issued against employment of such energy if consciousness is not rightly aligned. Morphologically our throat is akin to the *tube* in a jet plane – and it isn't even necessary to envisage the accompanying turbine to pursue the comparison further. The Pulso-Jet does without a turbine, achieving the necessary compression solely by the way the *tube* is shaped. Our throat does exactly the same too. We have no – or at most a minimal – physical sense of the energy unleashed in this tube. It is inconceivable that this should vanish, so we must assume its conversion into psychic energy. That happens whenever we use the pulso-jet of our throat for creating sounds, but of course most strongly of all when this utilisation is most complex and differentiated – during overtone singing. So even morphologically such singing entails development of spiritual energy.

IV
MUSIC : MATERIAL OR TRANSCENDENTAL?

Overtones and the sensorium for their perception play a minor part in Western music compared with most other cultures. Of course their existence is known, and their vibrations contribute to the creation of tone-colours. They cannot be avoided, and they automatically sound out, 'dictated' by the instrument being played. It was probably the introduction of tempered tuning in the eighteenth century that resulted in ever greater atrophy of awareness of overtones in Western music. That was inevitable because tempered tuning amounts to negation of natural tuning, which is postulated in every single note by way of the accompanying overtone series. It is almost as if a piece played in tempered tuning – and thus virtually all Western music – insists on correcting nature. Not a single note in such a piece is heard in its natural relationships – apart from the octave itself. Man's belief that he can do things 'better' reigns.

Tempered tuning probably also led – directly or indirectly – to the rising cadences so characteristic of Western music. For us it is self-evident that melodies generally tend to rise upwards. Any child called on to play a scale or a triad will start with the lowest note and move upwards. Hardly anyone who listens to music devotes attention to the fact that the situation is different in almost all the rest of the world. Descending cadences predominate there. Even cadences in the American Blues, which is a hybrid form, tend to move downwards – and that is even more evident in African, Indian, Amerindian, Balinese, and classical Japanese and Chinese music. Dane Rudhyar, the important American philosopher of music and composer, writes: 'The vocal and instrumental sounds we hear are only the resonance of matter . . . The audible sounds produced by this resonance *rise.*' Cultures whose cadences move upwards are 'matter-orientated'. Descending cadences, on the other hand, are derived from the overtone series – and thus ultimately from the cosmic and spiritual sphere as the dimension where harmonics arise. It could be said that such music descends to earth like a gift, like a blessing.

Rudhyar reminds us of the link between consciousness of overtones and devoutness – an experience so familiar to ethnomusicologists that it is almost a rule laying down that: The richer and more differentiated the overtones in a culture, the more profound and highly developed its spiritual potential.

Perhaps the situation can be seen as follows. Overtone-conscious cultures with downward moving melodies receive their music from above. The Western world derives its music from below, from the realm of matter, releasing such music in order to offer it to the heights.

V
THE FATAL CONNECTION : WESTERN SCIENCE AND WESTERN MUSIC

Astonishingly, the more rationally Westerners thought, the less interested they became in their music's overtones.

And another correlation: The more richly and consciously a music is endowed with overtones, the more timeless it is. The most timeless music in the West, scarcely influenced by the comings and goings of other styles, is Gregorian chant. It is also replete with overtones.

Ever since Twelve-Note and Serial music made their appearance, Western musical fashions and trends have changed so fast that one can hardly keep up. It must be realised that the composer creates his own 'tone row', his own 'scale', which determines musical developments in detail because it both negates (not for the first time in the West) and is in fact decidedly hostile to the overtone series.

The most timeless music on this planet comes from the great Indian classical tradition, which also disposes over the most differentiated awareness of harmonics.

In the development of electronic music there came a time in the fifties when some musicians and composers infringed the most important of overtones' laws – and they still do today. They no longer allowed overtones to 'come', to 'happen', but manipulated them instead, utilising every single overtone as if it were a primary note. There's no more 'opportunity' or 'adventure' in such music. It sounds absolutely dead, and no one wants to listen to it.

All that is basically only the outcome of a development that may have got under way a couple of centuries ago, but only now retrospectively reveals what was involved right from the start. For the great Western concert music of the Classical and Romantic periods, overtones are really only something additional that is included anyway. What counts and is desired is the primary note – struck, stroked, or blown. That, however, signifies that the note is primarily seen as an isolated phenomenon. Every note is separated from all the rest. It is detached from its 'participation' in other notes and abstracted. In other words, Western music has done with notes what science has done with nature since Descartes and Bacon – isolating, alienating, and sundering things from their natural context.

Musicologists apply the adjective 'functional' to the harmonic system used in our Classical and Romantic music. The link between 'functionality' and 'harmonics' – which would not be conceivable in any other culture – is revealing. What 'functions' is not the whole series of overtones but always just the 'intended' note with reference to the related chord. In these chords the musical process resists the overtones – as if Western music wanted to say: only notes created by man and his will to go his own way vibrate here; not the tones that accompany nature, cosmos, and universe. That tendency is (as previously mentioned) even more strongly emphasised in Twelve-Note and Serial music.

The workings of functional harmonics are somewhat mechanical in the Newtonian sense and in accordance with rational scientific thinking. They function like academic medicine's view of a person as merely a succession of chemical reactions, which can be manipulated by introducing the necessary chemicals – as if creating 'modulations' within functional harmony by interpolating notes from outside the scale.

There can be no doubt that classical and romantic harmony has functioned wonderfully well. Great, elevated music has come into being through that very system. Evaluations are not at issue here. The mechanistic and rational view of nature, and the accompanying science established by Descartes, Bacon, and Galileo, have also functioned marvellously. They made technical civilisation possible. The question at issue in our modern crisis is, however, what Jean Gebser calls the 'deficiency': the degeneration, exaggeration, and hypertrophy of mechanistic thinking. That is what afflicts us today after centuries when we predominantly enjoyed its advantages.

In music rich in overtones, the 'system' (as comprehended by Gregory Bateson, the great anthropologist and researcher into systems) creates the tones, whereas in Western classical music it is the notes that establish the 'system' – in accordance with the old rationalistic model where the particles are said to create the atom, the atoms the molecule, the molecules the cells, and so on. Physics' concept of the field helps here, but the question is whether the field creates the tones or the notes the field. In music with a wealth of overtones the former is the case; in conventional Western music the latter. There the whole regulates the parts, and here the parts constitute the whole. There the whole is more than the sum of the parts whilst here totality merely consists of adding up the individual parts.

In musical cultures where overtones are put up with as a 'necessary evil' every note is separated from all the rest. It is alienated – like man in contemporary societies. In such music each note is only a particle – like people in modern mass society. Each note's participation in all the rest is 'played down' – both metaphorically and literally. The note is – as American historian and mathematician Morris Berman put it – 'non-participatory', just like man in traditional Western science.

On the other hand, in cultures where the 'real' music occurs in the realm of overtones – in India, on Bali, in China, in traditional Japanese music, or in Africa – every single note entails the vibrations of all the rest: in the same way as modern holism shows that human beings resonate with the universe. Every note 'participates' in all the tones of the harmonic series, and has, as it were, an individual participatory consciousness – as a human being must also have in order to survive contemporary upheavals, and particularly ecological and political crises. For such a consciousness neither tones nor human beings are alienated. Instead of classical exposition and evolution, the appropriate music provides what the New Biology calls *natural drift*.

VI
WORLD MUSIC: DISCOVERING WHAT WE
HAVE IN COMMON

The development in recent years of awareness of overtones has been accompanied by the blossoming of what to us are unfamiliar instruments. First to appear were instruments from Indian classical music: sitar, sarod, shenai, nagaswaram, etc., which were increasingly employed in Western music, including pop, rock, and jazz. They made particularly and impressively clear what is meant by 'suppression of the overtones'. The West does of course also possess instruments which make a refined contribution to the culture of overtones – such as the violins constructed by the Amati family at Cremona during the sixteenth and seventeenth centuries. It can, however, justly be said even of them that they merely 'put up with' overtones, compared with a sitar, veena, or sarod which have more 'resonance strings' for the production of harmonics than Western instruments' 'playing strings'.

Today we no longer need look to Asia. The West has established its own overtone culture, which follows the example set by Asia's great music but is nevertheless completely Western. Jazz musicians headed the way, but by now the new awareness of overtones is to be found almost everywhere – in rock, pop, concert music, Minimal Music, and even among the avant-garde, where young composers derive material for a work or movement from one or more overtone series, and assign the various instrumental groups (strings, wind, percussion) to different harmonic series.

That is linked with the search for instruments rich in overtones where one can 'work' with such harmonics rather than just allowing them to be heard. Such instruments have rarely existed in traditional Western music, and, if at all, then among the percussion: gongs, cymbals, bells, glockenspiels, etc. Rather strangely, even though the Western world is capable of manufacturing anything it can use and sell, we have never been able to produce cymbals, gongs, and bells anything like as good as their oriental counterparts in terms of richness, fullness, and subtlety of sound. Gongs (the word is Malayan) first came from Indonesia and later from China. Even a Balinese village craftsman can still make better gongs and metallophones than financially powerful instrument-making firms in Europe and America. American and European specialists have travelled to Bali and Java to study the processes involved in manufacturing such instruments, but they were unable to get behind the secret. Bells used to come mainly from Persia and cymbals from Turkey. Even today the best manufacturer of cymbals in the USA is the successful Mr Zildjan, a Turk.

Ironically though, the wheel has turned full-circle. The West's growing awareness of overtones has been complemented by a sudden emphasis on manufacture of high-quality instruments accentuating harmonics. The best cymbals, for instance, come today from Switzerland, a country which for hundreds of years made the world's finest clocks, and was therefore particularly associated with mechanistic and rationalistic thinking. In the meantime the best clocks come from Japan – from that part of the world which for centuries thought little of rationalistic calibrations.

Many musicians have discovered the difficulties involved in production-line manufacture of high-class instruments for the cultivation of overtones. A piano can certainly be manufactured in a factory. The tempered tuning even demands that all instruments be made exactly the same. But series manufacture of a sitar or veena? That's hardly possible – even though it is attempted today: with unsatisfactory results. On the other hand, the industrial production of concert-grands has resulted in ever-increasing improvements in precision and sound-quality. The fact is that what takes place in the overtone series is something very personal, going back beyond the relationship between musician and instrument to the kinship between craftsman and material – as if some per-son's vocation were to make himself heard through sound (*per sona*).

The instruments in a *Gamelan* orchestra on Bali are not interchangeable. Each orchestra has its own tuning and its own culture of overtones. A craftsman or a workshop (usually an entire family) constructs *all* the instruments in an orchestra, precisely attuned to one another, rather than individual ones – and a *gamelan* orchestra can include around forty different instruments. When an instrument falls apart, Balinese master-musicians do not simply buy another. They insist that the replacement comes from the family workshop, the son, or the descendants of the man who originally produced all their instruments.

Never before in the Western world have so many new instruments been devised and constructed as today. Only a few copies of each prototype are made in most cases, and in many instances there is only the original. Musicians make such instruments for themselves – and watch over them like a precious secret. Just as the masters of Asian music have done for centuries – but once again it is important to stress that the young people who behave similarly in the West are not imitating 'Asian' customs. The initiative was entirely theirs. In that respect too the instruments they build and play are also becoming part of the current of 'World Music'.

It's not just chance that this term has suddenly become so important. The phrase 'World Music' is fashionable, but only because the West has all of a sudden discovered it. The music thus characterised is as old as the world itself. It's the only music that is above fashions, and truly timeless – which fundamentally provides the basis for all music. Karl Berger, one of today's best-known 'world musicians', says: 'What we do is to listen beyond superficialities to what all cultures have in common. We don't imitate anything. We also uncover within ourselves what we all have in common. It's just because we carry that within ourselves that it's common to all.' And Stockhausen too has proclaimed: 'Every human being bears the whole of humanity within himself or herself.'

14

TV REASSURES THAT SHOOTING DOESN'T HARM ANYONE

In my book *Nada Brahma* I attempted to show that modern television culture is a breeding-ground for aggressiveness because it is primarily directed towards the eye. Every evening aggression is incubated in millions of family homes, which provide all the cosiness and warmth necessary for such a process. Martin Grotjahn's investigation of 'The Impact of Television on the Collective Unconscious' contains the plausible view, largely ignored by makers of TV programmes: 'Television reassures us every day that shooting harms no one.'

The Schramm, Lyle, and Parker team of American psychologists compared a 'radio town' in the Rocky Mountains where atmospheric conditions made TV reception impossible with a normal 'television town' where people spend an average of six hours a day watching TV. In the 'radio town' criminality was much less predominant and family relations were considerably more harmonious. There were also fewer divorces and fewer problems between pupils and teachers in the state schools. So why does no one draw the conclusions when findings are so clear-cut?

The psychologists' 'Television in the Lives of Our Children' investigation shows that very much greater inner and social 'balance' prevails in the 'radio town'. A profound concord is to be felt between this finding and the fact that nature has located co-ordination of our sense of balance in the ear, the organ radio-listeners use to a greater extent than TV-viewers. It is there that our situation is 'weighed' and we discover whether we are 'balanced'.

That also throws light on what is involved in being 'hard of hearing' – a phrase used by Martin Luther in his translation of the Bible. It is applied to someone who can no longer hear well, who no longer really listens to other people (or his or her own voice) – and thus becomes 'hard' towards them. Hardness is therefore a vice for the ear. One registers with astonishment that the opposite is obviously the case for the eye. We talk about a 'cutting' or 'stabbing' look, and about 'a sharp eye'. Whatever cuts and stabs, and is sharp, must be hard. So the characteristic 'virtue' of the eye is 'hardness', and of the ear 'softness' and 'tenderness'.

Television, however, makes spectators of us. It does not want participation, and it desensitises. The Schramm–Lyle–Parker team analysed a hundred hours of programmes chosen at random. That included:

> . . . twelve murders, sixteen major gun fights, twenty-one persons shot, twenty-one other violent incidents with guns, fifteen fist fights, fifteen incidents in which one person slugged another, an attempted murder with a pitchfork, two stranglings, one stabbing in the back with a butcher knife, three suicides, four people pushed or falling from a cliff, two attempts made to run people down with automobiles, a raving psychotic loose in an airliner, two mob scenes (in one the wrong man is hanged), a horse grinding a man under its hooves, two robberies, a woman killed in a fall from a moving train, a tidal wave, an earthquake, a hired killer stalking his victim, and one guillotining.

Martin Grotjahn is convinced that such a flood of violence, murder, and crime must inevitably bring about 'indifference and alienation from one's own emotion':

> The constant exposure to crime as a banal everyday routine is causing callousness. It supports the attitude of modern man as an onlooker and not as a participant. . . . The secret decision of the viewer is unavoidable: This shall not happen again, the next time I shall carefully avoid participating in what is being shown . . . I will remain at a distance, uninvolved, alienated, always an onlooker, never a participant.

Such an attitude is, however, in the interest of the powers that be.

In *Nada Brahma* I discussed the strange phenomenon of the poor quality of TV sound despite the fact that we've long had the technology to make the sound as good as the picture without sets becoming very much more expensive. In the meantime the explanation has become obvious. We only want to hear as much as is absolutely necessary for understanding the picture. We want - to use the language of myth - Odysseus's chains and wax, which we stuff into TV loudspeakers rather than into our own ears.

The chains are the electric leads connecting TV sets - and thus viewers - with aerials and the electricity supply. Anyone who spends a lot of time in front of a TV set is chaining himself or herself down. It doesn't matter whether the programmes captivate or leave the viewer cold. Over the longer term the chains of indifference cut much more deeply.

15

LISTENING IS IMPROVISING

'The biggest thing in music is how to listen.'
David Friesen

I

LISTENING TO OTHERS MORE THAN TO ONESELF

Roberto Laneri, himself both improviser and composer, calls composing the 'ego-trip par excellence'. The musical activity most diametrically opposed to composing is improvising. We know that there are some musical cultures where the composer dominates - above all in Western music - and others where the improviser rules, as almost everywhere else in the world. However, we also know that both improvisers and composers exist in almost all cultures, and that there are borderline cases where it is often not possible to determine whether something has been composed or is being improvised. In most such cases it turns out that what was originally improvised has been repeated so often over the course of time that it has taken on the character of something composed even though not written down.

If we ask about the relationship between improvising and composing, on the one side, and the world of listening and seeing on the other, there is initially no doubt that both activities result in the creation of music and are therefore more closely related to hearing than to looking. Things become more interesting though when we attempt to refine such distinctions.

In a group of improvisers meaningful music comes into being by way of highly alert listening on the part of the individual musicians. It can even be said – and anyone who has played in such a group will confirm this – that you must listen to the other musicians more than to yourself. After all, you know what you're up to. You unconsciously (and yet with intensified awareness) strive for attunement with the other players, and often find that you reach the point towards which they are moving a bar, a breath, or a beat earlier. Whole studies and books have been written about the mysterious phenomenon of group or collective improvisation. In the fifties when I started writing about jazz, I followed the then current fashion and attempted to explain that mechanistically – and that is still the usual explanation put forward in most of today's conservatoires and schools of music. That posits a harmonic scheme, a framework of chords, where the improvising musicians 'meet up'. We know in the meantime that this explanation is not sufficient – even if a harmonic framework really does exist. It is even less adequate in the case of 'free' improvisation utilising modes and scales, ragas and harmonic emphases, centre notes, graphic scores and playing instructions, or even greater 'liberty'.

Mechanistic explanations are 'causal', thus implying that what a single musician has improvised or established as a basis provides a 'reason' for what the others play. That is not, however, possible because the concept of causality demands that time must pass between what the initiator does and the response of the other musicians. Now, there certainly sometimes is a time-lapse before a group picks up on what a specific initiative may imply, but the response is much more frequently immediate. The group 'vibrates' as a whole in 'collectively' changing musical lines, metres, rhythms, developments, and processes.

II
THE COLLECTIVE AS A SINGLE ORGANISM

One alternative to causality is synchronicity. C. G. Jung coined that term – strangely and yet characteristically when working together with atomic physicist Wolfgang Pauli, inventor of the 'Pauli Principle' and a man who also experienced in *his* sphere that things do not behave causally in the way that academic science believes, or used to believe. Synchronicity – says the dictionary – is the 'meaningful coincidence of two or more events that cannot be explained in causal terms'. The term is by now also used in cybernetics, biology, atomic physics, anthropology, ethnology, statistics, and the economic sciences. Everywhere people are discovering certain 'series' of numbers or events which, having recurred a few times 'by chance', tend from then on to repeat themselves more frequently than the laws of mathematical probability (with their logical and causal evaluation) would lead us to expect. A process 'develops' in such series and then fades away until a new 'series' arises 'by chance', returning more frequently than would be likely under the rules of probability. Many card-players – and adherents of games of chance in general – know that phenomenon. Croupiers at casinos tell of astonishing cases of synchronicity which seem utterly unbelievable to outsiders and yet are authenticated by the records. Synchronicity does not merely exist. Our consciousness also acts accordingly even though mental awareness may not be 'conscious' of its existence. We could hardly survive in city traffic if that weren't the case. The mafia bosses behind the casino business in Las Vegas, Reno, and Atlantic City have long given up relying solely on the mathematics of probability. They are far in advance of the majority of humanity in this respect, and employ experts in what they term 'serial happenings' in order to maximise their profits even more effectively.

The 'law' (if it can be termed such) of synchronicity also prevails within group musical improvisation. Such a group moves like a flock of migrating birds – or shoal of fish. Zoologists used to believe that there had to be a 'leader' whom the others followed. Today it is known that the only time there is occasionally a 'leader' is when two or three birds are flying together. When, however, a large formation of birds suddenly spontaneously changes direction, wheeling through an S-curve or abruptly almost reversing course, without disrupting their grouping, that is what the New Biology views as a single organism. No leader regulates the formation. The flock moves synchronistically. It is a 'system', the now indispensable term

introduced by Austrian biologist Ludwig von Bertalanffy and popularised by anthropologist Gregory Bateson.

A group of improvising musicians is also a 'system' in that sense.
If it's really 'together', it can react, move, and change as if it were a
single being. Like a flock of birds or shoal of fish. What happens in
such groups obeys the laws of synchronicity rather than those of
causality, and cannot therefore be explained down to the last detail.
Musicians can't do that either – but they do talk about the 'high'
which carries them along when a collective improvisation is particularly successful. Players in the Globe Unity Orchestra, a jazz
ensemble of European musicians established in West Germany, speak
about a 'sense of uplift'. Danish alto saxophonist John Tchicai once
said it was so wonderful that you could only compare it with the
joys of love-making – which also depend on synchronicity and
immediately become 'stale' if causality gains the upper hand.

III
WHY COMPOSERS CAN BE DEAF

Systems that seem to exist as a single organism cannot come into
being in music without intensified listening. One could almost speak
of 'inner listening', which rushes ahead of 'outer listening' in a way
that cannot be pinned down in words. This 'rushing ahead' is a
characteristic of musical synchronicity.

'Inner listening' of course also exists within a good string quartet
or an excellent chamber ensemble, but it is only of secondary importance in composed music since the musical flow is determined by
what is picked up visually from the notes the composer uses to
'inform' the musician – rather than by what is heard and felt
through the 'synchronistic system'. Synchronistic 'inner listening'
is here, as it were, something supplementary that brings the music of
the quartet or ensemble closer to perfection. That is why it is so
important for musicians to play by heart. The more they can do
without visual information, the more uninhibitedly they can
become a system that acts as a single organism. And yet – for that
very reason – it is certainly the case that inner listening (and
listening in general) is the primary consideration for the musician
involved in group improvisation.

Information gained through the eye predominates for the musician
who plays composed works. The fact that a player is not primarily
dependent on the ear accords with the process of composition. The

composer does not listen to other people – or at most in ways only indirectly influencing his style. He listens to himself – and looks at the notes he is writing down. He takes the music from the medium in which it unfolds, from time, making it into a category of space, tangible as a score. If it can be said that great architecture is 'frozen music' (Schelling), then composed music can be called 'musical architecture'. The transposition of composed music into space can go so far that it doesn't matter if a composer is deaf. He must primarily be able to see what he writes. Beethoven is the obvious exemplification of that – and one can hardly ignore the inner logic (and tragedy) involved in Beethoven of all composers, a man who went further than any predecessors in constructing his symphonies in the same way as an architect a cathedral roof and dome or a bridge, being almost completely unable to hear anything by the end of his life. It is probably also revealing that musicologists have never been able to determine with complete certainty exactly what was involved in the great composer's deafness. Beethoven himself was hesitant about saying anything, as if ashamed that he, the master of an art dependent on listening, could no longer hear properly. He must have felt the absurdity of that situation. The listener to music also feels it – otherwise there wouldn't have been so much written about this topic.

Composed music is music transposed into space. Whatever exists in space is visible. And what is visible tends to follow the dominance of the eye – especially in a civilisation where people have for centuries been shaped by such an ascendancy, during the very period when the phenomenon of composing established itself in the West. The supremacy of the visual is an everyday experience for every musician and musicologist. It is so much simpler – and quicker – to look in the score than to listen!

Of course most composers hear their music inwardly when they are writing down the notes – but some don't even do that. John Cage thus asked Morton Feldman: 'Do you hear the music you're writing down?' Feldman at first answered 'Yes', but Cage, referring to his own compositional experience, persisted: '. . . Is it as if you don't completely hear it?' Feldman then conceded: 'The truth lies somewhere in between. I write it down so as to hear it.' To which Cage responded: 'I don't hear anything.' Feldman: 'I don't really hear anything. I watch and observe it.' (Note the 'eye words'. And note too the insistence with which Cage conducts the conversation. One feels that he is ill at ease. He knows that something is wrong. He is making music – and yet listening has declined in importance!)

IV
COMPOSED MUSIC EXISTS IN SPACE

Stimulating insights regarding the transposition into space and visualisation of music are supplied by modern neurology. They come from Karl Pribram, one of the most innovative of researchers who is also a connoisseur of music. Musical ability is for most people situated in the right hemisphere of the brain (the hemisphere of feeling, intuition, and sensitivity) which regulates the left side of the body. One could almost say that, viewed figuratively, the heart-beat a baby hears is primordial music.

An amazing discovery has, however, been made about composers and professional musicians involved in Western concert music. In most of the people examined their musicality had moved to the left side of the brain, which programmes what we do with the right hand as well as our sense of form and design, visually and metaphorically. Musicality is thus, as it were, deprived of its natural feedback from the heart and feeling side, and transferred to the realm of logic and functionality which are usually in the left half of the brain. That part of the brain serves causality, and the right hemisphere synchronicity. Here we can sense particularly clearly what really happens during the composition of Western music. Space, form, functionality, logic, and purposefulness enter into music.

A close connection exists between dominance of the eye in the West and the fact that great Western music is primarily based on a composed score. Only musicians from a predominantly eye-regulated culture can rely so extensively on what they see when playing or writing concert music. For everyone else it is completely self-evident that the ear is in sole charge of programming music-making. Music can at most be transposed into space and made visible in dancing. Apart from that any association of music-making with spatial and visual dimensions would seem completely absurd to musicians in non-Western cultures – if they ever got round to thinking about something so bizarre!

Kevin Volans reports on *mbira* music in Southern Africa: 'Pieces are only learnt by way of listening . . .' – and he expressly adds 'and without watching'. I have often observed that on Bali, in North and South India, and over the years with hundreds of jazz musicians. They sing or play a melody or theme to one another: one, two, or at most three times – and then they have it. They also prefer that method even if the music has been written down. There are good reasons for the inadequate and often exceedingly amateurish nature of jazz musicians' notation (compared with classical players). They simply don't need such exact notation since they learn the music by ear after having played or sung it to one another.

A musician who learns by ear internalises music much more quickly than one who plays from notes – 'slipping' into the music as if it were his own, and soon becoming unable to separate it from that.

Many African musicians and black American bluesmen think it absurd to play someone else's music. If that is suggested, they ask: Why? I have my own! A further question is embedded in that declaration. How can someone else's music in any way involve me? In jazz too most musicians – today as earlier – tend to prefer their own themes. Someone who composes generally writes for musicians he knows well, for colleagues and friends, rather than for anonymous orchestral players, let alone for 'posterity'. He doesn't need particularly accurate notation since his composition primarily serves the function of further distilling the musicians' personal styles and inspiring their improvisations.

Whoever learns by listening, mainly playing his own music and doing without notation (or at most making reluctant and incomplete use of its possibilities), leaves music where it belongs: in time where listening is the prime sense.

Whoever learns a piece of music by reading it, principally playing the music of others and perfecting notation to an ever greater extent, transports music into an ultimately alien dimension: into space whose cardinal sense is seeing.

V
IMPROVISED MUSIC SAYS : WE!

We have discovered the following relationships:

Composed Music	*Collective/Improvised Music*
Space	Time
Eye	Ear
Seeing	Listening
Causality	Synchronicity
Logic	System
Left half of the brain	Right half of the brain

I	We
Isolation	Community
The West (especially in concert music)	The rest of the world (principally Asia and Africa, but also the majority of young people in the West)

(None of these terms is to be taken as an absolute. Reservations always apply.)

We can summarise as follows: Synchronicity is the causality of people who put the main emphasis on listening and improvising. And causality is the synchronicity of those who primarily see and compose. The former occurs more in time, and the latter more in space.

Improvised music says We! – to an even greater extent than the polyphony Adorno extolled. Composed music says I! The composer listens to himself and to his own inner voice. The improviser listens – firstly and primarily – to the people improvising with him, to his fellow human beings. The composer is alone. The improviser is part of a community.

Our age is becoming aware – hesitantly and much too slowly – of hypertrophy of the visual and the associated dangers, and more and more people are once again starting to recognise the ear as our most important and noblest sense. That *must* result in intensified consciousness, interest and joy, active involvement, and experience with regard to improvised group music. And that is exactly what is happening.

16

PUTTING TO THE TEST

I
SEEING = JUDGING : THE PRIMORDIAL SEPARATION

Seeing entails judging. The eye passes judgement. The judgement separates the judge from what is judged. Seeing involves keeping at a distance. Viewed literally – if I bring an object too close to my eyes, I can't see it clearly any longer. The outlines blur and the structures are no longer perceptible. When the object is one or two centimetres away from my eyes, it starts to get dark; and when it is right on top of them, things are completely black. This shows that in the moment of becoming one, the eye loses its function. The eye *must* in fact stop looking in order that this becoming one may be possible. That is why most people close their eyes when kissing and making love.

The eye needs distance in order to be able to judge. For our other senses, however, the closer the better.

The whole of Western philosophy – from the Greeks onwards – is a philosophy of passing judgement. It may have split up into a variety of directions, systems, and conceptual structures, but all schools of thought have one decisive factor in common: they pass judgement; they separate; they criticise.

Criticism has been a central concept in Western philosophy from Plato by way of Kant to the Frankfurt School. The word *criticism* derives from the Greek *krino*, which initially meant sever, divide, separate, select, choose, and prefer, but as early as Plato's time had come to signify accuse, pass judgement, decide, condemn, etc.

If therefore Western philosophy's love of wisdom and truth (which is what the Greek term *philosophia* entails) primarily involves separating, judging, and criticising, then it is a philosophy of seeing, serving the sense that is more predisposed to passing judgement than any other. The dominance of the eye is built into philosophy right from the start – and certainly in a positive sense too with its sublimity, diversity, originality, and stringency. Someone at the end of that line of philosophy, Jean-Paul Sartre, expressed what is entailed with his stupendous capacity for observing himself as if he were another: 'Never before have I sensed so clearly that I think with the eyes' – he wrote as a young soldier in Alsace at a decisive phase in his life when he was starting to philosophise.

Separation of the world into observer and observed, subject and object, which is the precondition for criticism, creates distance and remoteness. As we have seen, the eye creates – and needs – distance and remoteness. If it comes too close, the result is a *blur*, which is a central concept in the holography employed in neurology and physics.

We make mistakes if we are distant. We can best perceive something close at hand, but then the process of judging, the primordial separation, comes to an immediate stop. We simply know: That's the way things are. The closer we edge up on something, the more judging changes imperceptibly into experiencing. Our most powerful experiences come during states of oneness. Conversely, when oneness becomes closeness, closeness distance, and distance remoteness, then experiencing and participating are transformed into observing, judging, and condemning. We 'stand back' – and must do so in order to be able to see.

We cannot be deceived with regard to what we have experienced. We *know* that. But deception is possible as far as our judgements and observations are concerned. We can deceive ourselves from the distance the eye creates and needs. The danger of deception is increasingly reduced as we approach the closeness our other senses require.

II
THREE DAYS WITH BOUND EYES

It is possible to try out all of this for yourself. You can experience what this book is about. It can only be demonstrated in experience. While working on this book I took part in a group experience: for three days I couldn't see. Any blind person may laugh, but the people in the group who lost their sight for this period soon discovered it wasn't a joke. There were eleven of us – four women and seven men – entrusted to two Berlin therapists, one male and one female.

It may sound unlikely that someone who had for years been working on books about hearing should hit upon such an experience by chance, but I swear that really was the case. Friends had recommended the group to me but not revealed that I would have to run around for three days with my eyes bound. I didn't even realise that when the workshop started. I only noticed that when we arrived, care was taken to ensure we didn't see one another. No one knew what any of the others in the group looked like. I was told: We're now going to bind your eyes 'for a while'. I thought perhaps that meant for an hour. Then we would see one another. The others thought the same. None of us knew when our blindfolds would be taken off. On the first day we hoped it would be the following morning; in the morning we hoped it would be in the afternoon; on the second day the hope was of the third . . .

By the evening of the first day we already had a fairly accurate idea of the other people in the group – and of the two therapists and their staff, who guided and assisted us when we couldn't cope on our own. Like people who can see, we chose favourite partners among the group, which didn't just involve men selecting women and vice versa. They were simply human beings with whom we got on well.

There were a few rules. We weren't allowed to say anything about our profession, training, age, or possessions. What mattered was what we were, not our role in society. What counted was Being, not Having.

The room in which we spent most of our time was sufficiently big for us not to come into constant body-contact. When we encountered or bumped into one another, we first asked: Who are you? As early as the second day that was hardly necessary any longer. We recognised one another by voice and physique. Of course men first got to know women, but the women soon learnt to distinguish among one another, and the men picked up that ability too.

We were not allowed to take off our blindfolds during the night either. We all slept in one big room. Anyone who had to go to the lavatory was guided there by a sighted helper. By the second day most of us found the way by ourselves. When we poured out coffee or tea, we put a finger-tip in the cup and stopped pouring when we felt the liquid. We could distinguish without seeing between butter, cheese, honey, and jam. Many different dishes were available buffet-style. We chose what we wanted and passed on the dish to our neighbours, perhaps accompanying it with a recommendation or description so that they knew whether to expect something sweet or sour, liquid or dry, spicy or bland.

It was difficult to put up with not being able to see. During the first night one of the participants – a sportswoman – said she couldn't stand it any longer. She wanted to leave. The therapist had explained that we could go at any time but would not be permitted to return.

This woman thought she needed constant eye-contact. She was the only person who became aggressive as a result of not being able to see. The other ten of us observed that renunciation of the eyes made us less aggressive. The sportswoman was ultimately particularly glad that she had stuck things out.

It wasn't only human encounters that moved us. One of the therapists put a newly hatched chick into my hands. I made a cage out of my fingers and kept the chick there for about half an hour. I felt the tiny heaving body, the struggling legs pricking me, and I heard the cheeping which sounded fearful but then became ever calmer so that I suddenly sensed: the little creature feels at ease.

I'm sure that if I'd had use of my eyes I would have moved my hands much more, opening the fingers so as to see the chick better. I would thus have made it edgy and restless. It wouldn't have felt so secure.

We made figures out of modelling clay. One of the women participants produced an elephant. When we were able to see it on the evening of the last day, we were amazed at how carefully it was modelled. She had made only one mistake. The trunk was somewhat too thin and had fallen off. When she fixed it on again, she had attached it at the wrong end. I had produced a bowl, and when that got too boring I made a hole in its base. When I could see what I had done, it was shaped like an ear – and the hole I had bored with two fingers was also comparable to an ear.

At breakfast it was wonderful to find an egg in a big bowl, carefully shell it without breaking the skin, find the egg-spoon, put some salt on the edge of the plate marking where it was so that the marmalade didn't taste salty afterwards, and carefully eat the egg without the yolk overflowing from the egg-cup. Never before had I so consciously perceived the soft, elastic membrane enclosing an egg. I didn't just eat the egg: I had an intense experience. I understood why we call its membrane a 'skin' – as if it were the delicate skin of a body we love.

The subtle intensification of our senses, which increased from hour to hour, became exemplarily clear when one of the therapists asked us to sense our pulse without touching it. If during everyday existence we want to know our pulse-rate, we do what doctors do. The doctor takes our wrist, and if he is a conventional medic observes the strongest pulse-rate – but not the many different rates, nine in all, an acupuncturist can register. Now however – in our state of intensified capacity for perception – the therapist only needed to ask us to feel our pulse and make it the measure of our breathing. For instance, take eight pulse-beats for breathing in, and eight for breathing out. Every one of us was capable of feeling the pulsing as a gentle inner knocking throughout the entire body.

The experience of other impulses and stimuli we generally only perceive superficially was similarly intense: fleeting contact with someone else's skin, an encounter between two fingers, and stroking the back of a hand.

If we bump into someone on the street, we say 'Sorry' and carry on heedlessly. We have perceived nothing of the person concerned. But just fleetingly touching someone in the corridors of the house where we were becoming aware of the borderlands of experience helped us perceive a great deal of the essential nature of that person – in avoidance of contact, bodily movements, holdings back, and the way in which the other wriggled past between us and the wall.

At that moment we no longer had any tactile senses, we *were* our tactile senses. We experienced why these tactile senses are unique among all our senses in existing throughout our entire body rather than just in the head. In every pore, in every muscle, in every square centimetre of our skin. We received signals from everywhere. Of course they also reach us in our everyday lives, but we pay scarcely any attention to them there. Now, however, we became our sensory apparatus – a unified feeling and touching and perceiving where signals were themselves reality rather than informing us about reality.

It was marvellous to experience how considerately and carefully we treated one another. We listened intensively for one another. We achieved harmony. If we had been able to see, we would have been much less considerate. We really experienced – beyond the theoretical insights provided by psychologists in books – how much more lovingly we treat one another when we do not precipitately judge by way of visual appraisal.

We went out for a walk together, responding to the Berlin street sounds. We experienced the atmosphere in a cemetery without being able to see the place. At a metro station someone asked us why we were wearing blindfolds, and I told him we'd just had an operation. The man said he was very sorry and wished us a speedy recovery. We expressed our thanks, but had to laugh out loud.

At the cemetery I heard three different kinds of music, and could distinguish clearly between them. The guitar sounds came from high up on the right, obviously from an open window or a balcony. I sensed that this didn't involve a radio. Rather someone sitting there – perhaps a young woman – playing the guitar. Then there was funky, black rock music, moving quickly from right to left. I thought someone must be carrying a radio or cassette-recorder, but then excluded the radio because the local stations wouldn't broadcast George Duke or Herbie Hancock at two in the afternoon. The other music came from the cemetery church or chapel, and I understood that a funeral service was in progress. I really could hear and distinguish between all three kinds of music at the same time – each as what it was. I'm sure that if I'd been able to see at that moment I would either have missed hearing something, or have thought the superimposition of three incompatible kinds of music disturbingly chaotic. Now, however, I was following these different sources of music with the greatest of interest, enjoying each of them.

I banged into a tree, felt my way around the bark, and guessed it was a birch – which it was.

We listened, felt, tasted, and smelled with an intensity none of us had previously experienced in our lives. The most surprising thing was that at the end of the three days we also *looked* with similar intensity.

During the afternoon of the final day the therapist asked us to select an ideal partner. We sat in front of that person, looked at him or her, and at that very moment were allowed to take off our blindfolds. We then questioned our partner for ten minutes, following the Zen intensive technique of 'Tell me who you are'. We saw the other person more intensively, more thoroughly, and more lovingly than we would ever have done if we had seen whoever it was right at the start – saw him or her with what Goethe called the 'eyes of the spirit', and more clearly than if we had observed for a month with our 'everyday eyes'.

Everyone was expected to say something in conclusion – and we were now allowed to mention our lives in the world outside. One of the women felt that she had found the person with whom she got on best very much more quickly than if she had been able to see. She would never have chosen him if she had first seen him. She now thought he was someone very important for her. The eye would therefore have led her astray about this human being's qualities.

Other people from the group had similar things to say. A young man remarked that his mother had always said: Don't let your choice of partner be guided by externalities. Almost everyone has been given such advice, but hardly anyone follows it. These three days had, however, demonstrated that important encounters are blocked if one selects by appearance and judges accordingly.

I added that in Asia you learn that the Guru appears when he is needed. That had also been true of this workshop. When you need a group, you find one. It was only then that I revealed I was a writer who produces books on listening. I talked about my work on how the eye can be deceived. 'These three days were a test granted me. Perhaps they were a present. Now I know – more authentically than ever before – that what I have been writing about in recent years is "true". It was put to the test in this group.'

III
OF RAY CHARLES, ROLAND KIRK, AND
SLEEPY JOHN ESTES

In my workshops, seminars, and groups, I frequently ask participants to blindfold themselves so as to increase the receptiveness of their hearing, feeling, and other senses inclusive, ultimately, of seeing. There are often blind people present, who are particularly open to the world of hearing. During my time as a jazz producer I sometimes made records or radio and TV programmes with blind musicians who are frequently found in black music, and I assume that my present capacity for working with the unseeing was stimulated by that.

At the end of the fifties I made a TV show in New York with Ray Charles, the great singer who after the years of Cool Jazz reintroduced the blues into the world. When I came back into the studio after a break, the blind Ray was sitting at the piano. He said he'd 'combed' the place but hadn't 'seen' any conga drum, so could I get one from next door. The studio was pretty large, and stuffed with instruments and technical gear. Ray was nevertheless absolutely certain that there weren't any congas here. It seemed remarkable to me that he employed the word 'see' to describe searching through the place by feel, which must have taken him a long time.

In the early sixties I discovered the later celebrated Roland Kirk as an unknown street musician playing for pennies in Chicago's South-side black ghetto, and immediately brought him to Germany where I was then co-director of the annual Essen festival. This was the blind multi-instrumentalist's first television and festival appearance. He amazed his listeners by playing several saxophones simultaneously – mostly battered old objects he'd picked up in pawnshops and flea-markets, using individual parts for making new instruments.

Kirk's hotel room in Essen was strewn after just a few hours with innumerable parts, saxophone reeds, little screws, screwdrivers, and other tools. Everything was scattered all over the place so that even someone who could see would have had difficulty in finding what he wanted, but Roland sat calmly on a chair working away at his instruments, immediately laid hands on whatever he needed, and occasionally asked me to pass him something, giving precise instructions: on the right-hand side of the window-sill; or on the left of the bedside table next to the lamp; or at the foot of the bed. In all my years in the company of jazz musicians I'd seen many working away at their instruments, but few stripped them down as much as this blind saxophonist, who then reassembled them as quickly as someone who could see.

A few years later I presented Kirk at the Berlin Jazz Festival. I met him by chance one day at one of the city's metro stations. I was appalled to see this man who was now a 'star' blindly feeling his way up some steps. I asked him where he wanted to go. 'To Edith' came the answer – to a woman he had met in Essen who lived in Berlin. I asked whether Edith couldn't have come to fetch him. Oh no, he replied. He'd travelled this stretch with her yesterday, and now he 'knew' it. The following day I found out that he had managed to get to Edith's flat even though that necessitated changing trains two or three times in an unfamiliar city he'd arrived in a couple of days previously. He did that with the same self-assurance as all the people around him who could see. Kirk, too, employed the word 'see': 'I wanted to see Edith.'

Shortly before his death Kirk played in Radio City Music Hall as part of the New York Jazz Festival. I came through the door to the backstage area, talked to George Wein, the festival director, and hadn't yet noticed Roland when I heard: 'Hey Joe [as many musicians called me], please come over. I wanna talk to you.' I still don't know how that was possible. Roland was seven or eight metres away. We hadn't met for five years or so. I was deliberately talking to Wein in a low voice. There were at least twenty other people backstage, all chattering away excitedly as is usual on such occasions. Several musicians were tuning their instruments. Theatre staff were carrying around drum cases and electronic equipment . . .

While I was walking over to Kirk with a feeling of complete disbelief, I sensed that he didn't hear the general 'babble' as a confused mishmash of sounds but could pick up each individual voice and filter out what he didn't want to 'perceive'. He thus stored up the voices of people talking in the same way as we jazz people store up the sound of an important tenor saxophonist or trumpeter. Once we have it 'inside', we always recognise it.

In 1964 I presented Sleepy John Estes, the blind singer-guitarist, at one of my first 'American Folk Blues Festivals', which at that time moved through Europe each year, opening the ears of the young English pop scene, inclusive of Beatles and Rolling Stones, to the blues.

Sleepy (b. 1904) lived with his wife and his five children in a battered shed on the edge of a Tennessee cotton field. He became celebrated for his enormously expressive singing. Experts talked about him 'crying the blues'. His way of singing influenced many stars of white popular music – including Johnnie Ray and later Elvis Presley. For thirty years the blind Sleepy was accompanied and guided by Hammie Nixon, harmonica-player and gas station attendant at Brownsville, Tennessee – first through the southern states in the USA and then through Europe too. This guidance impressed me just as much as Sleepy's singing. Hammie looked after Sleepy so lovingly that he might have been his shadow. He carried his instrument case, took out the guitar, guided him to meals, to the lavatory, to his hotel in the evening, and helped him get ready for bed. And Hammie accompanied Sleepy on the harmonica in exactly the same way. With the fine-spun gentleness of the great New Orleans clarinetists rather than with the unexpected, sudden, and harsh phrases of the other great blues harmonica-players such as Sonny Boy Williamson.

When Sleepy and Hammie came into the studio, love was manifested. Not erotic love – rather the contrary: love in defiance of all erotic possibilities. Years later that experience led me to attempt something similar in my workshops. I had people whose eyes were bound led and looked after by others who could see – for one or two days, and sometimes only for a few hours. That may only have mediated the vaguest idea of the thirty-year-long relationship between Sleepy and Hammie, but the important thing is to have that experience. Participants reported that they thus experienced love with a directness that is ever-rarer in our society. Both recipient and donor were enriched by the happy experience of this love.

There was a moment in our Baden-Baden TV studio when Hammie was out of the room and Sleepy couldn't find his guitar. Sleepy quietly sang to himself one of his celebrated blues stanzas: 'Now when you lose your eyesight, your best friend's gone' – and he was heard by the previously mentioned Sonny Boy Williamson, probably the most celebrated harmonica player of the blues, who

responded with his own blues and the well-known line: 'Eyesight to
the blind.' Unfortunately we didn't record that. It happened during
a break in recording. But I'll never forget this brief sung dialogue:
the one lamenting the loss of his best friend along with his sight, and
the other affirming that the man grieving in fact possessed true
'sight' – as if there were no doubt about who was 'seeing' and who
'listening'.

Roland Kirk – who was blind like Sleepy John Estes but younger,
more positive, more powerful, and no longer merely 'cryin' 'n
sobbin' ' – didn't need any Sonny Boy Williamson. He himself asked
an audience of 2,000 in Berlin's Philharmonic Hall: 'Does anybody
here say I don't see?' And then into the disbelieving silence he threw
the words: 'I tell you, I see.' And from all around, first hesitantly
and then ever more powerfully, came shouts of 'Yes!' and 'Yeah,
man!'. And all of a sudden 2,000 people – or at least most of them –
comprehended what is involved in 'Eyesight to the Blind'!

17

Do You Hear
the Rushing of the River ?

A Meditation

'Meditation is simply what an individual at this present stage of
consciousness has to do in order to go beyond that stage . . . If we are
to contribute to evolution . . . then meditation . . . becomes . . . a new
categorical imperative.'

Ken Wilber

'The possession of many kinds of knowledge cannot be compared
with consciously renouncing the search for something specific. That
is best of all. There do not exist different kinds of spirit, and there are
no teachings that can be expressed in words. Since there is nothing

more to be said, the meeting is concluded' – said Zen Master Huang-Po, and sent his pupils to the meditation hall.

A meditation belongs in this book, as in its predecessor. I place this meditation – towards which everything else has been leading – at the conclusion. I only give the bare outline since teachers, courses, groups, and books providing an introduction to meditation are to be found everywhere today. It is best to sit in a traditional meditative posture. Anyone who cannot do that should at least make sure that the knees are as close to the ground as possible – lower at any rate than the navel. The upper part of the body should be upright, focused on the stomach, the *hara*, the centre of our existence, rather than on the chest. You should breathe regularly and tranquilly without interfering in the process. The breathing should be allowed to flow. You observe it in full consciousness, allowing yourself to be carried along.

Our meditation will focus on a *Mondo*, the Zen dialogue between Master and pupil providing in concentrated form both a task and indications as to how it may be solved.

> *'Do you hear the rushing of the river?'*
> *The Master asks his pupil.*
> *'Yes, Master,' answers the pupil.*
> *'That is the Way,' replies the Master.*

Meditating on this *Mondo* alongside a river offers a particularly profound experience. Sitting on a stone at the edge of a mountain stream. Beneath a waterfall. On the bank of a river. On the sea-shore where waves are breaking. But the river is everywhere. Even where you live. You only need put those questions, and the inner river, the *Nada*, will make itself heard.

There is a marvellous tradition of meditating beside a river. It is not just a matter of chance that the river is a favourite subject in Chinese and Japanese pen-and-ink drawings and paintings. Drawing, pen-and-ink work, and painting have long formed part of Zen. The artists have almost always been meditators. They preferred painting a river where they had also meditated. Painting *is* meditating.

Waterfalls and bridges are often depicted in Zen pictures. The waterfall is a leap within time – as in Science Fiction. At one moment you are still in this dimension, and then you are immediately in that – and yet you stay in the same river, the 'vehicle' and 'spaceship' for your journey.

The bridge already symbolises the outcome. The meditator has 'crossed to another shore'. Lao Tse 'crossed the river' before he dictated his *Tao Te Ching* to the gate-keeper. Bodhidharma 'crossed the river to the north'. This motif returns time and again in Zen stories. Someone always crosses 'the' river at some stage.

The river is a good 'vehicle' because it is beyond space and time. At its source, in its middle section, and at the estuary – as a trickle, a stream, and a river – it is always just 'the' river. Not just in China and Japan. This motif is to be found in our culture too – from Heraclitus to Hermann Hesse. You never step twice into the same river – and yet it is always the same. You are constantly travelling on – and yet you're always safe in the river. As one *Mondo* has it: 'The bridge flows on while the water stands still.'

'You must risk jumping into the water without knowing how you are supposed to swim,' says Krishnamurti. 'The beauty of meditation is that you never know where you are, where you are going, and what the objective is.'

Jump. Swim. Meditate. Become the river. Lay down this book. If you want, you can carry on reading later. This is the most important moment anyway. What you have to do is to meditate for twenty minutes.

> '*Do you hear the rushing of the river?*'
> '*Yes, Master.*'
> '*That is the Way.*'

Meditate on just that. To meditate entails paying attention and being attentive. Attentiveness involves doing nothing except: Sitting. Breathing. Being aligned and in the *Hara*. Hearing the text. Listening very closely to it. Being the text. Until it becomes a sound. Become this sound. The text then no longer begins with the word 'Do' and ends with 'Way'. All the words are in the river, and the river rushes along, and the river is nothing but a rushing.

Krishnamurti: 'Meditation is like a river. It cannot be tamed. It flows and flows and overflows its banks. It is music without sound. It is the silence in which the observer ceases to be immediately he plunges in.'

Understand what Zen means by attentiveness. A disciple came to Master Eko. The rain was pouring down. The disciple had meditated for seven long years. He expected a discussion about his spiritual way, hoping for profound analyses and conclusions. But Eko asked: 'Where did you leave your umbrella? To the left or the right of your shoes?' The disciple couldn't remember. He'd come to Eko full of excitement, concerned with much more important things than an umbrella.

So the Zen Master said: 'Meditate for another seven years.' The disciple: 'Just because of such a minor oversight?' Eko: 'Not knowing where one left one's umbrella is not a minor oversight.'

The river does not just rush onwards. It consists of millions of drops of water. Listen to each individual drop. The drops in a whirlpool or waterfall are as diverse for the river as the individuals constituting humanity. Be attentive. Listen to the individuality of every drop.

The river is the Way. You know – you've read – that it's more important to travel than to arrive. You need not know where the river enters the ocean. The river doesn't know that either. No one reaches the final objective. Anyone who thinks they'll get there deceives themselves. Even the great enlightened ones knew – and experienced – that the Way always continues further no matter how far they may have come. Even the Way followed by Buddha and Jesus leads further. You are wasting your time if you think about where it is leading. Thinking doesn't bring you any further since the Way is without end.

You can't meditate, you can't even live – let alone love – properly, if you're preoccupied about the future. Or about the past. So be where you *now* are: on the Way. On that stretch of the Way where you actually are at this very moment.

Don't be anywhere else. Be here. Krishnamurti, Alan Watts, Bhagwan, and others have popularised the concept of 'here and now' in the Western world – and that is a wonderful achievement, but such knowledge is thousands of years old.

Don't think that talk of the Way – the ancient Chinese *Tao* and the *do* in Japanese Zen – is just Asian nonsense. The word *via* (Way) appears 880 times in the *Vulgata*, the Latin translation of the Bible and the most influential book in Western civilisation. So wherever you go, you are therefore on the Way, even in the Western world.

Yet Eastern wisdom can help you. For instance the Chinese characters for *Way*. This runs *Head + Foot = Way*.

The old Taoists saw this as a sign indicating the Way. It says that if you follow the Way, head and foot will stop being two different things. The head will become the foot, and the foot the head, and both will become the Way. You will become the Way – from head to foot. You will become one. I – the I that is writing this book and is much too much of a head person (and perhaps must be in order to be able to write) – and many of my readers could also interpret the sign as follows: Send your head down to your feet, and get going at long last! That is the journey we spoke about in the introduction to this

Head

Foot

(Foot + Head =) The way

book, the real Way! This book provides an impetus towards setting out on that Way.

In the task we have set ourselves the river is the Way.

> *'Do you hear the rushing of the river?'*
> *'Yes.'*
> *'That is the Way.*

You hear – to adapt Martin Buber – the rushing of the river but don't know where this rushing really comes from: the river or yourself – the rushing of the blood in your veins and ears, your primordial *Nada*, the rushing of Being.

If you meditate for long enough, you will hear *Nada Brahma*. The *Shabda*. The *Naam*. The *Sangit*. The *Kirtan*. The river of sound. Thousands of people have experienced it in their own particular way. That is why there are so many names for it. Among Zen monks in Japan and China, among Sufis in Persia and Turkey, among

Hindus in India, among Sikhs in North India, among Tibetans in the Himalayas, among itinerant Russian monks, among Muslims in the Islamic world, among the monks on Athos . . .

> *'Do you hear the rushing of the river?'*
> *'Yes.'*

Meditate on that for a few months. You should do so at least once a day for thirty minutes, or meditate for two twenty-minute sessions, preferably in the morning and evening. Don't say: I can't do that. If you really can't do that, that's alright too – and you should meditate as often as you can. But you really know that you can!

You will soon feel – perhaps after just a few weeks – that something is changing. You are clearer, more precise, more present. You are less frequently frustrated, less aggressive, more open, more tolerant, more communicative. You sense that in other people rather than in yourself. You have fewer difficulties with them. You make their acquaintance more quickly and gain new friends. You're happier and laugh more often. You feel united with your fellow human beings. You become aware that *all* are your brothers and sisters. Those are the beginnings – a very modest start – of your experience that All Is One.

You stop being over-sensitive. You become *zen*-sitive: more alert, receptive, intuitive, compassionate. Your health may improve too.

Krishnamurti: '. . . Being completely open and self-abandonment – to the hills, the sea, human beings – are the true essence of meditation.'

When you have started to change, meditate for another month or two on your *Mondo* – and then switch to something else of somewhat greater potency. Your new task will be:

When you extinguish meaning and sound, what do you then hear?

That is a Zen *koan* from the eleventh century. *Koans* are formulae for meditation, absolutely comparable with mathematical formulae. When you have operated with them for a while, you will be convinced that they do work. Zen meditators have employed this *koan* for eight hundred years, and the Japanese are practical people concerned with what happens on this earth. They would simply forget such a formula if it didn't function. Since it hasn't been forgotten, you can be sure that you are now working with intense spiritual potency which thousands of people have tried out.

Meditating is not the same as believing. Meditation involves experiencing something for yourself. A *koan* is not a declaration of belief, just a technique for your consciousness, created by people who are geniuses as technicians of consciousness. They would never insist on you believing anything if you haven't experienced it for yourself. They have too much respect for you to try that. They don't command: Believe. They say: Experience.

You extinguish the river. Its sound. Its meaning. Every meaning. Even what I said about it. You obliterate all of that – and

> *What do* you hear *then?*
> > *What do you hear* then?
> > > *What do* you *hear then?*
> > > > What *do you hear then?*
> > > > > *What do you hear* then?
> > > > > > *What do you* hear *then?*
> > > > > > > What *do you hear then?*

Basically things are simpler now. You *only* put that one question. You listened to the river with both your ears. Now you cross over. You listen with the *Third Ear*. With your 'real ears'.

You 'uncover' Primordial Sound. You now hear nothing but that. You know that it can be heard. Ordinary people have heard it, so you can hear it too. There is a place within you that has long listened to it. Otherwise this book would not touch you. You would have given up reading it long ago.

Let your task remain:

> *What do you hear then?*

The rushing has risen out of the cochlea in your inner ear into a logarithmic curve – open, endless, approaching the vertical – which signals a crossing over: from the rushing of the river to the rushing that you *then* hear.

You hear it in your legs, which are painful from long sitting. Or they don't hurt any longer because they know you won't pay any attention. You hear it in your breathing, in your stomach, in your sex, in your finger-tips, in your toes. You *are* that rushing.

You are the rushing of the universe. The rushing of the big bang that was a primordial sound which is still resounding – in the cosmos; in the genes of everything alive on this planet; on every other star; in electrons and photons.

> *If you extinguish meaning and sound, what then do you hear?*

Yes, what do you hear then? Ask yourself that.daily. For twice twenty minutes – or once thirty minutes. That question can become your 'destiny' – 'in the single and preparatory intention of listening more intently' (Heidegger). Hearing more and more. Mounting the curve. Going beyond the comparative to the superlative. Listening – more listening – most listening.

What do you hear then?

At some stage you hear *it*. Perhaps just for a few seconds on the first occasion. Then ever more frequently. And for longer. Every time you hear it, you experience oneness. You hear – and *see* – oneness. You perceive it as you can never perceive with your normal senses. But this sense is also 'normal'. Otherwise we wouldn't have it. We have only let it atrophy. You perceive it as: the Truth. Now you can take it to yourself – Take the Truth – as if it were a material object: There it is.

You hear, you see, you experience, you taste, you smell, you know: You are the Universe. The universe is in you. You are in the universe. Everything is in you.

You can forget about all the clever books which tell you that. You've experienced it for yourself. And you experience it ever anew – as the most precious moments in your life. You have reached a peak of listening.

Time and again stories are told about Zen monks laughing. Now you know why they laugh, and the reason for this loud, resounding, echoing, triumphant, incomparably joyous and assured laughter. You think monks should be tranquil and quiet. But their laughter is like a rifle-shot. The most splendid laughter in the world.

I heard it for the first time in April 1962 when I bought a ticket for the *Ryo-an-ji*, the celebrated Zen garden at Kyoto. The monk selling tickets looked at the woman with me and laughed – just like a rifle-shot. At that time I didn't know what it meant. But the laughter remained in me. You don't forget that kind of laughter, and I remembered it years later when I discovered what is involved in Zen monks' laughter.

It's possible that you're now laughing like that yourself. You have good reason.

18

SONGS OF PRAISE

'Adoration can light a lamp by the way a sitar is played.'
(after an old Indian legend)

I
'GOD HUNGERS FOR SONGS'

No culture – from the Indians of the Upanishads to the Jews of the Psalms, from the Babylonians to the Aztecs, from the Egyptians to the Japanese, from the Sufis to the Balinese – has ever existed that did not experience music as a song of praise. Music was first created as a means of adoration. So as to sing the praise of the gods and God in joy and exaltation. That was the beginning, endowing music with energy. That energy powered music everywhere: in love and sorrow, in yearning and helplessness, in anger and pain.

That beginning is still to be sensed in music. Only to someone who needs negativity in art to legitimate his own denial does it sound naive to believe, towards the end of the twentieth century, that music is a song of praise. It certainly is in Stockhausen's 'Light' and Messiaen's 'Turangalila', in Coltrane's 'Love Supreme' and Miles Davis's 'Bitches' Brew', in Ali Akbar Khan's 'Karuna Supreme' and in Stravinsky's 'Symphony of Psalms'.

Music can still be the 'shaft formed from songs of praise' of which the Upanishads sing. This shaft drew the chariot of the sun, which couldn't cross the heavens without it.

Marius Schneider has shown that the Sanskrit root *bra* can mean both *grow* and *adore*. It is to be found in the names of both *Brahma* the God-Creator and *Brahman* the Cosmic Principle. So Brahma the God grew to the degree that his praises were sung. The universe expanded through song.

Martin Buber reminds us that the first myths were songs of praise. And Marius Schneider summarises: 'God hungers for songs'. After a life devoted to studying religions and spiritual traditions across the world, Schneider bases that view on all of humanity's myths and not just on the Vedic tradition. All myths maintain that the world grows by way of song and music. 'May my song, full of sweetness and fragrant oils, be a palatable repast for Indra' – invokes a singer of the Rig-Veda.

What music? In this book and its predecessor we have time and again come across the fact that our human and earthly music reflects the proportions of the cosmos. Not every numerical value is a tone but every tone is a numerical value; and we have discovered that nature prefers – to an extent exceeding all chance mathematical probabilities – those numbers which are simultaneously tones. The fact that 'the world is sound' isn't just a widespread myth or legend. It is also confirmed in the established findings of fundamental harmonic research and many other disciplines. We have found the world's tonal character confirmed in DNA genes and electron spins, in the solar wind and geomagnetism, in the weather, and in the song of flowers and plants.

That leads to another question. If our earthly music started as a song of praise and in many instances still entails adoration, and if human music is only a minimal part of the universe's music, must not cosmic music – the music of the spheres and galaxies, of planetary orbits, elementary particles, and genes – primarily be a song of praise too?

No one limited to earthly knowledge and insights is in a position to resolve this question once and for all, but we can glimpse the answer. Our final chapter presents evidence that may be of assistance.

II
THE 'PURPOSE' OF MUSIC

Of all the many non-human musics and harmonic processes discovered in nature, one is particularly close to us: the song of birds. This occurs in the same frequency area of audibility, and is so similar to human music that we have referred to it as 'song' since time immemorial. Musicians have been inspired by it for thousands of years. Not just flautists but also the creators of symphonies and works for organ: Beethoven in the 'Pastoral', Messiaen in many of his compositions, Respighi in his 'Pines of Rome', John Cage in his 'Song Books', or trombonist Albert Mangelsdorff in his improvisations. So might the singing of birds also be a song of praise? Can we discover whether that is the case?

Zoologists and ornithologists explain birds' 'music' as being – like everything else – a function of evolution. Bird-song is said to assure the reproduction and survival of the species. Anyone, however, who knows a bit about biology realises that nature possesses much more direct and simpler songless processes and mechanisms which bring about the desired outcome in far more predictable fashion.

Anyone who explains bird-song solely in terms of a biological function is somewhat akin to a scientist viewing human music as being biologically conditioned – which is not totally inconceivable. Imagine that an astronaut from a distant cosmic civilisation comes to our earth, attends a concert (perhaps a rock or jazz festival), can make little of the music, but observes that young people get to know one another, flirt, embrace and kiss, and then go home together. When he returned to his remote star, he would announce that the 'purpose' of music on earth is to serve preservation of the species.

When we smile at that idea, we realise that the evolutionary 'purpose' biologists attribute to bird-song is something supplementary. The scientists are right, but what they have discovered is no closer to the essential element than our astronaut's findings about earthly music. The scientists' discovery, which is open to logical demonstration, is only a secondary manifestation. Evolution *makes use* of bird-song – as sometimes also human music – as an additional means of attaining its objectives. It makes use of everything – including bird-song.

If scientists are permitted to take the postulate of evolution as their starting-point, then we must also be allowed to set off from the postulate of songs of praise. It immediately becomes clear that our postulate leads further, even in scientific terms. Its range is greater, and it even offers an opportunity for scientists' evolutionary interpretations. They cannot integrate adoration with their ideas, but there is room for scientific theories and deductions in the cosmos of people who start off with the hypothesis of thanksgiving. The narrowness of the scientific world-view and the consequences of such thinking became apparent as early as Schopenhauer, who thought the song of the nightingale 'an incomprehensible squandering of artistic talent on an ignorant creature'.

Anyone who observes and listens to birds singing – whether it be in a cage in the corner of a room, or, more convincingly, on a spring morning with a blackbird jubilating at the top of a tree whose first leaves are appearing – feels exactly what people in non-alienated cultures have felt since time immemorial. For the blackbird (or the lark or nightingale) singing serves exactly the same purpose as for us human beings – the purpose of making 'beautiful music'. Of expressing joy, adoration, and happiness – and of celebrating the festival of life. Nourishment for the souls of all those who hear them – which means *all* of nature's creatures including the human race. Food perhaps even for the Gods who – as Marius Schneider said – 'hunger for songs'.

III
'DO YOU KNOW HOW MANY MOSQUITOS
DANCE . . .?'

Let's go a step further. Human music and bird-song constitute a specific form of a principle to be observed everywhere in nature – even outside the musical and auditory sphere. Zoologists tell us about dances of joy involving baboons and chimpanzees. They maintain that such dances are necessary for purposes of reproduction, but apes can copulate even without such loud jumpings around. It may be obvious that the dancing does ease propagation, making it more intensive and joyous. Human dancing and music can do the same. But no evolutionist has ever proved that the 'purpose' of these dances is copulation – 'proved' in the way that scientists use the word when attacking something which doesn't fit into their theories.

Poets celebrate the dancing of mosquitoes: 'Do you know how many mosquitos dance / in the bright heat of the sun?' – and have viewed that as a dance of joy ever since antiquity. Zoologists also try to interpret this as a function of preservation of the species, but here too the opposite interpretation is more likely. Nature probably uses the dance as a source of additional impulses for maintaining a species that would survive even without it.

Zoologist Jane van Lawick-Goodall filmed a chimpanzees' 'rain-dance' at the Gombe Reserve in East Africa during and after a heavy downpour. This was most certainly not a 'sexual' dance. The male apes rolled exuberantly and joyously down a slope, ran up to the top again, and rolled down once more. They tore branches off trees – the kind of palm branches that human beings also wave around on ceremonial occasions – and whirled them through the air, vocalising enthusiastically. The female apes were not in sight. Jane van Lawick-Goodall was absolutely sure that this dance proclaimed joy. The chimpanzees were 'celebrating' the rain.

If such a 'rain-dance' has once been observed, it probably occurs frequently – and not just among chimpanzees. Are mosquitoes expressing their joy when they whizz through the air after summer rainfall, dancing around one another in complex choreographies? Are elephants also communicating delight when their huge bodies and trumpeting trunks take on an almost floating lightness and gentleness in a dance? Are kangaroo-rats doing the same when throughout the night their powerful back legs drum rhythms exactly paralleling what may perhaps be heard just a few kilometres away in a Yoruba ceremony? If those Africans are proclaiming joy, love, and interconnectedness with nature, might it be that similar rhythms beaten out by rats contain the same message? It is after all the same music.

Wolves and coyotes (observed and filmed by Jim Nollmann), and whales and dolphins (documented by John C. and Antonietta Lilly) sing together with human beings. The human sings first – and then the animals join in. Nollmann and the Lillys also tried singing wrong notes, but then the wolves, coyotes, whales, and dolphins remained silent. They exercised the same criteria as human beings, and often reacted more quickly and sensitively to wrong notes than the humans making music together. So it really is the same music!

IV
Waltzing Whales

Whales offer striking evidence of danced and sung music in nature. Whales' songs are filled with emotion which some human listeners find very affecting as if they were hearing their own species. Fishermen in Southern California or off Newfoundland say that you become melancholy and can even cry when you hear these songs. Musicians such as Judy Collins, Alan Hovhaness, Paul Winter, and Paul Horn have based their own compositions and improvisations on such sounds.

The sounds made by whales are more differentiated in pitch and intensity than human speech. Even here, of course, zoologists believe that whales' songs prepare the way for mating. It has also been discovered that such sounds are employed for echo location. They don't, however, need to be anything like so differentiated for either purpose. Young Californian zoologists have in fact recently conceded that they are an 'extra bonus' on nature's part, which cannot be explained in biological or evolutionary terms. They even contradict positivistic interpretations since the echo location would function much more reliably with simpler sounds than the whales' highly varied songs.

Whales' sensitivity to sound and musicality is also demonstrated in the way they move along in triple time. They break surface to a stressed 'one' and disappear again after two more unstressed beats. Or else they reverse the process: diving on 'one' and covering three times the distance under water during the unstressed beats. Both upward and downward movements are structured in triple time.

You could say that whales waltz along – not horizontally like human beings but vertically from above to below. They cover huge distances in that way – around 16,000 km a year from, for instance, Alaska down to Baja California in Mexico and back up to the North.

V

THE UNIVERSE DANCES

In his *On the Nature of the Psyche*, C. G. Jung reports on the Elgonyi, a tribe on the southern slope of Mount Elgon in East Africa. He observed that

> . . . people came out of their huts before sunrise, holding their hands – into which they spat or blew – in front of their mouths. Then they raised their arms and held the open hand towards the sun. I asked them what that signified but no one could give me an explanation. They had always done so, having learnt it from their parents. The medicine man was said to know what this meant. So I asked the medicine man. He knew just as little as the others but assured me that his grandfather would have known. People simply did that at every sunrise . . .

That is the real tradition of which dance, music, and proclamations of joy are a part. 'People' simply do things that way. Among the Africans on Mount Elgon parents learnt it from the previous generation – just like the dancing mosquitoes, trumpeting elephants, and singing birds; the marriage ceremonies among bees, ants, and termites; the 'spawning dances' (an expression coloured by evolutionary thinking, but I make use of it since no other exists) among fish; and hundreds of similar phenomena – including, of course, the concerts put on by human beings. None of these phenomena is necessary for perpetuation of the species, but they create a framework in which procreation can be differentiated – becoming richer, easier, more joyous and lively because such phenomena themselves embody those characteristics. They differentiate the 'environments' of reproduction.

Love is the name we give to the most differentiated procreative 'ambience'. That is the objective towards which differentiation strives – and where and with whom it is achieved remains open. Is it always attained among human beings? Certainly not. How do we know that only human beings are able to achieve – or strive to achieve – love?

'The dance' is obviously to be found everywhere right down to the level of amoebas and cells. Physicists even employ the term 'dance' with regard to the behaviour of particles in the atomic nucleus. It is possible that this 'dance' is the primordial dance, shaping and conditioning all the other dances – and music, the acoustic equivalent of the dance – in nature and the universe. And the song of the nightingale too. And the St Matthew Passion.

Since particles dance, *everything* that constitutes this universe dances. The dance of the god Shiva constantly creating the universe anew.

VI
THE LADDER OF LOVE

'Energy is Eternal Delight' runs a celebrated phrase by William Blake (1757–1827), the English poet and painter who at the end of the eighteenth century foreshadowed Art Nouveau and Freud and Jung's unravelling of symbols.

When children play joyously together, we can see energy and delight becoming one. We sense it too when people dance the night through – even though they become tired after just two hours of their everyday work which demands much less of them. Everyone experiences it when making love. And it is impossible to believe that we are so cut off from nature that what applies to us is not also true of the rest of creation. For the chimpanzees which shriek with joy as they roll down a slope. For the larks that sing as they ascend into the heavens. For the vines that shoot up in arabesques, developing that vitality, energy, pleasure, and enchantment we later feel in our heads when we drink the wine. For the dance of the photons, without location or mass and nevertheless energy. Here in the smallest particles in the universe – energy begins. Together with: delight, joy, pleasure, happiness . . .

'Energy is Eternal Delight' – and by energy Blake meant bra, bringing about growth through songs of praise. The energy of the cosmos.

It has long become apparent that no contradiction exists between the idea of songs of praise and the idea of love (even if biologists do prefer to see it as procreation). Both serve higher development in more than just a biological sense. As Teilhard de Chardin showed, they increasingly counter entropy, death, and decline.

Tantric and ancient Javan tradition tell of a 'Ladder of Love'. When a woman loves a man, she loves *all* men in this one man. When a man loves a woman, he loves *all* women in this one woman. Together they love *all* human beings, they love *all beings*. By loving all beings, they love *to be* – Being as the primordial ground of the cosmos. They love Essence and Being. They love the creative power and energy of the universe which many of us call God. They *love* – purely and simply. Who they in practice love is merely a matter of preference, depending on their individual fate and its ramifications.

On every rung of the 'Ladder of Love' the word *love* can be exchanged without any loss of meaning for the word *praise (laud)*. Richard Fester has shown that in many languages the words for love, laud, and live derive from the same root. For early human beings living entailed loving and lauding.

The ladder continues upwards. It is impossible that it should stop with human beings. It leads both above and below – into both the macro- and the micro-cosmos. Into the universe!

This ladder of adoration is reflected in the harmonic structure which may have been known since Pythagoras but has never before been uncovered in such abundance as at the present time. And yet what has been found to date is only a minimal part of what remains to be discovered. The more the avant-garde of physicists and cosmologers is gradually joined by the majority of scientists in breaking free of mechanistic, materialistic, and evolutionistic thinking, the more their senses will become attuned to tracking down the musical, rhythmic, and dance-like ground-pattern of the universe. The more science is impelled by both sides of the brain (rather than just by the left hemisphere), the more self-evident will it become for researchers to direct their attention towards and catch up on the previously neglected 'aesthetic' element, *listening* and *yielding to* what can be intensely heard through the ears but was *overlooked* during the centuries of mechanistic observation of nature.

It can already be concluded that whales' songs and 'waltzes', the songlines and sound-waves singing birds project into the morning air, the triumphant trumpeting of elephants, and the patterns and curves created by colourful fish in tropical waters are paradigms –

audible and visible emanations of a fundamental pattern of behaviour within the cosmos, shining through in both the microcosmic and macrocosmic worlds in the dance of photons and the bongo-rhythms beat throughout the universe by pulsars millions of light-years away. We encounter these paradigms everywhere. In the waves of the sea, the patterning of shells and coral, and in human symphonies. Music and dance, love and praise, are concealed everywhere.

Blake's 'Energy is Eternal Delight' is to be observed everywhere. And as Heraclitus declared:

> 'The hidden harmony
> is mightier
> than what is revealed.'

Poets speak of the 'celebration of life'. That is so omnipresent that we can conclude: celebration is not just a characteristic of life, and not even a function of life; Life itself *is* celebration.

Living is *lauding* is *loving*. But what about all the dissonance? After all we see daily that life also involves damning, hating, and vomiting. And anxiety, fear, anger, rage, murder, war, disease, old age, suffering, hunger, pain, death – all 'revealed' in exactly the way Heraclitus used the word. By contrasting the manifested and the concealed, Heraclitus made clear that what is 'hidden' is mightier (see also Chapter 4, 'Thinking through the Ear'). Is harmony therefore also concealed within dissonance? Do the limits to our perception become more immediately clear here than anywhere else?

We have seen that chaos does not exist. Cyberneticists' research into that area concludes that what seems chaos to us is *also* order. The problem is that we cannot – as yet? – perceive it as order. If the overtone scale is the only true and natural musical scale, then we should take account of the fact that *all* notes are present there. But we first register the notes that seem harmonious to us – and I deliberately use the visual word 'seem' to imply the possibility of deception. Then come the less harmonious notes, which are more distant, but the idea of the overtone scale also entails climbing upwards. The few people who have really done so have uncovered 'hidden harmony'. They know that nothing is unharmonious. The harmony close at hand may be more manifest, but the hidden harmony is mightier.

Our task is therefore to listen more intensely, hearing beyond what is manifest. We should not be satisfied with finding harmony there. We have to find harmony where we are as yet unable to hear it – or see, feel, taste, or smell it – but where, as Heraclitus tells us, it is nevertheless hidden. That is yet another expression of this book's social and political relevance.

I concluded *Nada Brahma* with the 150th psalm. Giving voice to praise receives more powerful expression there than almost any-where else in world literature. When I started writing *The Third Ear*, I had no idea that I would once again – despite following a very different course – end with praise and adoration. The journey may not have been as direct as in *Nada Brahma* but it accords with contemporary indirectness and the hidden nature of the harmony extolled by Heraclitus. That is why a contemporary version of the psalmist seems appropriate in conclusion of this book – and I find Nicaraguan-born Ernesto Cardenal's variation the most beautiful of all.

Psalm 150

Praise be to the Lord of the Cosmos
    Space is His Temple
    extending over billions
    of light-years.

Praise be
    to the Lord of the Stars
    and of interstellar space.

Praise be
    to the Lord of the Milky Ways
    and what lies between.

Praise be
    to the Lord of the atoms
    and to the emptiness surrounding them.

Praise Him
    with violins, flutes,
    and saxophones.

Praise Him
    with clarinets and English horn,
    with French horns and trombones,
    with flugelhorns and trumpets.

Praise Him
    with violas and violoncelli,
    with pianos and pianolas.

Praise Him
    with Blues and Jazz,
    and symphony orchestras,
    with negro spirituals
    and Beethoven's Fifth,
    with guitars and xylophones.

Praise Him
    with record players and cassette recorders.

Let everything that hath breath,
    every living cell,
    praise the Lord.

Hallelujah!

NOTES

Considerably more extensive notes and a more comprehensive bibliography are to be found in the German edition of this book. 'B' refers to the Bibliography.

Introduction

P.2. *Sense of balance.* More precisely: Receptors ensuring balance are distributed all over the body – down to the soles of the feet. But the receptor in the ear's semicircular canal is *primus inter pares.*

Ear more accurate than the eye. The ear (even of someone only moderately musical) 'measures' the correctness of an octave down to the last oscillation. The eye (even of an experienced painter) cannot avoid mistakes of up to 200 nm (nanometres) when evaluating colours. More detailed information is presented in Chapter 1. Other issues just touched on here are also treated in detail elsewhere in the book.

5. *Jean Gebser* (B).

Marilyn Ferguson (B).

6. *Krishnamurti.* Occasionally it has not been possible to track down quotations. In those few instances quotations have been retranslated into English.

1. Ear and Eye

12. *The deaf and blind.* Cf. psycho-physicist S. S. Stevens in the Time-Life book *Sound and Hearing* (B): 'How valuable the sense of hearing is becomes apparent when it is lacking. A child born blind . . . usually overcomes its difficulties. A child born deaf can be lost to humanity . . . It is hearing and the speech thus made possible that endow a person with the unique capacity for communication.'

13. *We see a colour.* . . . More information about the eye's inaccuracy and susceptibility to making mistakes (compared with the ear) is presented in *Nada Brahma* (B) Chapter 9. That deals too with the 'harshness' and 'cutting' nature of the eye – as reflected in linguistic usage. Someone can have a 'piercing' gaze but certainly not a 'penetrating' ear – or anything remotely similar as far as the ear is concerned. The chapter also covers the eye's aggressiveness and the corresponding attribute among people who mainly take in the world through their eyes.

14. *Both ear and eye can evaluate.* The previously mentioned chapter in *Nada Brahma* provides further information and additional quotations from science and research.

15. *Leibniz*. The original Latin is so perfect that it is worth quoting: 'Musica est exercitium arithmeticae occultum nescientis se numerare animi.' (G. W. Leibniz: *Epistolae ad diversos*, Vol. I, Leipzig 1734).

16. *Superlearning/Losanov method*. See Sheila and Nancy Ostrander/Lyn Schroder: *Superlearning*.

17. *Auditive and visual sphere*. On the establishment of relationships between various kinds of waves (here electromagnetic and sound vibrations) see the note to p. 87/88.

20. *Paul Parin, Fritz Morgenthaler, etc.* (B).
   Gregory Bateson. The Ecology of Mind (B).

21. *Plato. Politeia*.
   Jean Gebser. The Ever-Present Origin (B).

22. *Petrarch*. Quoted from Jean Gebser, op. cit.

26. *Prayer*. It is characteristic of the Christian world's hostility towards the body that communication with the Godhead takes place almost exclusively through prayer. Not through the body – as in yoga, tantra, and African religions. Not through dancing – as in the Old Testament still, primordial Christianity, Africa, the Aztecs, Incas, and in American Gospel Churches. Not through the breath – as in Indian Prana techniques and many meditative cultures (since every breath we take links us – more directly than anything else – with the Divine and the universe). Not through movement. Not through the unconscious and its uncovering. Everything – or almost everything – only through the mind. One could call that the reduction of religiosity to its absolute minimum.

27. *Early man as primarily a listener*. Bachofen (B) is not alone there. See also Jean Gebser (B).
   Krishnamurti (B).

28. *Richard Fester* (B).
   The ear establishes a more correct relationship. See also Chapters 2 and 10. Those show that the ear's perceptions accord better than the eye's with the findings of the New Physics. Our visual sense corresponds better with classical Newtonian physics. We now know, however – see such physicists as Heisenberg (B) – that the Newtonian concept is a 'special case' and only 'explains' a minimal part of the infinite universe. Classical physics is 'eye physics'. The celebrated postulate 'Measure everything that is measurable' was never really followed. In the majority of cases the old physics measured what was *optically* accessible. The minimal sector thus explained was that of the eye.

32. *The Tibetan Book of the Dead* (B).

2. We See Three Dimensions

34. *Lincoln Barnett.* Quoted from Roberto Laneri, *Prima Materia* (Dissertation, University of California, San Diego 1975).
36. *Balance receptors.* See also note to p. 2.
37. *Wataru Ohashi* (B).
38. *Alfred A. Tomatis* (B). I only discovered the work of this great French researcher into the ear and hearing after finishing writing *Das Dritte Ohr.* Tomatis' research provides fascinating scientific confirmation – from the realms of ontology, neurology, and evolutionary studies – of my own findings, but I can only follow this up in greater detail in future publications.

3. The Ear Goes Beyond

39. *René Chocholle.* Quoted from Dopheide (B).
41. *The ear* consists of the outer, middle, and inner ear. The outer ear ends at the highly sensitive tympanic membrane. Behind that is the middle ear with the three tiny bones which transmit and intensify the membranal vibrations. The fluid-filled inner ear contains the semicircular canals and the spirally arranged cochlea duct which 'encodes' sound, transforming it into nerve impulses. The organs of balance (situated in the semicircular canals) and the organ of Corti, the actual means of hearing (discovered in 1851 by Italian-born Alfonso Corti), are also in the inner ear. Simplifying somewhat, it can be said that vibrations of air operate in the outer ear up to the tympanic membrane; mechanical processes – magnified by the malleus, incus, and stapes – predominate in the middle ear; and these suddenly and mysteriously break off at the inner ear's 'oval window', and are transformed into electricity. These electric signals – about which we still know little – in turn stimulate the auditory nerve. Over the course of just a few millimetres the ear thus transforms mechanical into electrical vibrations. The fluid with which the inner ear – and above all the cochlea – is filled acts as a kind of shock-absorber. The most mysterious process is the 'encoding'. If the vibrations were simply transmitted, magnified, and transformed, the signals could become distorted as in corresponding forms of communications technology. If, however, the information transmitted merely consists of the presence or absence of a signal . . . then minor mistakes are unimportant. All that matters is that the coding gets through – and is understood and decoded in the brain. That, for instance, explains how we can recognise even a much distorted familiar voice over the telephone. The coding process is clearly mathematical so it is independent of distortions and approximations, and it can be assumed that evolution established this for autonomy's sake. (After S. S. Stevens (B).)
    W. D. Keidel (B).

43. *G. von Békésy*. In W. D. Keidel (B).
45. *Now, Past, Future*. See also *Nada Brahma* (B) Chapters 2 and 6.
46. *231 different notes in an octave. Compensatory hearing*: after Rudolf Haase, especially 'Der meßbare Einklang' (B). On 'Compensatory hearing', known since the Baroque era, see Chapter 9.

4. Thinking through the Ear

49. *Upanishads* (B).
50. *Richard Fester* (B).
51. *Huang-Po* (B).

6. Listening Words

61. *Heidegger. On the Way to Language* (B).
61. *Rupert Sheldrake*. In a discussion at the 'Other Realities' conference at Alpbach/Tyrol in 1983.
63. *Hegel* (B).

7. Landscapes of the Ear

67. *Greater authors*. Scarcely any of world literature's great authors was so dedicated to 'investigating with the ear' as Marcel Proust, who literally 'yielded to' his world. Samuel Beckett writes about Proust withdrawing to his cool room in Combray where he extracted the quintessence of a scorching hot morning from the scarlet, star-shaped *pounding* of a hammer on the road and the *chamber music* created by flies in the darkness. When he lies in bed at daybreak, *sounds, bells,* and *street cries* tell him all about the weather, temperature, and what is to be seen.

8. Ears That Do Not Hear

72. *Max Picard* (B).
    Meister Eckhart (B).
73. *Los Angeles Airport*. From Steven Halpert (B) together with the later reference to vacuum cleaners (section IX).
    American acousticians. See Murray Schafer (B).
77. *Decibel. Deci* signifies a tenth, and *bel* stands for Alexander Graham Bell (1847–1922), the inventor of the telephone. A sound whose intensity is a thousand times greater than another is merely 30 dB 'louder' – and if the intensity is a hundred thousand times more the dB

reading only increases by 50. A single decibel is intended to character-
ise the least perceptible noise.
78. *René Chocholle, Fritz Winckel*. Quoted from Dopheide (B).

9. The World Is Sound

85. *Dane Rudhyar* (B).
86. *Tritone*. One can speculate endlessly about the tritone. There exist
both the minor tritone (45:32 = 1.40625) and the major tritone (64:45 =
1.4222). The difference between them is the 'syntonic comma' known
as the 'Diaschisma' (2048:2025 = 1.011358). Truly precise division of
the octave lies between the major and minor tritone. This ratio practically never occurs in music, which indicates that the octave *cannot* be
bisected. The oneness it symbolises is indivisible. The word 'symbolises'
is, however, confusing. Oneness *is* indivisible. The fact that the octave
cannot be bisected provides convincing demonstration.
86. *Plus and minus spin*. As explained by Nobel laureate Maria Goeppert-
Mayer. 'Spin' can be crudely defined as a particular kind of particle
rotation.
Tempered tuning. Introduced in the West by Andreas Werckmeister in
1691. In China Prince Chu Tsai Yü calculated the nine exponentials a
hundred years earlier (1595).
87. *Planetary frequencies*. Kepler postulated a fundamental tone (the
low G for Saturn), and from that calculated the corresponding proportions or intervals. Anyone who octavises does not need to make any
such assumption. See Chapter 11, especially pp. 120/121.
Cousto (B). *Exactly ten octaves*. Cousto calculated 141.27 Hz in the
30th octave for Mercury, the innermost planet within our solar system,
and 140.24 Hz in the 40th octave for Pluto, the most distant planet in
the galaxy. The planets closest to and most removed from the sun are
therefore separated by exactly ten octaves.
If you want to reach the visual sphere. It goes without saying that this
involves moving through various kinds of waves – from the realm of
sound-waves to that of electromagnetic light-wave radiation. It is,
however, equally true that the law of octavising – like all harmonic
laws – takes precedence over this. If the phenomenon of vibrations
and waves is universal, and if all such oscillations demonstrate a preference – far beyond what is statistically to be expected – for whole-
number harmonic relationships, that of necessity implies the fact that
harmonic regularities transcend and permeate *all* kinds of vibrations
and waves. The phenomenon of waves is, however, itself also more
universal than is revealed to limited human perception. The various
kinds of waves and vibrations mainly seem so different to us because
people use ears, feelings, eyes, or various forms of complicated technical procedures or measurements for observing them. Even if we do

establish that the planets move around the sun in integral harmonic progressions, we create a relationship between two completely different kinds of 'vibrations', 'waves', and 'frequencies' – between those of planetary orbits and those of our earthly, audible music. That is what we do if, for instance, we octavise and transpose from the sphere of audible vibrations into the electromagnetic realm or the resonance of the DNA spiral. By doing so we are thinking 'ana-logically'. (See Chapter 5.)

88. *Earth, sun, and moon tone.* Their greatest impact results from being octavised to the point of audibility and used for meditation, which is why I produced the 'Primordial Tones' cassettes. Each of these tones stands for the quality the associated heavenly body represents in our consciousness. The sun tone for light, warmth, joy, abundance of life, and masculinity; the moon tone for love, sensitivity, creativity, and femininity; the earth tone for Mother Earth's power, providing a sense of reality, a 'sure footing', and grounding a meditator yoga-style. Meditations can be accompanied by some appropriate idea – such as 'I am Light' for the sun tone or 'I am Love' for the moon tone (as suggested in greater detail in the booklet accompanying the cassettes). For couples meditating, which can also be of a Tantric nature, there is a sounding together of sun and moon, or of Mars and Venus (on the 'Primordial Tones II' cassettes). The sounds of the heavenly bodies – and particularly of the earth, sun, and moon – are 'primordial tones' in terms of being archetypal. We – the genes for everything alive – have been 'receiving' them on this planet for millions of years. They are impressed on our genes and our unconscious – operating like Jungian archetypes. When we hear such tones – octavised to the point of audibility – we once again recognise them as something we have known right from the very beginning. Perhaps that is the explanation for their strength of impact during meditation. Primal tones are not just used by individual meditators. They are also employed in workshops and seminars by many therapists and psychologists, who are unanimous about their effectiveness. ('Primordial Tones I' with Earth, Sun, and Moon Tones, and the Shiva-Shakti Sound. 'Primordial Tones II' with Jupiter, Venus, and Mars Tones, and the Karuna Sound. Distributed by: Beyond, 648 N. Fuller, Hollywood, CA 90036, USA. Element Books, Longmead, Shaftesbury, Dorset, England.)

90. *Dorothy Retallack.* From Peter Tompkins/Christopher Bird (B). See also *Nada Brahma*, Chapter 5.

91. *Concert pitch in the Baroque and Early Classical periods.* From *Riemann Musik Lexikon* (B. Schotts Söhne, Mainz 1967).

91. *Sannyasin colour.* That is a different orange 'tone' to the colour attained by octavising the earth-day (702 nanometres). Strikingly many orbital frequencies lead – when octavised into the visual sphere – to orange-red: Venus (616 nm), Jupiter (742.6 nm), Uranus

(657.5 nm), Neptune (645 nm), and, as previously mentioned, the Earth and Moon. If, however, these frequencies are octavised into the audible sphere, the outcome is clearly distinguishable tones, ranging from an F sharp to a B (i.e. four semitones), which can therefore be precisely delineated in words. The greater precision of hearing – and its reflection in language – once again becomes apparent in this context.

93. *Greek melodies descended*. See Chapter 13.

93. *Kepler. Harmonices Mundi Libri V*.

96. *Power supply system*. José Delgado, a Spanish-American scientist, has demonstrated in a series of much-remarked experiments the extent to which even weak electric fields affect our emotions and well-being. Fields 'no stronger than what is radiated by a neon light' influenced the behaviour patterns of such different species as apes, human beings, fish, and dogs. 'Aggressive fish became placid in a field with the right frequencies. Apes could be made frantic, loving, peaceful, or high-spirited just by manipulating a dial.' While academic scientists were – as always – still doubting such findings, the American Army leapt on Delgado's research to put it to military use.

96. *Ultra-sound*. According to findings by Dr R. Mendelsohn, lecturer in preventive medicine, Illinois University.

101. *Hans Jenny. Cymatics* (B).
   George Leonard (B).

101. *Heisenberg* (B).

103. *Myths, legends. . . .* See *Nada Brahma*, Chapter 11.

103. *Paramahamsa Muktananda* (B).
   Feyerabend (B).

104. *Itzhak Bentov* (B).

10. Total Listening

105. *Meister Eckhart* (B).

106. *David Bohm's holomovement* is in my opinion best expounded in Ken Wilber, *The Holographic Paradigm* (B) – with contributions by David Bohm, Karl Pribram, Renée Weber, Fritjof Capra, Marilyn Ferguson, etc. This chapter makes considerable use of that book. Many of my quotations derive from either Wilber's book or Bohm's contribution to the Alpbach/Tyrol 'Other Realities' forum in 1983. Also of importance are: David Bohm, *The Implicit Order* (B); Bob Toben, *Space-Time and Beyond* (B); Werner Heisenberg, *Physics and Beyond* (B); David Bohm *et al.*, *On the Intuitive Understanding of Known Locality as Implied by Quantum Theory* (Birkbeck College, University of London, 1974); J. A. Wheeler, *Superspace in the Nature of Quantum Geometrodynamics* (Benjamin, New York, 1967); and Fritjof Capra, *The Tao of Physics* (B), *The Turning Point* (B), and lectures during his 1984 visit to Germany.

109. *Ch'an-sha Ching-ts'en.* Japanese name Chosha Keijin. Quoted from Yoel Hoffmann (B).
109. *Sarfati, Wheeler, Feynman, Gödel.* Quoted from Bob Toben (B).
113. *Satprem* (B).
115. *Eugene Wigner.* Quoted from Bob Toben.
116. *Karl Pribram, John Battista.* There are contributions by both Pribram and Battista in Ken Wilber, *The Holographic Paradigm* (B).

11. Audible and Inaudible Sound

119. *Upanishads* (B).

Bats. Even when it is completely dark, bats can avoid a wire less than a millimetre thick without being able to see it – thanks to echo-location in the sphere of ultra-sound. They can thus locate even the smallest of insects, catching up to 500 in a single hour. Bats 'see' with their ears. They can therefore hunt at times of day when birds are unable to do so.

Some kinds of bat – for instance the leaf-nosed bat – have such big ears that they look like additional wings or sails. Bats' supersonic cries come from a huge vocal cavity, capable of uttering 200 or more impulses per second. Their intensity can be so great that they correspond to a four-turbine jet flying past about one and a half kilometres away – and yet human beings cannot hear bat-cries. Scientists who have transposed such cries into the sphere of audibility speak of them being 'horrible' and 'unbearably loud'. The volume guarantees that these cries are reflected by almost any surface. The bats' ears respond to reflections a hundred billion times weaker than the sounds sent out. Bats can therefore make precise distinctions between whether they have located a grain of sand or a living insect.

Until just a few years ago, bat research was handicapped by scientists' inability to imagine that these creatures could possibly 'see' without some optical aid, or that echo-location in many cases functioned more accurately, quickly, and in more foolproof fashion than visual location. Insects and birds, which can see, can be led astray by various decoys, but that is not true of bats dependent on hearing.

Science is traditionally (and excessively) fixated on optical phenomena, so only in recent years did it learn to understand the diversity of bats' capacities for perception – around a century later than comprehension of the optical possibilities open to birds.

119. *Shah Niaz.* Quoted from Kirpal Singh (B).

Music for Hearing 'Audible and Inaudible Sound'
The Harmony of the World – A Realisation for the Ear of Johannes Kepler's Astronomical Data from *Harmonices Mundi 1619* by Willie

Ruff and John Rodgers: Saturnus–Jupiter–Mars–Terra–Venus–Mercurius (Yale University LP 1571, available from: W. Ruff, School of Music, Yale, New Haven/Conn. 065 20).

Earth's Magnetic Field – Realisations in computed electronic sound by Charles Dodge, produced at the Columbia University Computer Center (Nonesuch Records H-71 250, New York). Solar Wind and Earth's Magnetic Field.

DNA Suite by Dr David Deamer – 'A musical translation of DNA sequences' (Cassette Science and the Arts, 144 Mayhew Way, Walnut Creek/Cal 94 596).

Primordial Tones – presented by J. E. Berendt. The Tones of Earth, Sun, Moon, and the Shiva–Shakti Sound (Sun and Moon together): meditation for individuals or couples. Hans Peter Klein and Cornelia Kühler, Sandawa-Monochord. (USA: Beyond, 648 N. Fuller, Hollywood, CA 900 36 – England: Element Books, Longmead, Shaftesbury, Dorset.) 2 cassettes and accompanying booklet.

12. Why Women Have Higher Voices

129. *Wolf D. Keidel* (B)
129. *120–180 Hz.* According to Cousto the range for the male spoken voice is *c.* 120–180 Hz, and for the female *c.* 200–250 Hz. This entails a logarithmic function so the Hertz number doubles every octave.

Scientists with little feeling for the dimension of hearing. The case of Alexander Bain (1818–1903), a celebrated English physiologist and psychologist, makes clear the degree to which awareness of hearing atrophied in the dominant form of science. Even around the turn of the century Bain could still maintain in all seriousness that binaural hearing played absolutely no part in sound location, and that assertion was accepted (in the twentieth century!) by almost the entire scientific community – so little were scientists aware of conscious, attentive, alert, and critical hearing. (See also note for p. 119 on *Bats*.)

Vocal pitch. Dictionaries of music usually give the following vocal ranges: Bass C – f; Tenor c – c″; Alto e – e″; and Soprano g – f″ (each with corresponding range above and below. Descriptions differ because what is important is where a voice feels 'at home', not its deepest or highest note).

131. *Weber-Fechner Law.* Named after philosopher and physicist Gustav Theodor Fechner (1801–1887) and physiologist Ernst Heinrich Weber (1795–1878). Fechner discovered a way – based on work by Weber – of precisely calculating the difference between pitch and volume. For him – and for science in general since that time – this was a difference between quality and quantity. Pitch entails quality and volume quantity. Expressed mathematically, the law says that perception

intensifies with the logarithm of the stimulus. Later research considerably differentiated the law (by replacing Fechner's addition of sensations by multiplication) but confirmed the principle. Interestingly, Fechner chiefly valued his law because it seemed to prove the indestructible oneness of mind and matter, implying an exact mathematical correlation between subjective relationship and the physically measurable – that very correlation denied by mechanistic and materialistic science. That science adapted the law after its own fashion. It ignored the philosophic content and was fascinated by the possibility of measuring human perceptions. To a certain extent one can say that Fechner's law brought about the opposite of what he hoped. (After S. S. Stevens (B).)

High voices dominate. Here is more evidence uncovered by science:

1. The nerve fibres which convey sound-signals from the ear to the brain are linked with different parts of the brain – depending on the kind of frequencies carried. High tones end up deep in the cortex while low notes finish up close to the brain's surface. Here too it is obvious that evolution wanted to take high notes 'deeper', thinking them more important than low tones.

2. Scientists at Harvard University in the USA have established a subjective pitch scale. Test subjects were given the task of tuning an electronic piano (by turning specific knobs) so they felt that the notes were equidistant. This subjective tuning in no way accorded with the physicists' and piano-makers' 'objective' scale. What are called *Mel* units (from *melody*) were established so as to measure intervals in the new scale. These investigations revealed that an octave around middle C ranged over some 200 Mel whereas an octave at the upper end of the scale covered around 700 Mel. The experiments confirmed what many musicians have long maintained: the upper octaves sound 'more expansive' than the lower. They therefore allow – and encourage – much more meticulous differentiations, which signifies that early human beings must have listened more attentively to higher than to lower sounds.

3. Experiments by John William Strutt Lord Rayleigh, an important English physicist (1842–1919) who won the Nobel Prize in 1904, point in the same direction. He showed that the sound of a tuning-fork (or similar source of sound) of low pitch is much more difficult to determine with accuracy than that of a high note or spoken word. (After S. S. Stevens (B).)

134. *René Chocholle*. From Dopheide (B).
137. *Richard Fester* (B).
138. *J. J. Bachofen, Erich Neumann, Mircea Eliade, C. G. Jung.* See (B).
138. *Ken Wilber* (B).
138. *Mountains of corpses in the matriarchy.* Heide Göttner-Abendroth has shown that the death of the hero-lover of the matriarchy's Great God-

desses is a 'pattern' found in almost all cultures. Among the Greeks, Artemis, daughter of Zeus and 'eternal virgin', killed Actaeon with an arrow because he saw her naked. Aphrodite tore her beloved Adonis apart after transforming him into a boar. According to Cretan legend, Erechtheus is killed annually by Athene's stroke of lightning. Demeter, grieving for the loss of her daughter Core, forbade plants to grow until the whole of humanity died. Hera had Iacchus, the son of Demeter and her brother Zeus, dismembered. In another version, Demeter turned her youthful hero into a goat, which was then torn apart by the maenads. The Minoan Zeus was chopped up with a double-headed axe by his mother and first lover, the Earth Goddess Rhea. And Hera gave Heracles (whose name signifies 'Glory of Hera') his twelve labours only because she hoped they would kill him.

Things were even worse in Egypt. Hathor, the daughter of Re the Sun King, changed herself into the lion-headed Goddess Sachmet and became so frenzied that she wanted to eat up the entire human race. Isis had Re bitten by a snake. In Sumerian Babylon the Great Goddess Inanna-Ishtar tore apart her hero Tammuz, and condemned Gilgamesh to death because he rejected her love. Every king was dependent on the Great Goddess's approval and inevitably ended up as a sacrificial victim. In Asia Minor the Sun Goddess Arinna let vegetation dry up throughout the earth just because Telepinu left her. In Phrygia Cybele castrated Attis with her own hands, and in her cult the male priests had to whip and – taking over her role – emasculate themselves. In pre-Israelite Palestine the Goddess Anat cut open her lover Mot with a sickle, decapitated him, and scattered his flesh on the fields. The wrathful and revengeful Semitic and Jewish Jahweh – 'Eye for eye, tooth for tooth' – was only a patriarchalisation of Iahu, the Great Goddess of the Orient whose symbol of the 'Sublime Dove' degenerated into the ascetic and misogynous 'Holy Spirit' in Israel and Christianity.

In India Sarasvati, the matriarchal River and Water Goddess, had Sun God Indra chained and dragged off to another country. She also robbed Rudra of his manhood. The Great Goddess Kali has become the epitome of terror, and is often depicted bathing in blood.

Among the Celts, Dana – the Danae of the North after whom Denmark is named – struck down her lover Dagda with a flash of lightning. Ireland and Wales were totally devastated at the whim of Branwen, the Primordial Mother, whose lover and brother, Bran, was castrated. The Irish Moon Goddess Morrigain transformed her youthful lover Pwyll into a stag and killed him – like Artemis on Crete. Among the Germanic peoples of Scandinavia, Jörd, the Earth Mother, had the men who pulled her chariot swallowed up by the sea. Freya, the Goddess of Love, Beauty, and Fertility, transformed her brother-husband Freyr into a boar, and then killed and cooked him – as Aphrodite did to Adonis in Greece.

Heide Göttner-Abendroth also maintains that terror of death is a patriarchal idea. Under the matriarchy death was indissolubly linked with rebirth – with 'Dying in order to Become' – which women constantly experience in their own bodies. Man tends to repress death; woman accepts and transforms it. Viewed in that light, the blood that flowed in the Great Mother's cults was a stream of life.

140. *Androgyny.* An impressive vision of the new androgynous human being is presented by June Singer, American anthropologist and psychotherapist, in her book, *Androgyny* (B).

143. *X chromosome.* X chromosomes' potential to exist on their own implies *parthenogenesis* (= virgin birth), i.e. procreation without a male. That *must* have existed at some stage or else such an idea would not haunt so many of humanity's cults and religions. At some time it was 'fed' into the 'computer' of human genes.

144. *Husband.* Richard Fester elucidates the genesis of this word in great palaeo-linguistic detail (B).

145. *Anatomy of our teeth.* See Kushi (B).

147. *Domination from female roots.* See the language tables in R. Fester, *Ur-Wörter der Menschheit* (B).

E. Reclus. Quoted from Richard Fester, *Ur-Wörter der Menschheit* (B).

149. *American behavioural researchers.* Such as Anneliese Korner: 'Sex Differences in Newborn with Special Reference to Differences in the Organisation of Oral Behaviour' in: *Journal of Child Psychology and Psychiatry*, 14/1973.

13. Overtones Open the Door

153. *Roberto Laneri. Prima Materia* (unpublished dissertation, University of California, San Diego, 1975). My collaboration with Roberto Laneri in numerous radio and concert performances inspired many passages in this chapter.

156. *Harmonics create tone-colour.* The process is more complex than the sentence indicates. The overtone series generated by good musical instruments are highly complicated structures which cannot always be easily deciphered. The manufacturers of electronic musical instruments have nevertheless succeeded in decoding such harmonic series for almost all instruments so that their sounds can now be produced electronically (albeit for the most part without great authenticity).

No music without overtones. René Chocholle. From Dopheide (B).

161. *Dane Rudhyar.* (B).

I have listed below a selection of instrumental pieces and vocal music rich in overtones.

Tibet – from *An Anthology of the World's Music.* Tantric Rituals – recorded in North India in 1968 (Anthology Record & Tape

Corp., 135 West 41st St, New York/N.Y. 10036) (Singing by Tibetan monks including some impressive OMs)

Cho-Ga, Tantric and Ritual Music of Tibet – Tibetan Monks from Northern India and Nepal (Dorje-Ling Records, Box 1420, San Rafael/CA 94902)

Tibetan Ritual Music – Lamas and Monks of Tibet (Lyrichord LLST-7181)

Michael Vetter. Overtones – Voice and Tambura (Harmonia Mundi/Wergo-Spectrum SM 1038/39 – 2 LPs)

Michael Vetter. Tambura Preludes – Pro-vocationes (Harmonia Mundi/Wergo-Spectrum SM 1041/2 – 2 LPs)

Michael Vetter. Missa Universalis – Overtone Mass (Harmonia Mundi/Wergo-Spectrum SM 1051)

Roberto Laneri. Two Views of the Amazon (Harmonia Mundi/Wergo-Spectrum SM 1046)

The Harmonic Choir and David Hykes. Hearing Solar Winds (Harmonia Mundi 558 607)

David Hykes and Harmonic Choir. Harmonic Meetings (Celestial Harmonies CEL 013/14 – 2 LPs)

David Hykes and Harmonic Choir. Current Circulation (Celestial Harmonies CEL 010)

Katsuya Yokoyama Plays Classical Shakuhachi Masterworks. 'Zen' (Harmonia Mundi/Wergo-Spectrum SM 1033/34 – 2 LPs)

Shomyo Buddhist Ritual from Japan. Dai Hannya Ceremony – Shington Sect. (UNESCO Collection Musical Sources – Philips 6586021)

Bali. Gamelan, Ketjak, Geng Gong, Legong, etc. (Recorded on Bali by J. E. Berendt – in the 'Song and Sound the World Around' series: Philips 6303172)

Kohachiro Miyata. Shakuhachi (Nonesuch 72076)

Goro Yamaguchi. Music of Shakuhachi (Nonesuch 72025)

Tibetan Bells II – Henry Wolff and Nancy Hennings (Celestial Harmonies LC 7869)

The Singing Bowls of Tibet (Saydisc Records, Badminton/England SDL 326) (Tibetan temple bowls from genuine 'holy' metals: gold, silver, copper, lead, tin, iron, zinc, and bronze)

Paul Horn. Inside the Great Pyramid – recorded in the grave chambers of the pyramid of Gizeh (Kuckkuck 060/061 – double album)

Paul Horn. Inside – recorded live in the Taj Mahal (Kuckkuck 062)

Songs of the Humpback Whale (Capitol ST-620)

'And God Created Great Whales': Concerto for Whales and Symphony Orchestra by Alan Hovhaness (Columbia 30390)

Missa Gaia. Earth Mass by *Paul Winter.*

Chorus of the St John the Divine Cathedral, New York, Paul Halley (Organ), Paul Winter (Saxophone), David Friesen (Bass), Brazilian Percussion, Whales, Wolves, Dolphins, Birds, etc. – recorded live in the Cathedral of St John the Divine and in the Grand Canyon (Two records. Living Music Records, 65^G Gate Five Rd, Sausalito, CA 94965)

14. TV Reassures That Shooting Doesn't Harm Anyone

167. *Martin Grotjahn* (B).
167. *Wilbur Schramm, Jack Lyle, and Edwin B. Parker. Television in the Lives of Our Children* (Stanford University Press, Palo Alto 1964).

15. Listening Is Improvising

169. *David Friesen.* One of the best American bass players from the younger generation, quoted from the record sleeve to Mal Waldron/ David Friesen: 'Encounters' (Muse Records MR 5305).
171. *C. G. Jung and Wolfgang Pauli's 'Synchronicity'.* Excellently explained by Heisenberg (B).
173. *John Cage/Morton Feldman.* 'Musik Texte' 5/July 1984.

Only a few of the many possible records could be selected. The music of any good improvising group (as extensively available on the record market) illustrates the ideas presented in this chapter.
Oregon. 'Distant Hills' (Vanguard VSD 79342)
Oregon. 'Music of Another Present Era' (Vanguard VSD 79326)
Oregon. 'Out of the Woods' (Elektra/WEA 53101)
Oregon (ECM 1258)
Condona – with Collin Walcott, Don Cherry, Nana Vasconcelos (ECM 1132)
Condona 2 (ECM 1177)
Condona 3 (ECM 1243)
Paul Winter Consort (Living Music LMP-1, double album)
Paul Winter Consort. 'Common Ground' (A & M SP 4698)
Kenny Wheeler – Sextet with Evan Parker, Eje Thelin, etc. (ECM 1156)
To Hear the World in a Grain of Sand – World Music Live at the Donaueschingen Festival 85 – Luis DiMatteo, Vikah and Prakah Maharaj, Lennart Aberg, Bernd Konrad, Connie Bauer, Tom van der Geld, Rudy Smith, David Friesen, Dom Um Romao, Andrew Cyrille, produced by J. E. Berendt (Soulnote SN 1128)
Vocal Summit – Lauren Newton, Urszula Dudziak, Jeanne Lee, Jay Clayton, Bobby McFerrin: 'Sorrow is not for Ever – Love Is' produced by J. E. Berendt (Moers Music 2004)
Globe Unity Orchestra. 'Intergalactic Blow' (ECM 60039)
John Handy – Ali Akbar Khan – with L. Subramaniam. 'Rainbow' produced by J. E. Berendt (MPS/Polydor International 821885-1)
Dissidenten and Lemchaheb. 'Sahara Elektrik' recorded in Morocco (Shanachie Records 64005)

16. Putting to the Test

177. *Most people close their eyes.* The Tantric demand that the eyes should be kept open so as to look closely and intensely at one's partner doesn't contradict this sentence but rather complements it. That amounts to the opposite of normal seeing with its 'just looking around' and 'seeing is seeking'. That involves finding: additional penetration and reception.

177. *Sartre, Jean-Paul* (B).

182. *Zen intensive.* A meditation technique developed by Bhagwan Shree Rajneesh among others. A couple ask one another the old Zen question of 'Who am I?', changing roles every ten minutes. This is most effective if persisted in for days with only absolutely essential breaks. Advanced practitioners of the 'Zen Intensive' even do without sleep and work through the night.

17. Do You Hear the Rushing of the River?

186. *Ken Wilber. Up From Eden* (B).

187. *Huang-Po* (B).
Meditative posture. Lotus position in: *Nada Brahma* and many books on meditation (B).

187. *'The' river.* After H. Hesse's *Siddartha*, quoted and commented on in *Nada Brahma* (B).

188. *Krishnamurti* (B).
Zen Master Eko. From Yoel Hoffmann (B).

189. *Via = Way 880 times.* From W. Johnson (B).

190. *Martin Buber* (B).

18. Songs of Praise

194. *Adoration can light a lamp.* The Vedic legend from which this chapter's motto derives tells of a tiny village in the Himalayas. It was winter and bitterly cold. People were freezing and hungry. The snow lay up to the roof-tops. Wood was wet and none of the villagers had been able to light a fire for months. One day a travelling musician who'd lost his way suddenly appeared. The villagers were so poor that they had hardly anything to offer him, but they were good people and gave him a bowl of soup and a place to sleep under the stairs. In the evening the musician played on his sitar. The villagers gathered around. Some sang, others danced, and spirits rose. The musician improvised throughout the night, and then towards morning – and people scarcely believed their eyes – a light suddenly started burning,

for the first time since the beginning of winter. That light was then used to start fires in village hearths. The sitar player had fanned the fire into flames by the very warmth – the fervour and power – of his music. The legend also tells that the musician had ignited a flame in people's hearts many hours before it began to burn in the lamp.

bra = grow, adore. The Sanskrit syllable *bra* or *bri* appears in the Hebrew of the Old Testament in the crucial first sentence 'In the beginning God created the heaven and the earth': *'Bershit Bara Elohim Et Haschamajim We-Et Ha-Aretz'.* It appears twice with the first word repeated in the second since the Aleph can be an a, e, i, o, or u. The Hebrew *bara* means to create. The same root is to be found in the Greek – *bryo* (e.g. embryo) or the English *bear.* Its highest expression is in *Brahma* and *Brahman*, which is also reflected in *pray, prescere* (Latin), etc.

194. *Martin Buber* (B).
    The world grows by way of song and music. See *Nada Brahma*, Chapter 11.

195. *The song of birds.* The affinity between bird-song and human music includes the fact that birds also love man's music-making. A personal observation: song-birds sometimes fly through an open window into my work-room – but only when music is being played. They once came three times when Artur Schnabel was performing the Waldstein Sonata.

197. *Procreation not the purpose.* Wilhelm Reich circumscribed the importance of reproduction particularly convincingly. After his experiments with muscular spasms and development of a 'four-stroke formula for the orgasm' (Mechanical tension – electrical charge – electrical discharge – mechanical relaxation), he summarised: 'Sexuality does not therefore serve procreation. Reproduction is an almost chance outcome of the process of tension/charge in the genital sphere. That is depressing for eugenic moral philosophy but true . . . Procreation is a function of sexuality, and not vice versa as hitherto thought . . .' (Wilhelm Reich: 'The Discovery of the Orgone I' (B)). Viewed cybernetically, reproduction is part of a feedback control system, i.e. it is both cause and objective, and in both respects bound up, forwards and backwards, with similarly influenced factors. That is an all-embracing, 'systemic', 'holistic' view, which differs in essential respects from the way of seeing, fixated on *ratio* and purpose, pursued by the traditional sciences (and morality).

197. *'Do You Know How Many Mosquitos Dance . . . ?'* Song by Wilhelm Hey.

198. *Echo location.* Not just with regard to obstacles or distance above the sea-bed, but also for the location of food – and with dolphins (especially porpoises) as well as whales. These creatures are large and fast with dolphins attaining speeds of 32 km per hour. Blue whales (over 30 metres long and up to 120 tons in weight) are the largest animals ever to

have existed on earth. In order to navigate such a large weight at considerable speeds, or to slow down suddenly, whales must be able to locate obstacles and prey far in advance. They thus orientate themselves by way of sound and ultra-sound – within the human range and far beyond: up to 170,000 Hz. In that way they can 'see', and catch, fish only a few centimetres long. Researchers have covered dolphins' eyes with suction-discs but the creatures had no difficulty in finding rubber rings thrown into a pool. In another experiment they distinguished between two steel balls differing slightly in diameter – a test where even the human eye could go astray. The dolphins' keepers, who could see, weren't sure about distinguishing between the two balls, but the animals dependent only on hearing made no mistakes. Porpoises caught in a net never touch the mesh, which they can locate acoustically with absolute assurance. They establish where the floating net, attached to corks, comes to an end, and jump out of it. (After S. S. Stevens (B).)

199. *C. G. Jung.* 'The Nature of the Psyche' in: *Structure and Dynamics of the Psyche* (B).

201. *Teilhard de Chardin* (B).

Counter entropy. These forces counter universal 'thermo-death' which the second law of thermodynamics sees as unavoidably bringing about the 'end of the world'. The fact that mechanistic scientific thinking should have chosen such a negative name for something so positive as negentrophy – in fact the most positive force of all – is particularly revealing. On the questionable nature of the scientific concept of entropy, see also *Nada Brahma*, Chapter 7.

201. *Love, laud, and live.* Be-*lieve* also belongs in that sequence.

203. *Ernesto Cardenal. Psalms* (B).

Psalm 150. How marvellous that Johannes Kepler, the thinker and researcher who made harmonic thought 'respectable' for modern science, also returned time and again to the idea of 'Songs of Praise'. He thus wrote:

God is our Lord,
Great is His Power,
And His wisdom is without end.
Praise Him, sun, moon, and planets,
No matter in what language
Your hymn of praise may sound out to the Creator.
Praise Him, ye heavenly harmonies,
And ye witnesses and verifiers
Of His revealed truths.
And thou, my soul,
Sing the Lord's glory thy life long.
All things,
The visible and the invisible,

Are from Him and through Him and to Him.
To Him alone be Power and Glory
From Eternity to Eternity.

I have proclaimed to humanity
The glory of Thy Works
To the extent that my finite mind
Could grasp Thy Infinitude.

Johannes Kepler

BIBLIOGRAPHY

Adorno, Theodor W., *Philosophy of New Music* (Continuum 1973; Sheed 1987)

Bachofen, Johann Jakob, *Myth, Religion, and Mother Right* (Princeton U.P. 1967)

Bateson, Gregory, *Steps to an Ecology of Mind* (Ballantine 1975; Paladin 1973)

——*Mind and Nature* (Bantam 1979; Fontana 1985)

Benenzon, Rolando O., *Music Therapy Manual* (C. C. Thomas 1981)

Bentov, Itzhak, *Stalking the Wild Pendulum* (Bantam 1979; Wildwood House 1978)

Berendt, Joachim-Ernst, *The Jazz Book – from Ragtime to Fusion and Beyond* (Lawrence Hill 1982; Paladin 1984)

——*Nada Brahma* (Destiny Books, 1987)

Berman, Morris, *The Reenchantment of the World* (Cornell U.P. 1981)

Blofeld, John, *Mantras: Sacred Words of Power* (Unwin 1978)

Bohm, David, *Wholeness and the Implicit Order* (Ark 1983); see also Wilber, Ken

Buber, Martin, *The Way of Response* (Schocken 1966)

Capra, Fritjof, *The Tao of Physics* (Bantam 1977; Fontana 1983)

——*The Turning Point* (Simon & Schuster 1982; Fontana 1983)

Cardenal, Ernesto, *Psalms* (Crossroad 1981; Sheed & Ward 1981)

Charon, Jean, *The Unknown Spirit* (Coventure 1983)

Colegrave, Sukie, *The Spirit of the Valley* (Virago 1979)

Cousto, Hans, *The Octave – The Origin of Harmony* (Life Rhythm 1988)

Curtius, Ernst Robert, *Essays on European Literature* (Princeton U.P. 1973)

Diamond, John, *Life-Energy in Music* (Zeppelin 1983)

Dopheide, Bernhard, *Musikhören – Hörererziehung* (Wissenschaftliche Buchgesellschaft, Darmstadt 1975)

Eckhart, Meister, *Meister Eckhart – Sermons and Treatises* (Element 1986)

Eliade, Mircea, *The Myth of the Eternal Return* (Princeton U.P. 1954)

Enomiya Lassalle, Hugo M., *Zen. Way to Enlightenment* (Taphingen 1968)

Ferguson, Marilyn, *The Aquarian Conspiracy* (J.P. Tarcher 1981; Paladin 1982)

Fester, Richard, *Ur-Wörter der Menschheit* (Kösel, Munich 1981) – and many other books published in Germany.

Feyerabend, Paul, *Against Method* (Schocken 1978; Verso 1978)

Garfield, Patricia, *Creative Dreaming* (Ballantine 1976)

Gebser, Jean, *The Ever-Present Origin* (Ohio U.P. 1986)

Gibran, Kahil, *Thoughts and Meditations* (Citadel 1984)

Govinda, Lama Anagarika, *Creative Meditation and Multidimensional Consciousness* (Theosophical Publishing House 1976; Allen & Unwin 1977)

Grotjahn, Martin, *The Voice of the Symbol* (Mara 1971)

Haase, Rudolf, *Der meßbare Einklang – Grundzüge einer empirischen Weltharmonik* (Edition Alpha, Klett, Stuttgart 1976) – and many other books published in Germany and Austria.

Halpern, Steven, *Sound Health* (Harper & Row 1987)

Hamel, Peter Michael, *Through Music to the Self* (Element 1978)

Hegel, Georg Wilhelm Friedrich, *The Phenomenology of Spirit* (Oxford U.P. 1979)

Heidegger, Martin, *Basic Writings* (Routledge 1978)

——*On the Way to Language* (Harper & Row 1982)

Heisenberg, Werner, *Physics and Beyond* (Harper & Row)

Heraclitus, *Cosmic Fragments* (Cambridge U.P. 1954)

Herder, Johann Gottfried, *Über den Ursprung der Sprache* (Freies Geistesleben, Stuttgart 1965)

Hesse, Hermann, *The Glass Bead Game* (Bantam 1970; Picador 1987)

——*Musik*, selected by Volker Michels (Suhrkamp, Frankfurt a, M. 1972)

Hoffmann, Yoel, *The Sound of the One Hand* (Basic Books 1975)

Hoyle, Fred/Wickramasinghe, N.C., *Evolution from Space* (Simon & Schuster 1984; Paladin 1983)

Huang-Po, *The Zen Teaching of Huang-Po* (Grove 1959; Buddhist Society, London, n.d.)

James, William, *The Varieties of Religious Experience* (Penguin 1982)

Jantsch, Erich, *The Self-Organising Universe* (Pergamon 1980)

Jaynes, Julian, *The Origin of Consciousness in the Breakdown of the Bicameral Mind* (Houghton Mifflin 1976)

Jenny, Hans, *Cymatics* (Schocken 1975)

Johnston, William, *Silent Music* (Harper & Row 1979; Fontana 1976)

Jonas, Doris F./Jonas, A. David, *Other Senses, Other Worlds* (Stein & Day 1976)

Jung, C.G., *The Structure and Dynamics of the Psyche* (Routledge 1960)

Kakuska, Rainer (ed.), *Andere Wirklichkeiten* (Dianus-Trikont, Munich 1984)

Kapleau, Philip, *The Three Pillars of Zen* (Doubleday 1980; Rider 1980)

Kayser, Hans, *Akroasis: The Theory of World Harmonics* (Plowshare 1970)

Keidel, Wolf D., *The Physiological Basis of Hearing* (Thieme-Stratton 1983)

Kepler, Johannes, *Gesammelte Werke* (Beck, Munich 1938)

——*Weltharmonik in 5 Büchern* (Beck, Munich 1938)

Khan, Hazrat Inayat, *Music* (International Headquarters of the Sufi Movement, Geneva 1959)

——*The Music of Life* (Omega Press 1983)

Krishnamurti, Jiddu, *The Second Penguin Krishnamurti Reader* (Penguin 1970)

——*Meditations* (Gollancz 1980)

Küng, Hans, *Eternal Life?* (Doubleday 1984; Fount 1985)

Kushi, Michio, *The Book of Macrobiotics* (Japan Pubns, Inc. 1987)

Lao Tse, *Tao Te Ching* – New translation by Gia-Fu Feng & Jane English (Random 1972; Wildwood House 1973)

—— *Tao Te Ching* – Richard Wilhelm (Arkana 1985)

Leonard, George, *The Silent Pulse* (Dutton 1978)

Lilly, John C., *The Centre of the Cyclone* (M. Boyars 1973)

Long, Max, *Introduction to Huna* (Esoteric Pubns, n.d.)

May, Robert, *Sex and Fantasy* – *Patterns of Male and Female Development* (Wideview Books 1981)

Mellers, Wilfred, *Man and His Music* (Barrie & Jenkins 1988)

Michell, John, *City of Revolution* (Abacus, n.d.)

Miller, Alice, *Thou Shalt Not Be Aware* (Farrar, Straus & Giroux 1984; Pluto 1986)

Muktananda, Paramahamsa, *Kundalini* (S.Y.D.A. Foundn. 1980)

Neumann, Erich, *The Origins and History of Consciousness* (Princeton U.P. 1954; Routledge 1982)

—— *The Great Mother* (Princeton U.P. 1964)

Ohashi, Waturu, *Do-It-Yourself Shiatsu* (Dutton 1976; Unwin 1979)

Ouspensky, P.D., *In Search of the Miraculous* (Harcourt Brace Jovanovich 1965; Arkana 1988)

—— *Tertium Organum* (Random; Routledge 1982)

Parin, Paul/Morgenthaler Fritz/Parin-Matthey, Goldi, *Fear Thy Neighbour As Thyself* (U. of Chicago Press 1980)

Picard, Max, *The World of Silence* (Regnery-Gateway)

Plato: *Phaido* – *Philebus* (Penguin 1970)

Prigogine, Ilya/Stengers, Elisabeth, *Order Out of Chaos: Man's New Dialogue with Nature* (Shambhala 1984; Flamingo 1985)

Rajneesh, Bhagwan Shree, *The Hidden Harmony* – Heraclitus (Rajneesh Foundation, Poona 1976)

—— *Philosophia Perennis* – Pythagoras (Rajneesh Foundation International 1981)

—— *The Book* – Series I, II, III (RFI 1984)

Reich, Wilhelm, *The Function of the Orgasm. The Discovery of the Orgone* (Condor 1983)

Reps, Paul, *Zen Flesh, Zen Bones* (Penguin 1971)

Róheim, Geza, *Animism, Magic, and the Divine King* (International Universities Press 1972)

Rudhyar, Dane, *The Magic of Tone and the Art of Music* (Shambhala 1982)

Sartre, Jean-Paul, *War Diaries 1939–1940* (Verso 1984)

Satprem, *Sri Aurobindo or the Adventure of Consciousness* (Institute for Evolutionary Research 1984)

Schafer, R. Murray, *The Tuning of the World* (Knopf 1977)

Schonberger, Martin Maria, *Verborgener Schlüssel zum Leben* – *Weltformel I-Ging im Genetischen Code* (Barth-Scherz, Munich/Berne 1973)

Schultz, Joachim, *The Movement and Rhythms of the Stars* (Floris 1986)

Shah, Idris, *The Sufis* (Octagon 1982)

Sheldrake, Rupert, *The New Science of Life* (J.P. Tarcher 1983; Paladin 1987)

Silesius, Angelus, *The Book of Angelus Silesius* (Wildwood House 1976)

Singer, June, *Androgyny* (Doubleday 1977; Routledge 1977)

Singh, Kirpal, *Naam or Word* (Sant Bani Ashram 1975)

Steiner, Rudolf, *The Philosophy of Freedom* (Rudolf Steiner Press 1964)

——*Goethe's Conception of the World* (Haskell 1972)

——*Anthroposophy: An Introduction* (RSP 1983)

——*The Inner Nature of Music & the Experience of Tone* (RSP 1983)

Stevens, S.S., *Sound and Hearing* (Time-Life Books)

Suzuki, Daisetz T., *Mysticism: Christian and Buddhist* (Mandala 1980)

Suzuki, Daisetz, T.; Fromm, Erich; Martino, Richard, *Zen Buddhism and Psychoanalysis* (Harper & Bros. 1960)

Teilhard de Chardin, Pierre, *The Future of Man* (Harper & Row 1969; Fontana 1968)

——*Christianity and Evolution* (Harcourt Brace Jovanovich 1974)

Tibetan Book of the Dead – edited by W.Y. Evans-Wentz (Oxford U.P. 1980)

Toben, Bob, *Space-Time and Beyond* (Dutton 1982)

Tomatis, Alfred A., *La nuit utérine* (Editions Stock, Paris 1981)

Tompkins, Peter/Bird, Christopher, *The Secret Life of Plants* (Harper & Row 1984; Penguin)

Upanishads (Penguin 1970; Wildwood House 1978)

Watson, Lyall, *Supernature* (Hodder 1986)

Wilber, Ken (ed.), *The Holographic Paradigm and Other Paradoxes* with contributions by David Bohm, Fritjof Capra, Marilyn Ferguson, Karl H. Pribram, Renée Weber, etc. (Shambhala 1982)

——*Up from Eden* (Shambhala 1983; Routledge 1983)

Wittgenstein, Ludwig, *Tractatus logico-philosophicus* (Humanities 1972; Routledge 1962)

INDEX OF NAMES

SUBJECT INDEX